Praise for *The Beginner's Guide to Nation-Building*

No challenge in international relations today is more pressing or more difficult than that of supporting weak states. James Dobbins, one of the leading practitioners of the art, offers a set of clear, simple prescriptions for helping to build a stable peace in the wake of conflict and disorder. Drawing on the often painful lessons of recent history, Dobbins brings a new level of rigor and openness to this essential subject, and provides a useful tool for all in the United Nations who are engaged in meeting this challenge.

—Kofi A. Annan, United Nations Secretary-General

I cooperated closely with Ambassador Dobbins in facing the challenges of postconflict stabilization in the Balkans and then Afghanistan, and came to greatly value his expertise. This latest RAND study draws upon that expertise and demonstrates his deep insights into the field of nation-building.

—Joschka Fisher, Visiting Professor at Princeton University, former German Foreign Minister and Vice Chancellor

Cogent, concise, and yet remarkably comprehensive in both its thematic and country coverage, *The Beginner's Guide to Nation-Building* distills the lessons from 24 historical case studies. The resulting wisdom—detailed, accessible, sobering, and instructive—should guide every policymaker who considers or prepares for such bold intervention, and every student and analyst who attempts to assess it. This is (and will likely remain for some time) *the* essential manual for rebuilding war-torn states.

—Larry Diamond, Senior Fellow, Hoover Institution, Stanford University

The value in this Guide is as much in the questions it forces policymakers to ask as in the recommendations it offers. If policymakers had asked before going into Iraq who would maintain law and order, how quickly could local police and military maintain the peace, how would local governance be established, or what would be the source of creating jobs—and found that they had few answers—then perhaps the whole mission would have been radically reassessed. The Guide also presents a challenge to our civilian institutions and the U.S. Congress. If we hope to manage the international consequences posed by conflict abroad, then we must build civilian capacities to support governance, the rule of law, and job creation, just as we would never expect to fight a war without training and equipping our soldiers.

—*Carlos Pascual, Vice President of the Brookings Institution,*
former Coordinator for Stabilization and Reconstruction,
U.S. Department of State

I know of no challenge in international affairs as demanding as that of state-building—what in the U.S. is called nation-building—and none where it is as imperative to learn from our experiences—good as well as bad—during the last few years. James Dobbins has not only guided U.S. policy on some of these operations, but has also led the groundbreaking work by RAND to draw the necessary lessons from them. This book will be required reading for policymakers and practitioners alike.

—*Carl Bildt, Swedish Foreign Minister, former Prime Minister,*
and first High Representative in Bosnia-Herzegovina

THE BEGINNER'S GUIDE TO
NATION-BUILDING

James Dobbins, Seth G. Jones
Keith Crane, Beth Cole DeGrasse

Prepared for the Smith Richardson Foundation

NATIONAL SECURITY
RESEARCH DIVISION

The research described in this report was sponsored by the Smith Richardson Foundation and was conducted under the auspices of the International Security and Defense Policy Center within the RAND National Security Research Division (NSRD). NSRD conducts research and analysis for the Office of the Secretary of Defense, the Joint Staff, the Unified Commands, the defense agencies, the Department of the Navy, the Marine Corps, the U.S. Coast Guard, the U.S. Intelligence Community, allied foreign governments, and foundations.

Library of Congress Cataloging-in-Publication Data

The beginner's guide to nation-building / James Dobbins ... [et al.].
    p. cm.
    Includes bibliographical references.
    ISBN 978-0-8330-3988-0 (pbk. : alk. paper)
    1. Nation-building. 2. Nation-building—Case studies. 3. Peace-building.
  4. Democratization. I. Dobbins, James, 1942–

JZ6300.B44 2007
327.1—dc22

2006100823

Cover Photo Credits (clockwise from top left):
AP Photo/Hidajet Delic; AP Photo/Karim Kadim;
AP Photo/Jozo Pavkovi; Photo Courtesy of www.defenselink.mil

The RAND Corporation is a nonprofit research organization providing objective analysis and effective solutions that address the challenges facing the public and private sectors around the world. RAND's publications do not necessarily reflect the opinions of its research clients and sponsors.

RAND® is a registered trademark.

Cover Design by Stephen Bloodsworth

© Copyright 2007 RAND Corporation

Published 2007 by the RAND Corporation
1776 Main Street, P.O. Box 2138, Santa Monica, CA 90407-2138
1200 South Hayes Street, Arlington, VA 22202-5050
4570 Fifth Avenue, Suite 600, Pittsburgh, PA 15213-2665
RAND URL: http://www.rand.org/
To order RAND documents or to obtain additional information, contact
Distribution Services: Telephone: (310) 451-7002;
Fax: (412) 802-4981; Email: order@rand.org

Foreword

The U.S. occupation of Iraq was marked by a series of unanticipated challenges and hastily improvised responses. U.S. officials did not foresee the looting that accompanied the fall of Baghdad, were not prepared for the disintegration of the Iraqi army or the collapse of most other Iraqi institutions, failed to appreciate the impact of years of sanctions and misgovernment on the Iraqi economy, and were surprised by the emergence of organized resistance. U.S. troops stood by while Iraq's public property was ransacked. U.S. occupation authorities moved to disband the Iraqi military and dismiss thousands of senior Iraqi officials. Washington first assumed that Iraq's reconstruction would be largely self-financing, and then initiated the largest bilateral U.S. aid program in history. Responsibility for managing this rebuilding effort was assigned to the U.S. Department of Defense, an agency without modern experience in postwar reconstruction.

A casual observer might conclude that the United States lacked experience in the field of nation-building. Appearances to the contrary, however, Iraq was not the first but the seventh society in a little more than a decade that the United States had entered to liberate and rebuild. In 1991, the United States liberated Kuwait. In 1992, U.S. troops went into Somalia, in 1994 into Haiti, in 1995 into Bosnia, in 1999 into Kosovo, and in 2001 into Afghanistan. Six of these seven societies were Muslim. Thus, by the time U.S. troops entered Iraq, no country in the world had more modern experience in nation-building than the United States. No Western military had more extensive recent practice operating within Muslim societies.

How could the United States perform this mission so frequently yet so poorly? To answer that question, one must recall the controversy that surrounded the practice of nation-building when that activity emerged in the early 1990s as the leading post–Cold War military endeavor. Between 1945 and 1989, the United States launched a new military intervention about once per decade. With the end of the Cold War, the United States suddenly found itself leading a new multinational military intervention nearly every other year. The pace of UN peacekeeping accelerated even faster, from one new mission every four years during the Cold War to roughly one new mission every six months ever since. For both the United States and the United Nations, these missions also became increasingly lengthy undertakings, the average lasting five to ten years. As a result, by the early years of the current decade, the United States found itself having to maintain three or four such missions simultaneously, while the UN was struggling to oversee as many as two dozen active operations at the same time.

The character of international peacekeeping also changed. During the Cold War, most U.S.-led interventions involved either prolonged hot wars, as in Korea and Vietnam, or relatively brief incursions, as in Panama and Grenada. Most UN peacekeeping missions were quite limited in size and purpose. With the dissolution of the Soviet Union, constraints imposed by superpower competition on both UN- and U.S.-led military operations fell away. As a result, the objectives of these missions gradually became more ambitious. No longer were U.S. and UN forces being used simply to freeze local conflicts in place by separating combatants, monitoring ceasefires and patrolling demilitarized zones. Both U.S.- and UN-led military interventions took on increasingly ambitious goals, seeking to reunite divided countries by disarming and demobilizing former combatants, holding elections, and installing democratic governments. Interpositional peacekeeping had given way to nation-building.

Early setbacks, including the Clinton administration's efforts in Somalia and the UN's mission in the former Yugoslavia, caused many Americans to become skeptical of the utility of such operations. Congress balked at the expense involved in funding a rising number of U.S.- and UN-led operations. Facing mounting domestic resistance, the Clinton administration pulled back from its expansive rhetoric in favor of "assertive multilateralism." Thereafter, that administration justified each successive intervention not as the new norm for multilateral action, but as an exceptional response to unique circumstances.

The Clinton administration consequently made only limited efforts to create an ongoing doctrine for the conduct of such missions, to build a portfolio of best practices, to establish an enduring division of labor among U.S. government agencies, and to build a cadre of experts available to move from one operation to the next. The President did issue a directive (Presidential Decision Directive 56) establishing an interagency process for managing operations of this sort.[1] But neither the Department of State nor the Department of Defense established any standing machinery for carrying them out. Service in such missions was not career-enhancing. No special training was provided. Neither department published guidelines for the conduct of these operations.

The Bush administration entered office even less inclined than its predecessor to make nation-building a national priority. President George W. Bush went on record during the 2000 presidential campaign opposing the use of U.S. armed forces in such missions. His emphasis was on building a leaner, more agile military capable of fighting and winning the nation's wars, by which he meant conventional wars, more quickly and economically. In consequence, the slow improvement that had been registered in U.S. nation-building performance through the 1990s, from the low point of Somalia to the increasing professionalism shown in Haiti, then Bosnia, and finally Kosovo, was reversed first in Afghanistan and then even more markedly in Iraq.

As the situation in Iraq worsened, the administration itself finally recognized and even acknowledged these early failings. The Departments of State and Defense and the White House have all taken initiatives to build U.S. capacity to conduct nation-building operations. The Department of Defense has issued a directive making stability operations, that department's term for nation-building, a core mission for

---

[1] See Presidential Decision Directive 56, "Managing Complex Contingency Operations," Washington, D.C.: White House, May 1997.

the U.S. military, henceforth supposedly to receive the same priority as preparation for major combat. The Department of State has established an office to prepare for and manage the civilian aspects of such operations. Five years after setting aside his predecessor's directive establishing the interagency structure for the conduct of these missions, President Bush issued one of his own.[2]

The U.S. government is not alone in seeking to promote a more professional approach to nation-building. The United Kingdom, Canada, and Germany have recently set up offices similar to that established in the Department of State to manage their countries' participation in postconflict stabilization and reconstruction. World leaders, meeting in late 2005, agreed to establish a comparable capacity at the global level, in the form of the Peacebuilding Commission. That new institution is intended to better integrate the efforts of the UN and its family of agencies with those of international financial institutions, major donor countries, and troop contributors in the conduct of such missions.

Western governments thus increasingly accept that nation-building has become an inescapable responsibility. However, Western publics remain skeptical. The popular conception of such missions continues to be shaped by early failures in Somalia and Yugoslavia. Developments in Iraq have only served to reinforce that skepticism.

This is unfortunate, since the overall nation-building record is encouraging. The United States has taken on the largest and most difficult nation-building challenges. Roughly half its operations have produced both sustained peace and continued democratic governance. The UN success rate, in generally more permissive environments, is actually somewhat better. Bosnia, Kosovo, Cambodia, Namibia, El Salvador, Mozambique, Sierra Leone, and Liberia are all at peace today because U.S., NATO, or UN peacekeepers came in, imposed order, separated combatants, disarmed and demobilized contending factions,

---

[2] See National Security Presidential Directive 44, "Management of Interagency Efforts Concerning Reconstruction and Stabilization," Washington, D.C.: White House, December 7, 2005.

organized elections, installed representative governments, and promoted economic and social reconstruction.[3]

Research from other perspectives substantiates the utility of nation-building. Paul Collier of Oxford University and the World Bank, with coauthor Anke Hoeffler, has found international military interventions to be the most cost-effective means of promoting sustained peace and economic growth in societies emerging from conflict.[4] In the absence of such an intervention, he notes, most of those nations would eventually relapse into civil war. The University of British Columbia, in its *Human Security Report 2005*, finds that, over the past 15 years, the number of wars around the world has declined by half. The number of dead, wounded, and displaced as a result of these conflicts has been reduced by an even greater proportion.[5]

Each nation to be rebuilt may be unique, but the nation-builder has only a limited range of instruments on which to rely. These are largely the same from one operation to the next. This guide is organized around the main components from which nearly all nation-building missions are formed, including soldiers, police officers, civil administrators, and experts in political reform and economic development. It describes how such contingents are best recruited and organized, how much of each will be required, how long they will be needed, and how they have been best employed in prior operations. Each chapter ends with a section on sizing or costing, showing how to estimate how much of that particular capacity is likely to be needed, and how much it may cost. The intent is not to suggest that nation-building can be reduced to a few simple formulas or that success depends on simply marshalling the necessary resources. Matching aspirations to resources is essential to success, however. This guide is intended to assist in that process.

---

[3] Paul Collier and Anke Hoeffler, "The Challenge of Reducing the Global Incidence of Civil War," Copenhagen Consensus Challenge Paper, Oxford: Centre for the Study of African Economies, Oxford University, April 23, 2004; James Dobbins, Seth G. Jones, et al., *The UN's Role in Nation-Building: From the Congo to Iraq*, Santa Monica, Calif.: RAND Corporation, MG-304-RC, 2005.

[4] Collier and Hoeffler (2004).

[5] Human Security Centre, University of British Columbia, *Human Security Report 2005: War and Peace in the 21st Century*, New York: Oxford University Press, 2005.

Preface

This guidebook presents a doctrine for conducting effective nation-building operations. It is designed to be an accessible handbook that describes effective policies for rebuilding a nation after—and, in some cases, during—a conflict. It is based on historical research into the conduct of such operations by the United States, Europe, the United Nations, and other states and organizations over the past 60 years. The doctrine identifies the most important components of nation-building operations; describes how these components are interrelated; establishes the best practices, size, and costs associated with each component; and draws upon national, international, and nongovernmental sources of expertise and capacity in each of these fields. The doctrine is prescriptive enough to guide specific operations, but adaptable enough to cover diverse and varied situations worldwide.

This guidebook is designed to assist the aspiring nation-builder. It is also intended to assist legislators, journalists, and academics in evaluating current or prospective operations of this sort. It brings together the best practices from the 16 case studies presented in the RAND Corporation's history of nation-building, which comprises the 2003 *America's Role in Nation-Building: From Germany to Iraq*, and the 2005 *The UN's Role in Nation-Building: From the Congo to Iraq*; an additional eight case studies, currently under preparation, are included in this guidebook.[1]

---

[1] James Dobbins, John G. McGinn, et al., *America's Role in Nation-Building: From Germany to Iraq*, Santa Monica, Calif.: RAND Corporation, MR-1753-RC, 2003; Dobbins, Jones, et al. (2005).

This research was sponsored by the Smith Richardson Foundation and conducted within the International Security and Defense Policy Center of the RAND National Security Research Division (NSRD). NSRD conducts research and analysis for the Office of the Secretary of Defense, the Joint Staff, the Unified Combatant Commands, the defense agencies, the Department of the Navy, the Marine Corps, the U.S. Coast Guard, the U.S. Intelligence Community, allied foreign governments, and foundations.

For more information on RAND's International Security and Defense Policy Center, contact the Director, James Dobbins. He can be reached by email at James_Dobbins@rand.org; by phone at 703-413-1100, extension 5134; or by mail at the RAND Corporation, 1200 South Hayes Street, Arlington, VA 22202-5050. More information about RAND is available at www.rand.org.

Contents

Figures

Tables

Summary

Nation-building, as it is commonly referred to in the United States, involves the use of armed force as part of a broader effort to promote political and economic reforms with the objective of transforming a society emerging from conflict into one at peace with itself and its neighbors In recent years, the frequency of such operations has greatly increased. During the Cold War, the United States embarked on a new military intervention on the average of about once per decade, while the United Nations launched a new peacekeeping mission on the average of once every four years. Few of these U.S.- or UN-led operations developed into full-blown nation-building missions. Since the end of the Cold War, the pace of U.S. military interventions has risen to about one every two years, while the frequency of new UN peacekeeping missions is up to nearly one every six months. The duration of these missions has also risen, with most now lasting five to 10 years. The effect is thus cumulative: The United States finds itself overseeing three or four such interventions simultaneously, while the United Nations must manage up to two dozen different missions at the same time.

The character of these undertakings has also evolved. During the Cold War, UN troops were usually deployed to separate combatants, to police demilitarized zones, and to monitor ceasefires. In recent years, the objectives for these missions have expanded to include reuniting divided societies, disarming adversaries, demobilizing former combatants, organizing elections, installing representative governments, and promoting democratic reform and economic growth. U.S.-led operations have also become larger, longer, and more ambitious in scope.

Despite some notable setbacks, the overall impact of this heightened international activism has been beneficial. International military interventions have proved to be the best, and indeed the only, reliable means of preventing societies emerging from civil war from slipping back into conflict.[1] Since the end of the Cold War, the number of civil wars around the world has reduced by half. The number of people being killed, maimed, or driven from their homes as a result of armed conflict has also, at least until recently, dropped even further.

Despite this wealth of experience, the U.S.-led occupation of Iraq has been marked by a myriad of unforeseen challenges and hastily improvised responses. Observers might be forgiven for thinking that the United States had never mounted such an operation. Yet, Iraq was the seventh major U.S.-led intervention in little more than a decade, having been preceded by operations in Kuwait, Somalia, Haiti, Bosnia, Kosovo, and Afghanistan. Of those seven societies, six are Muslim, Haiti being the sole exception. At the commencement of the Iraq occupation, therefore, no Western military had more modern experience operating in Muslim societies than the U.S. Army and no country had more experience managing large nation-building enterprises than did the United States.

Unfortunately, neither the U.S. military nor the government as a whole had made a systematic attempt over the preceding decade to reflect on the experience of those earlier operations and apply these lessons in preparing for what was likely to be their biggest and most difficult such challenge to date, in Iraq.

This attitude has changed. The administration has acknowledged early missteps in Iraq and has begun to put in place institutional arrangements designed to ensure a more professional approach to such contingencies in the future. Other governments, notably the UK, Canadian, and German governments, have set up similar structures. The UN has established the Peacebuilding Commission for the same purpose. These various initiatives are premised on the view that nation-building has become an unavoidable burden, that its practitioners need to do a better job of applying the lessons from prior missions

---

[1]   Collier and Hoeffler (2004).

to an evolving doctrine for the conduct of future ones, and must build cadres of experts available to go from one operation to the next.

This guidebook is a contribution to that effort. It is organized around the constituent elements of any nation-building mission. These include the military and police contingents, the civil administrators, and the experts on political reform and economic development. It describes how each of these components should be organized and employed, how much of each is likely to be needed, for how long, and how much this may cost. These lessons are drawn largely from the 16 case studies presented in earlier RAND work on nation-building,[2] and an additional eight that are currently under preparation for a forthcoming volume that builds on the prior research.

Mission Planning

Planning is a routine military activity, but one less developed among civilian authorities. The lead-up to most nation-building missions affords ample time for detailed planning, which should involve both the civilian and military components of the mission. Among the first issues to be addressed are the mission's objective, the intended scale of commitment, and the institutional arrangements for managing the intervention.

Setting the mission objective requires looking beyond its immediate purposes to appreciate the impact that an external military intervention will have on both the society in question and the surrounding region and to plot an outcome commensurate with the likely scale of commitment.

Most interventions are launched for some immediate, usually negative purpose, e.g., to halt aggression, civil war, famine, genocide, or the proliferation of weapons of mass destruction. This purpose may be achieved quite quickly, but the intervening authorities will then be left with the more difficult, time-consuming, and expensive task

---

[2]   Dobbins, McGinn, et al. (2003); Dobbins, Jones, et al. (2005).

of refashioning the society in which they have intervened. The intervention itself will change power relationships within that society and among its neighbors. Those advantaged by the intervention may begin to abuse their positions. Those disadvantaged may move to frustrate the intervening authorities' purposes.

Co-Option Versus Deconstruction

Broadly speaking, there are two alternative approaches to instigating reforms that can turn a violent society into one at peace with itself and its neighbors. One might be labeled *co-option*, under which the intervening authorities try to work within existing institutions and to deal, more or less impartially, with all social forces and power centers, to redirect their ongoing competition for power and wealth from violent to peaceful channels. The alternative approach might be labeled *deconstruction*, under which the intervening authorities first dismantle an existing state apparatus and then build a new one, in the process consciously disempowering some element of society and empowering others.

Most UN peacekeeping operations aspire to the first approach. Most U.S.-led peace enforcement missions adopt something closer to the second. A near-perfect exemplar of the co-option strategy would be the UN mission in El Salvador in the early 1990s. The embodiment of deconstruction would be the U.S.-led occupation of Germany in the late 1940s. Most missions fall somewhere between these poles. Peacekeeping, impartiality, and co-option are clearly the less costly approach. But peacekeeping alone will not halt aggression, civil war, genocide, or nuclear proliferation, nor can the intervening power remain impartial in conflicts to which it has become a party.

Where to position any given intervention along this spectrum from deconstruction to co-option depends not just on the needs of the society being refashioned, but on the resources the intervening authorities have to commit to that task. The more sweeping a mission's objectives, the more resistance it is likely to inspire. Resistance can be overcome, but only through a well-considered application of personnel and money over extended periods of time. In planning any mission, therefore, it is essential to ensure a match between ends and means. Missions that aim to impose peace upon unwilling parties and alter long-standing power relationships are likely to require much greater resources than are operations designed to perpetuate existing truces while drawing contending factions into peaceful but potentially mutually advantageous power-sharing relationships.

Mismatches between inputs, as measured in personnel and money, and desired outcomes, as measured in imposed social transformation, are the most common cause for failure of nation-building efforts. In estimating the resource demands of such operations, this guide provides ranges that encompass both approaches. The intent is to assist those planning missions in increasing the necessary personnel and money if committed to promoting sweeping change or to dial down the objective if resources are likely to be limited.

Institutional Frameworks and Consultative Forums

All nation-building missions involve a mix of national, multinational, and international actors. The nature of that mix is determined largely by the purpose and scope of the operation. Even nationally led interventions, such as the U.S. invasion of Iraq or the Australian intervention in the Solomon Islands, quickly find roles for other national partners, for the UN, and for other organizations. At the other end of the spectrum, no UN-led mission is likely to get very far without the cooperation of regional states and the backing of major powers.

The UN provides the most suitable institutional framework for most nation-building missions, one with a comparatively low cost structure, a comparatively high success rate, and the greatest degree of international legitimacy. The United Nations does not do invasions, however, and seldom deploys more than about 20,000 troops in any given operation. For missions that require forced entry, or that demand more than a reinforced division of troops, a coalition led by a nation or by an alliance such as NATO will probably be necessary, at least for the first phase of the operation. However, although NATO is militarily much more potent than the UN, it possesses none of the other attributes needed for successful nation-building. Thus NATO-led military operations will always require the UN or other national and international actors to provide the various civil components without which no nation-building mission can succeed.

Nation-building always requires the integration of national and international efforts. Larger missions require several layers of consultative machinery to operate effectively. The first, inner circle should include the major powers that care most about the success of the enterprise and are prepared to commit personnel and money to it. The second circle should involve the major financial donors. The third should involve the neighboring powers. Without such coordination, international efforts are likely to be disjointed, with the various organizations concerned competing for turf while shirking the riskier or less rewarding tasks.

When nations disintegrate, the competing contenders for power inevitably turn to external sponsors for support. Faced with the prospect of a neighboring state's failure, the governments of adjoining states seek to develop local clientele and back rival aspirants to power. It is, therefore, practically impossible to put a broken state back together if its neighbors are committed to frustrating that effort. Much as one may regret and deplore such activity, neighbors can be neither safely ignored nor effectively barred from exercising their considerable influence. The adjacent states, after all, suffer the consequences of state failure and civil conflict most directly. They must shelter the refugees and cope with the endemic diseases, increased criminality, spread of terrorism, and disruptions to their commerce generated by such conflicts. They cannot afford to remain uninvolved. It has always proved wise, therefore, to find ways to engage them constructively, no matter how unhelpful their activities may have been in the past. Failure to do so can condemn to failure even the most generously resourced operation.

Setting Priorities

The prime objective of any nation-building operation is to make violent societies peaceful, not to make poor ones prosperous, or authoritarian ones democratic. Economic development and political reform are important instruments for effecting this transformation, but will not themselves ensure it. Rather, such efforts need to be pursued within a broader framework, the aim of which is to redirect the competition for wealth and power, which takes place within any society, from violent into peaceful channels.

The first-order priorities for any nation-building mission are public security and humanitarian assistance. If the most basic human needs for safety, food, and shelter are not being met, any money spent on political or economic development is likely to be wasted. Accordingly, this guidebook is organized around a proposed hierarchy of nation-building tasks, which may be prioritized as follows:

- *Security*: peacekeeping, law enforcement, rule of law, and security-sector reform
- *Humanitarian relief*: return of refugees and response to potential epidemics, hunger, and lack of shelter
- *Governance*: resuming public services and restoring public administration
- *Economic stabilization*: establishing a stable currency and providing a legal and regulatory framework in which local and international commerce can resume
- *Democratization*: building political parties, free press, civil society, and a legal and constitutional framework for elections
- *Development*: fostering economic growth, poverty reduction, and infrastructure improvements.

This is not to suggest that the above activities should necessarily be initiated sequentially. If adequate funding is available, they can and should proceed in tandem. But if higher-order priorities are not adequately resourced, investment in lower-order ones is likely to be wasted.

Seizing the Moment

The weeks immediately following the arrival of foreign troops tend to be a time of maximum possibility. The appearance of an intervening force normally produces a combination of shock and relief in the local population. Resistance is unorganized, spoilers unsure of their future. The situation is highly malleable. But the capacity of intervening authorities to capitalize on these opportunities is usually limited by the absence of many mission components. To take advantage of what has been called the "golden hour" that follows the end of major combat operations, the intervening authorities need to have at their disposal upon arrival a minimum set of assets: enough troops, police, civil administrators, and humanitarian provisions to secure and supply at least the capital. These can be followed quickly by judicial and penal experts with funded plans for the disarmament, demobilization, and reintegration of former combatants and the training or retraining of the police force.

Soldiers

Soldiers are among the first elements of any nation-building mission to arrive. They are often called upon initially to perform many functions that would be better fulfilled by civilian experts, were such experts available in sufficient numbers. Their first priority, however, should be to establish a modicum of security in what may be a chaotic situation. Success in this task will be key to obtaining the population's support for the operation and introducing the civilian components of the mission in adequate numbers. Until individuals feel safer with the external military presence, they will not collaborate in reporting on criminals, terrorists, and other spoilers. Unless goods, services, and people can again circulate normally, political and economic reforms cannot begin to take hold. Intervening forces will normally require help from the local police and at least the passive cooperation of the local military in establishing a secure environment. Even when available, however, indigenous security services will usually prove incompetent, corrupt, or abusive, requiring close oversight, mentoring, and institutional change.

Once a minimal level of security has been established, the disarmament, demobilization, and reintegration of former combatants should be the next priority. Agreement among the contending parties to take part in such a process is often a prerequisite for deployment of an international force. In heavily armed societies with a long tradition of gun ownership, depriving individuals of their small arms may prove impractical. At a minimum, heavy arms should be gathered, stored, or destroyed, and the display of small arms by any except state security forces should be banned. Armed units should be broken up, and individuals should be offered alternative livelihoods. It is important that the mission arrive with a plan and adequate funding to perform these tasks.

In societies with wide scale unemployment, it will not be possible to find long-term positions for all former combatants. At a minimum, the reintegration program should supervise and support these individuals for a period long enough to allow units to be broken up and the ties among their members to be loosened.

The military component should establish extensive links with the civilian population. One avenue is through active intelligence collection, surveillance, and reconnaissance. The second is a program of civic action, through which military units support humanitarian and reconstruction assistance. Such tasks fall primarily to the civilian agencies, but the military can often supplement those efforts in useful and visible ways. This must be pursued with some sensitivity, recognizing that humanitarian organizations attach great importance to maintaining their impartiality in conflict environments and will resist close association with an intervening military force, even one operating on behalf of the UN.

While most postconflict societies will have more soldiers than they need, they will probably have fewer police officers than required. Even as armies need to be scaled back and reformed, police forces need to bolstered and also reformed. The military contingent of the mission is often involved in the former process and sometimes in the latter, although police training functions are better assigned to civilian police when available.

Forced entries are often the prelude to demanding peace enforcement operations. The entries themselves may not prove particularly difficult—indeed, in recent decades these have invariably been achieved rapidly and with minimal loss to the entering force. By contrast, the postcombat stabilization and reconstruction phase has been much more time-consuming and costly.

Stabilizing an internally divided society without significant indigenous capacity for security can require an external military force of 10 to 20 soldiers per 1,000 inhabitants. In circumstances in which the parties to the conflict have jointly sought external intervention and are prepared to collaborate with it, that requirement can be potentially reduced to one soldier or fewer per 1,000 inhabitants. Where only this lower force ratio is likely to be achieved, deployment should normally be conditioned upon prior agreement among the contending parties to disarm and disengage.

The cost for fielding a U.S. or NATO force is about $200,000 per soldier per year. The cost of fielding the typical UN peacekeeping force is about $45,000 per soldier per year. High-end peace enforcement operations require a military staffing level, on average, 10 times higher per inhabitant than do standard peacekeeping missions. Clearly, then, peace enforcement is appropriately a last rather than first resort, to be employed only if the stakes are great and the intervening powers highly committed.

Police

Public security is the first responsibility of intervening authorities. That security is sometimes imperiled by contending armies and is always threatened by criminals, gangs, and violence-prone political groups. International military forces are best suited for dealing with the first sort of threat, police with the rest.

Military police are better than standard infantry for some public security functions—such as crowd control—but less well suited than civilian police for criminal investigations or community policing. On the other hand, most international civilian police forces are not well equipped to deal with organized crime or large-scale violence. In many ways, the ideal police forces for nation-building missions are gendarmerie-type units that combine military discipline with a high level of investigative, forensic, and intelligence collection skills. Unfortunately, only a few countries maintain such forces and, consequently, they are always in short supply.

UN peacekeeping forces typically deploy about one police officer for every 10 soldiers. These international police forces monitor, mentor, and train local police forces. Where the local police force has disintegrated entirely, international police may need to undertake law enforcement functions themselves. This requires a much larger contingent of international police, something feasible only for very well-resourced operations in smaller countries.

Local police will need to be quickly vetted and closely supervised. In the medium term, they will need to be thoroughly reformed or replaced entirely. In the longer term, the new or retrained police will need to be mentored, supported, and held accountable. The intervening authorities should arrive with plans, funding, and personnel to begin performing at least the first two functions immediately.

Like the UN, the European Union has developed the capacity to deploy significant numbers of international police officers. The UN currently deploys over 7,000 police officers to postconflict areas; the EU has set a goal of being able to deploy up to 5,000. The United States currently deploys some 300 international police officers, mostly in Kosovo. It continues to rely on private contractors for this purpose. This arrangement is clearly inferior to a system wherein the deployed police would be U.S. government employees, rather than contractors, with the greater degree of reciprocal loyalty, discipline, and commitment that relationship implies. In both Afghanistan and Iraq, the United States has failed to deploy any civilian police whatsoever.[3]

---

[3]   International police are uniformed police officers who monitor local police or who themselves enforce the law. Civilian instructors in police training establishments, who may be former police officers, are not normally included in this category.

Most postconflict societies require at least two of their own police officers for every 1,000 inhabitants. The intervening authorities should anticipate the need to rebuild, reequip, and, for the first several years at least, pay a police force of this magnitude. The annual cost per local police officer will be approximately three times that country's per capita GDP. International police, by contrast, cost about $150,000 per person per year. Where the responsibilities of international police are limited to oversight, mentoring, and training of local police, one for every 10,000 inhabitants may be adequate. Where they assume a direct law enforcement role, one for every 1,000 inhabitants may be needed.

Rule of Law

In most nation-building operations, efforts to rebuild the judiciary and corrections systems have taken second place to police reform. This is unfortunate and counterproductive. Police who lack prisons in which to put criminals and judges before whom to bring them will inevitably be left with the invidious choice of either punishing miscreants themselves or letting them go. Either alternative will corrupt and demoralize the best-trained force.

A first-order issue to be addressed in most nation-building missions is what law to enforce. The usual answer is to take the country's most recently promulgated criminal code, purge it of obviously abusive statutes, and employ it as the law of the land. In some cases, the intervening authorities may have to go further into the past to find a criminal code acceptable to the population. Occasionally, it may have to promulgate laws of its own. These are decisions that should be made as part of the preparation for the mission so newly arriving troops and police have a clear idea of what rules are to be enforced.

In societies emerging from prolonged civil war, the legal system will likely have ceased to function. There will be an absence of judges, and those who are available may be unqualified. Courts and prisons may have been destroyed, and those that survive may have been stripped of essentials. As with the police, the short-term objective will be to vet the judiciary and corrections staff and oversee their activities, in the medium term to reform and rebuild both these institutions, and, in the long term, to foster the development of a rule-of-law culture. These activities should proceed in parallel with police reform.

Establishing the balance between retribution and reconciliation in societies emerging from conflict or tyranny presents a particular challenge. Whom to punish and whom to forgive, whom to exclude from the new dispensation and whom to co-opt into it are choices that cannot be entirely avoided.

War crime tribunals provide a judicial vehicle for holding accountable those most responsible for past atrocities. The local society will seldom be capable of mounting a credible legal process. International tribunals, on the other hand, are hugely expensive and may lack legitimacy in the eyes of the affected populations. Mixed tribunals, in which international and local judges sit together, can help to address some of these difficulties.

Lustration represents an administrative approach to the same problem. Here the intention is to assess group, rather than personal, responsibility. The objective is not so much to punish as to exclude the affected group from future influence, usually by barring them from public employment, and sometimes stripping them of other civil rights. Denazification in post–World War II Germany, demilitarization in Japan, and debaathification in Iraq are examples of this process.

Truth commissions lie near the opposite end of the retribution/reconciliation spectrum. These are nonjudicial inquiries into past abuses with a view to assessing blame but not levying penalties. In going this route, society is saying, "We are prepared to forgive, but not to forget."

It is clearly easier to exact retribution in circumstances in which the conflict has produced clear winners and losers, particularly if the losers have lost so badly as to preclude any further resistance. This is seldom the case. In other circumstances, any effort to impose accountability for crimes committed in the course of conflict, whether through judicial or administrative processes, may occasion more resistance than the intervening authorities are capable of suppressing.

War crime tribunals are sometimes employed by the international community as an alternative to intervention, rather than as an adjunct. In such instances, tribunals serve principally as a means of assuaging the international community's conscience without requiring it to commit the personnel and money needed to actually stop the crimes it abhors and punish the perpetrators. Proponents argue that the simple threat of judicial action at some indefinite point in the future will curb abusive behavior. There is scant empirical support for this thesis.

In the context of nation-building, war crime tribunals and lustration should be employed only in those rare situations in which the intervening authorities are equipped to enforce the outcome and ready to deal effectively with the resultant resistance. Applied in any other circumstances, the effect is likely to be an increased polarization of the society in question and an eventual resumption of violence.

Humanitarian Relief

Humanitarian operations often precede nation-building missions, initiated in response to the conflict and sustained in many cases throughout its course. Thus, while the arrival of peacekeepers may signal the opening of an operation for most of its constituent elements, it can signal the beginning of the end for those engaged in lifesaving humanitarian relief efforts, as displaced persons are helped to return to their homes, as refugee camps are closed, and as public services are restored.

Most major humanitarian relief agencies are professionally staffed, highly experienced, and comparatively well resourced. Funding for nation-building is almost always in short supply, but humanitarian relief is the aspect donors are the most inclined to fund. As a result, relief efforts are usually among the least problematic of any nation-building mission. We have found no mission whose overall success was compromised by inadequacies in this aspect of its operations. On the other hand, there are many examples of situations in which the intervening authorities' failure to establish a modicum of public security has made it impossible for humanitarian agencies to complete their tasks or even to sustain lifesaving assistance to threatened populations.

In cases in which the intervening authorities quickly establish a reasonably secure environment, relief operations usually proceed smoothly. Refugees return, sometimes with surprising rapidity. Public services are gradually restored, including public health services. The economy revives. Within a year or two, most humanitarian agencies can pack up and move on to another emergency or shift their emphasis from lifesaving to developmental activities.

Coordination between military forces and humanitarian organizations is never easy. The number of such organizations has grown vastly in recent years; not all are of the highest distinction. Humanitarian organizations seek to remain impartial, even when the United Nations is positioned on one side and local outlaws on the other. This may seem anomalous, as the same donor governments are often funding the humanitarian efforts and staffing the intervening military force. Humanitarian organizations feel strongly, however, that their ability to gain access to exposed populations depends on maintaining strict impartiality. Accordingly, representatives of such organizations carefully limit their interactions with international peacekeepers, even when they look to these forces for security.

Coordination becomes particularly difficult when the intervening authorities have failed to establish a secure environment. Then, the usual division of labor between international military forces and humanitarian organizations is difficult to maintain. Humanitarian organizations may find themselves unable to provide relief in very dangerous areas. International military units may feel compelled to step into this void and begin delivering relief supplies, in the process blurring the distinction between combatant and humanitarian worker. While such arrangements are better than a complete absence of humanitarian relief, it is generally best if the military and the humanitarian organizations each concentrate on their respective primary tasks: maintaining security or delivering assistance.

Governance

A society emerging from conflict may be able to wait for democracy, but it needs a government immediately if there is to be any law enforcement, education, or public health care. National governments are usually responsible for regulating and, in some circumstances, providing electricity and telecommunications. In most instances, municipal governments provide water and sanitation.

Although intervening authorities may sometimes serve initially as the government, they will never be in a position to deliver these services independently. They must rely on host country nationals and local institutions to provide public services. The intervening authorities may provide funding, guidance, and oversight, but the teachers, health workers, and most of the police force must be drawn from the host country.

The intervening authorities select people and organizations to deliver these services. These individuals and organizations are provided with funds and influence. The intervening authorities must be attentive from the start to ensure that such choices do not discriminate unhelpfully against groups, especially those that were party to the conflict. The intervening authorities need to choose partners carefully with a view to creating a government and distribution of power that will be sustainable when the authorities leave.

Many services can best be provided at the local level. Rebuilding government from the bottom up allows new leadership to emerge, including individuals unassociated with the recent conflict. On the other hand, empowering local officials before the national government has been reconstituted can feed sectarian conflict in circumstances in which the relationship between the center and the periphery is unsettled.

The intervening authorities will have to meet much, and perhaps all, of the initial costs of restoring basic government services. The requirement for financing public health, education, and general government administration can be expected to run about 10 percent of the country's preconflict GDP.

Economic Stabilization

The resumption of commerce requires the availability of a reasonably stable medium of exchange. Sustained growth is virtually impossible in periods of very high inflation. Although donors may finance the resumption of government services initially, it is important to quickly reconstruct the host state's capability to allocate that funding and oversee its expenditure and to expand its capacity to collect its own sources of revenue. The more money that is pumped into government, the greater the opportunities for corruption, control of which requires institutions for auditing and accountability and the creation of a professional civil service.

To meet these needs, early attention should be given to creating or strengthening a central bank, ministry of finance, and civil service commission. Occasionally, the decision is made to adopt a foreign currency as the medium of exchange. More often, there is a preference to keep a national currency to preserve the option of adjusting the exchange rate to better manage economic activity. Among the most difficult tasks facing the central bank is ensuring that commercial banks become and remain solvent.

Donor budget support is required to keep government expenditures and revenue in balance, thereby avoiding the need to print more money. Donor conferences are the usual vehicle for ensuring an adequate flow of funding. It is usually best to hold at least two such meetings, the first for immediate humanitarian, security, and economic stabilization needs, and the second, a year or two later, to focus upon longer-term development. The World Bank and the United Nations Development Programme should be asked to prepare a needs assessment in preparation for these conferences. The International Monetary Fund should take the lead in establishing or reforming the central bank and providing the wherewithal to manage the currency.

Democratization

The prime objective of a nation-building intervention is to leave behind a society at peace with itself and its neighbors. Democratization alone will not ensure this outcome. On the contrary, elections may be polarizing events in already divided societies. In the context of nation-building, the process of democratization should be seen as a practical means of redirecting the ongoing competition for wealth and power within the society from violent into peaceful channels, not as an abstract exercise in social justice.

Representative institutions based on universal suffrage usually offer the only viable basis for reconstituting state authority in a manner acceptable to most of the population. In considering constitutional design, a first step is to analyze the sources of violent conflict in the society. An exceptionally strong and committed intervening authority may be able to dispossess one group and empower another in an enduring fashion. In most circumstances, however, success in nation-building will depend more on co-option than on the exclusion of potential spoilers. In societies divided by sectarian strife, it may be necessary to craft power-sharing arrangements that limit the authority of the majority and provide guarantees to minority parties beyond those found in more developed democracies.

Democracies come in many shapes and sizes. Left to their own devices, intervening powers will tend toward replicating their own institutions, while local populations will be inclined to opt for a system with which they are familiar, even if that system has served them poorly in the past. In most cases, it will be better to adapt the familiar to new circumstances, rather than import wholly new arrangements unfamiliar to host country citizens.

Ideally, national elections should be preceded by the disarmament, demobilization, and reintegration of former combatants; the growth of civil society; the establishment of independent media; the development of political parties; and the holding of local elections. This sequence may not always be fully achievable. In some instances, the intervening authorities may be too weak to resist the call from dominant elements in the society for early elections, or to administer the society without the support of a government legitimized through the electoral process.

The UN is the best source of expertise on the development of transitional and permanent political systems. The Organization for Security and Co-operation in Europe (OSCE) has developed considerable expertise in the promotion of civil society, the establishment of independent media, and the development of political parties, though its activities thus far have been limited to Eurasia. Several nations, including the United States and Germany, maintain publicly financed party-based organizations that specialize in helping foster the development of political parties in emerging democracies. IFES (formerly the International Foundation for Election Systems) has organized elections in dozens of countries around the world under the most challenging of conditions.

Infrastructure and Development

Postconflict societies are attractive candidates for development assistance. Dollar for dollar, aid to nations emerging from war will result in much higher levels of growth than will the same amount provided to more settled societies. Postconflict societies also can use more assistance, as measured as a share of GDP, than more settled societies can. Whereas most developing societies cannot usefully absorb assistance representing more than about 20 percent of their annual GDPs, postconflict nations can make good use of aid representing up to 40 percent of their GDPs, and, in the first year following conflict, up to 70 percent.

The quality of policies adopted by the intervening authorities and the host government will be as important as the volume of assistance in determining the latter's utility. Controlling inflation, financing the government's budget (in the early years via large-transfer payments from international donors), creating regulatory and tax systems conducive to growth, reducing or eliminating subsidies, attracting investment, and operating utilities and state-owned enterprises on a sound, market-oriented basis will be essential to fostering sustained growth.

Reforms of this nature will necessarily occasion resistance. The process needs to be managed in ways that draw the society's major contending factions into a process of peaceful competition and away from a return to violent conflict.

The term *reconstruction*, when used to describe the reform of post-conflict societies, conveys the sense that physical rebuilding of homes, factories, roads, and power plants destroyed in the war is the prime need. This is misleading. Even more than infrastructure, nations emerging from conflict need better institutions. In most cases, these institutions need to be refashioned, not just rebuilt, since it is the old institutions that will have failed in the first place. This is as true in the economic sphere as in the political.

As regards physical infrastructure, the intervening authorities should give priority to fixing those related to security, health care, education, power, water, and sanitation in an effort to raise these services to something approaching prewar levels. The focus should be on emergency repair, not new investment. The improvement, as opposed to the repair, of infrastructure should be funded through project financing by international financial institutions like the World Bank or other lenders rather than through bilateral grant assistance. Project financing imposes disciplines that are too frequently absent from schemes funded with grant assistance, requiring, as the former does, all the parties to address issues of size, cost, and repayment in light of demand, anticipated revenues, and rate setting.

Security is an essential precondition for productive investment. Money spent on infrastructure and development will be largely wasted if people, goods, and services are subject to high levels of abduction, theft, or attack.

Conclusion

The ultimate objective of any nation-building mission is to leave behind a society likely to remain at peace with itself and its neighbors once external security forces are removed and full sovereignty is restored. Some level of democratization and economic development is likely to be essential to this desired result. Neither endeavor, however, can ensure peace, and either, if pushed injudiciously, can exacerbate rather than ameliorate the tendency toward renewed violence so prevalent in postconflict societies. If peace is to be created, security is key. Only when a modicum of security has been restored do prospects for democracy and sustained economic growth brighten.

Most historical nation-building operations have fallen into one of two categories. Peacekeeping missions have been mounted on the basis of prior agreement among the warring parties. Peace enforcement operations have been launched despite the opposition of one or more indigenous factions. Interventions of the first type have typically been led by the UN; those of the second by a major global or regional power. Peace enforcement operations typically require 10 times more personnel and money than do peacekeeping operations.

The expense of nation-building is shared among troop contributors, aid donors, and the international community as a whole according to various burden-sharing formulas. The costs of UN-led peacekeeping operations are spread most widely. Those for peace enforcement missions fall more heavily on the lead nation and its principal allies. Peace enforcement is thus not only much more expensive than peacekeeping; it is particularly so for the lead nation.

As a practical matter, therefore, full-scale peace enforcement actions are feasible only when the intervening authorities care a great deal about the outcome, and even then, only in relatively small societies. Thus, the effort needed to stabilize Bosnia and Kosovo has proved difficult to replicate in Afghanistan or Iraq, nations that are eight to 12 times more populous. It would be even more difficult to mount a peace enforcement mission in Iran, which is three times more populous than Iraq, and nearly impossible to do so in Pakistan, which is three times again more populous than Iran. Considerations of scale therefore suggest that the transformational objectives of intervention in larger societies need to be sharply restrained on account of the much more modest resources, relative to the population, likely to be available for their achievement.

Even the lighter, more consensual approach to nation-building epitomized by UN peacekeeping represents an expensive enterprise, although not more expensive than allowing a conflict, once halted, to be renewed. Put differently, conflicts impose greater costs on the international community than the expense necessary to ensure that the cycle of violence, once halted for whatever reason, is not renewed.[4]

Just as no war plan survives contact with the enemy, no nation-building plan can survive contact with the nation being built. The true test of any such planning process, therefore, is not its capacity to foresee every twist and turn of the operation, but rather its success in matching ends to means.

---

[4]   Collier and Hoeffler (2004, p. 3); Dobbins, Jones, et al. (2005, p. 247).

Acknowledgments

We are grateful to Marin Strmecki for identifying the need for this guidebook, Nadia Schadlow for helping to make it happen, and the Smith Richardson Foundation for supporting this work throughout its development. We thank the United States Institute of Peace for allowing Beth Cole DeGrasse to participate in the project, and for the research support provided by Yll Bajraktari and Emily Hsu. Nora Bensahel, Larry Diamond, Nancy Lindborg, William L. Nash, Gary Milante, Robert M. Perito, and Karin von Hippel read all or portions of the manuscript and provided helpful comments. We thank the following individuals at the United Nations for their assistance: David Harland, Paula Souverijn-Eisenberg, Antero Lopes, Chika Onaka, and Tim Irwin. Several RAND colleagues also offered helpful insights, including Terrence K. Kelly, Andrew Rathmell, and Olga Oliker. Nathan Chandler and Anga Timilsina provided key research support and collected data for the charts and graphs, and Joy Merck provided valuable administrative support.

Abbreviations

BBC	British Broadcasting Corporation
DDR	disarmament, demobilization, and reintegration
DFID	UK Department for International Development
GDP	gross domestic product
GPS	global positioning system
HIV/AIDS	human immunodeficiency virus/acquired immunodeficiency syndrome
HUMINT	human intelligence
IFES	formerly the International Foundation for Election Systems
IMF	International Monetary Fund
INTERFET	International Force East Timor
KFOR	Kosovo Force
MP	military police officer
NATO	North Atlantic Treaty Organization
NGO	nongovernmental organization
OCHA	United Nations Office for Coordination of Humanitarian Affairs

OSCE	Organization for Security and Co-operation in Europe
SWAT	special weapons and tactics
UN	United Nations
UNDP	United Nations Development Programme
UNESCO	United Nations Educational, Scientific and Cultural Organization
UNHCR	United Nations High Commissioner for Refugees
UNICEF	United Nations Children's Fund
UNMIK	United Nations Interim Administration Mission in Kosovo
UNSOM	United Nations Operation in Somalia
UNTAET	United Nations Transitional Administration in East Timor
USAID	U.S. Agency for International Development
VAT	value-added tax
VIP	very important person
WMD	weapons of mass destruction

CHAPTER ONE

Preparing for Nation-Building

It is rare for nation-building missions to be launched on short notice, in response to unforeseen developments, and thus in circumstances that preclude methodical planning. The 1961 UN intervention in the Congo and the 2001 U.S. invasion of Afghanistan were two such cases. More often, the probability of an operation can be foreseen months in advance. The U.S.-led interventions in Haiti, Bosnia, Kosovo, and Iraq fall into this category, as do most UN missions. In such circumstances, advance planning can greatly improve the prospects of success at acceptable cost. Preparations are most useful when they extend beyond the military sphere to encompass the many civilian components essential to the success of any mission. This presents a challenge, as civilian agencies involved are both numerous and diverse and are also less accustomed to the discipline of planning.

Planning for nation-building missions tends to bring together three types of people. First are the regional experts, those who understand why the society in question is in conflict. These experts often find it difficult to envisage substantial change and are consequently pessimistic about the degree of change that may be possible. The second category is made up of experienced nation-builders. These individuals may know little of the society in question but do understand the process by which transformation can be attempted. They are likely to advise that change for the better is possible, but time-consuming and expensive to effectuate. The last group is composed of those who know little of the society in question or of the nation-building process. People in this third category are most prone to believing that change can be achieved quickly and easily.

Members of this last category are also normally in charge. A decision to launch any military intervention is a matter of great consequence, after all, to be made not by military or civilian experts but by political leaders. Such leaders cannot be expected to possess expertise about the region or nation-building. Nor can the general public, which these leaders represent and to which they are accountable, be expected to have this expertise. Sound decisionmaking therefore requires that political leaders consult both categories of experts: those who understand why the nation in question has failed and those who understand how to rebuild it. This chapter discusses the issues they should consider during the consultative process.

Setting the Objective

Military interventions are usually launched with proximate, basically negative objectives. Typically, such operations are intended to stop undesirable events, such as attacks on civilians, genocide, famine, civil war, or the proliferation of weapons of mass destruction (WMD). Once these proximate objectives are achieved, the intervening authorities will face a host of new, sometimes unforeseen, though seldom entirely unforeseeable, challenges. The United States invaded Germany and Japan to defend itself against attack. NATO intervened in Kosovo to protect the Albanian majority from Serb oppression. The United States invaded Iraq to dismantle its WMD programs. Presidents Franklin D. Roosevelt and Harry S. Truman did not intend to commit the United States to a long-term engagement in Europe and Asia, structured around alliances with revitalized German and Japanese nations. NATO did not intend to spend the next decade in Kosovo protecting the Serb minority from Albanian retribution. The Bush administration did not anticipate the disintegration of Saddam Hussein's army, the rise of an insurgency, or the eventual need to referee a widening civil war.

All these twists of fate might have been predicted, but none were, at least not by those planning the respective interventions. Such predictions would have required an ability to look beyond the proximate objectives of each operation. It would have required recognition that the very act of intervention alters, often radically, the power balance and social dynamic in the subject nation and its region. By virtue of an intervention, losers suddenly become winners, and winners become losers. Those who find themselves advantaged by the intervention may exercise their new power without restraint, profoundly embarrassing their rescuers. Those who find themselves disadvantaged are prone to become spoilers, intent on frustrating the intervening authorities' purposes.

Interventions have external reverberations as well, creating new power relationships among neighboring states, motivating some to support spoilers and oppose the efforts of the intervening authorities. As the United States committed itself to German reconstruction, the Soviet Union moved to block or diminish the effectiveness of U.S. policy. NATO's intervention in Kosovo emboldened the Albanian minority in Macedonia to demand a greater share of power in that state. U.S. interventions in Afghanistan and Iraq greatly enhanced Iran's regional influence. These were probably predictable consequences, although they were not widely predicted, at least by those planning the interventions. As the United States and the rest of the international community gain more experience with such interventions, the capacity to look several moves ahead and to understand how interventions will reshape the domestic and external environment of the nations being rebuilt needs to improve.

Sizing the Commitment

Most nation-building missions aim to halt a conflict, if one is still under way, and to forestall a resumption of fighting while promoting the emergence of an indigenous government ultimately capable of resuming full responsibility for the security and well-being of its population. Democratic elections almost always play a role in establishing or consolidating such a government. Unless political and economic reforms have preceded elections, however, balloting may simply reflect, and even harden, existing social divisions. On the other hand, the more ambitious the reform agenda of the intervening power, the more resistance is likely to be engendered. Getting this balance right is the essence of a well-planned operation.

When nation-building missions founder, the problem can usually be traced to a mismatch between aspirations and commitment. Somalia is a good case in point. In 1992, the United States deployed a powerful force of over 20,000 U.S. soldiers and marines with the exclusive purpose of protecting the flow of humanitarian relief. This mission was accomplished without engendering significant resistance. In 1993, Washington reduced its military presence in Somalia by 90 percent, from over 20,000 to some 2,000 troops, but assigned this residual force the objective of supporting a less capable UN peacekeeping force in an effort to promote grassroots democracy, thereby challenging every warlord in the country. This mismatch between rising mission requirements and declining military capabilities produced early and dramatic results. U.S. and UN forces were confronted, bloodied, and ultimately withdrawn, their mission unaccomplished.

As noted, the more sweeping an intervening authority's objectives, the more resistance its efforts are likely to inspire. Resistance can be overcome, but only through the application of personnel and money employed wisely over extended periods of time. In planning any mission, therefore, it is essential to ensure a match between ends and means. Missions that try to impose peace on unwilling parties or aim to alter long-standing power relationships are likely to require much greater resources than are operations that seek to perpetuate existing truces while co-opting contending factions into peaceful but potentially mutually advantageous relationships. Peace enforcement missions of the first type typically require 10 times more personnel and money than those at the peacekeeping end of the scale.

Most modern U.S.-led nation-building missions have been of the more demanding variety. Most UN-led missions have been of the less demanding peacekeeping variety. Of course, those planning a new mission are unlikely to have complete freedom to choose the sort of operation to mount. Peacekeeping alone will not halt genocide, turn back aggression, or prevent the proliferation of WMD. Nevertheless, the distinction between peacekeeping and peace enforcement represents a spectrum, not a binary opposition. Even in circumstances in which a forced entry may be a necessary prelude to the nation-building mission, the intervening authorities are likely to have some latitude to determine how extensively to reorder the targeted society. That decision will in turn help determine how large a pool of spoilers the intervention will create. That calculation should in turn influence how large a commitment of personnel and money will be needed to deter or suppress the resultant resistance.

It is not always possible to scale commitments to match aspirations. If resources are limited, as they normally are, ambitions may have to be scaled down accordingly. Even where ambitious attempts at social engineering are desired, costlier and less costly alternatives may be available. Here a comparison of U.S. approaches to post World War II Germany and Japan is instructive. In Germany, the state was dismantled and subsequently refashioned from the bottom up. Every single institution of government was abolished and later recreated. In Japan, by contrast, nearly all the state institutions were preserved and subsequently reformed from within. The former approach resulted in more thoroughgoing social transformation (Germany is reconciled with its neighbors and its history; Japan is not), but also required much more personnel, money, and time to achieve.

A similar contrast between the rival strategies of co-option and deconstruction can be observed in U.S. efforts in Afghanistan and Iraq. The United States did not invade Afghanistan as part of a grander scheme to promote democracy throughout Central Asia. U.S. efforts were focused on preventing Afghanistan from again becoming a launching pad for global terrorism. Accordingly, U.S. authorities chose to work with neighboring governments and local Afghan warlords to oust the Taliban, chase down al Qaeda, and install a broadly based successor regime in Kabul. Only gradually, and somewhat reluctantly, did Washington assume wider responsibilities for peace enforcement and democracy-building in Afghanistan, and then only in response to strong urgings from within and without Afghanistan.

By contrast, U.S. objectives in Iraq were much more ambitious from the beginning. That country was intended to become a model for the region. The invasion is to this day presented by Washington as a first step in the democratic transformation of the greater Middle East. Rather than working with neighboring governments and local power brokers to form a successor government to Saddam's regime, Washington chose to mount a formal occupation with the intention of introducing major political and economic reforms before holding elections and restoring Iraqi sovereignty. However, U.S. planning in Iraq assumed that the occupying force that would oversee this immense experiment in social engineering could be smaller than the initial invasion force designed to topple Saddam and seize the country.

In the end, Washington miscalculated the resources needed for both these nation-building missions. This miscalculation has proved particularly costly in Iraq, where the much more ambitious effort at reform occasioned much greater resistance. Afghanistan, although by no means a model, does demonstrate that lower aspirations can allow for reduced commitments.

Choosing an Institutional Framework

Modern nation-building requires a mix of military and civilian capacity and national, multinational, and international participation. It therefore necessitates trade-offs between unity of command and broad burden-sharing. Both are desirable, but each can be achieved only at some expense to the other. For dangerous, highly demanding operations in which forced entry and conventional combat are likely to be necessary, the desire for unity of command normally prevails and nationally led coalitions of the willing are the preferred instrument. For sustained, long-term commitments in reasonably secure environments, considerations of burden-sharing are more likely to predominate, leading to a more prominent role for international institutions. This mix can shift over time. A number of missions have begun with a nationally led entry phase, followed by an internationally led consolidation and transformation phase.

Transition from a nationally led entry force to an internationally led peacekeeping mission can secure greater legitimacy and local acceptance for the intervention, as well as broader burden-sharing. Sometimes these sequential handoffs result in several external forces operating in the same area with different missions and different rules of engagement. This occurred in Somalia, Sierra Leone, and Afghanistan. This is an unsound practice, engendering duplication and risking confusion, miscommunication, and, in some instances, unnecessary casualties. A better model is that followed by the United States in Haiti in 1994 and by Australia in East Timor in 1999, in which the U.S.- and Australian-led entry forces, respectively, were drawn down and incorporated into the subsequent UN-led peacekeeping force.

Many international institutions have the capacity to contribute to nation-building operations, but only a few are structured to deploy military forces. These include the United Nations, NATO, the European Union, and the African Union. The UN has the widest experience. NATO has the most powerful forces. The EU has the widest panoply of civil capabilities. The African Union possesses none of these advantages.

Among international organizations, the United Nations has the most widely accepted legitimacy and the greatest formal authority. Its actions, by definition, enjoy international sanction. Alone among organizations, it can compel its member governments to fund operations, even requiring contributions from those opposed to the intervention in question. The United Nations has the most straightforward decisionmaking apparatus, and the most unified command-and-control arrangements. The UN Security Council is smaller than its NATO, EU, or African Union equivalents. It takes all decisions by qualified majority; only five of its members have the capacity to block decisions unilaterally. Once the Security Council determines the purpose of a mission and decides to launch it, further operational decisions are left largely to the Secretary-General and his staff, at least until the next Security Council review, generally six months thereafter. In UN operations, the civilian and military chains of command are unified and integrated, with unequivocal civilian primacy and a clear line of authority from the UN Secretary-General through the local civilian representative to the local force commander.

The UN is a comparatively efficient and cost-effective force provider. In its specialized agencies, it possesses a broad panoply of civil as well as military capabilities needed for nation-building. All UN-led operations (up to two dozen are routinely under way at any one time) are planned, controlled, and sustained by a few hundred military and civilian staffers at UN headquarters in New York. Most UN troops come from developing countries whose costs per deployed soldier are a small fraction of those of any Western army. In 2006, the United Nation deployed over 70,000 soldiers and police officers in 19 countries at a cost of some $5 billion per year. This made the UN the second largest provider of expeditionary forces in the world, after the United States but ahead of NATO, the EU, or the African Union. In one year, the cost to the UN of these 19 missions was approximately equivalent to what the United States spent in one month in Iraq.

Needless to say, the UN also has its limitations. While the UN Security Council is more compact than its NATO and EU counterparts, it is regionally and ideologically more diverse, and therefore subject to blocking in the face of strong East-West or North-South differences, as proved to be the case with Kosovo in 1999. On the other hand, the Kosovo operation was the sole occasion, since 1989, when either NATO or the EU agreed on an intervention but the UN Security Council did not. Since 1989, the UN Security Council has agreed to launch more than 40 operations, while the NATO Council has agreed to three and the Council of the European Union to two. In 2002, the United States and the United Kingdom calculated that they actually had a better hope of securing UN support for their invasion of Iraq than they did of gaining endorsement from either NATO or the European Union.

The broad latitude enjoyed by the UN Secretary-General and his local representatives in the operational control of blue-helmeted operations facilitates unity of command, but also serves to limit the willingness of some nations to contribute. NATO and EU procedures offer troop-contributing members much greater day-to-day influence over the use of their contingents than do those of the UN. Western governments accordingly favor these institutions for peace enforcement missions where the level of risk to their units is high.

· Similarly, the austere nature of UN headquarters staffing for peacekeeping operations keeps costs down but limits the organization's capacity to plan and support large or highly complex missions. As a practical matter, the United Nations' capacity to mount and sustain expeditionary forces tops out at about 20,000 soldiers, or a reinforced division. These forces always require permissive entry. The United Nations does not do invasions, although it has frequently authorized others to conduct them.

NATO, by contrast, is capable of deploying powerful forces in large numbers and of using them to force entry where necessary. But NATO has no capacity to implement civilian operations; it depends on the United Nations and other institutions or nations to perform all the nonmilitary functions essential to the success of any nation-building operation. NATO decisions are by consensus; consequently, all members have a veto. Whereas the UN Security Council normally makes one decision with respect to any particular operation every six months and leaves the Secretary-General relatively unconstrained to carry out that mandate during the intervals, the NATO Council's oversight is more continuous, its decisionmaking more incremental. Member governments consequently have a greater voice in operational matters, and the NATO civilian and military staffs have correspondingly less. This level of control makes governments more ready to commit troops to NATO for high-risk operations than to the United Nations. It also ensures that the resultant forces are often employed conservatively. National caveats limiting the types of missions to which any one member's troops may be assigned are a fact of life in all coalition operations, but have lately proved even more pervasive in NATO than in UN operations. NATO troops are much better equipped than most of those devoted to UN operations and are correspondingly more expensive. The resultant wealth of staff resources ensures that NATO operations are more professionally planned and sustained, but the proportion of headquarters personnel to fielded capacity is quite high and correspondingly more costly.

EU decisionmaking in the security and defense sector is also by consensus. The European Union has a leaner military and political staff than NATO does, in part because it can call on NATO, if it chooses, for planning and other staff functions. The EU, like the UN, but unlike NATO, can draw upon a wide array of civilian assets essential to any nation-building operation. Like NATO soldiers, EU soldiers are much more expensive than their UN counterparts. EU decision-making mechanisms, like those of NATO, offer troop-contributing governments more scope for micromanaging military operations on a day-to-day basis than do the UN's.

Half or more of all nation-building operations take place in sub-Saharan Africa. Several African organizations, most recently the African Union, have organized peacekeeping missions. No African Union member country has the capacity to conduct large-scale expeditionary operations. The African Union's efforts therefore tend to be even more dependent on U.S. and European support than are those of the United Nations. In consequence, the United States and its European allies may end up paying a larger share of the bill for African Union operations than for UN operations, despite their lack of membership in the former organization. While African Union interventions may be more acceptable to the host countries than ones headed by the UN, NATO, or the EU, this is probably for the wrong reason; the receiving government has opted for the weaker presence and less exigent oversight.

Establishing Consultative Forums

No international organization, not even the United Nations, possesses all the capabilities needed for effective nation-building. The United Nations has the ability to perform military, humanitarian, and political tasks, but generally shares responsibility for reconstruction and economic development with institutions such as the World Bank and the International Monetary Fund (IMF), which are outside the UN family of agencies. NATO has an even more limited palette of capabilities, basically providing only military forces. The World Bank, the IMF, regional development banks, and the European Union all have substantial capabilities in the area of reconstruction and the provision of financial assistance. Coordination among these various organizations depends heavily on guidance from their principal member states. It usually makes sense, therefore, for the governments with the greatest stakes in a mission to meet regularly to coordinate plans and ensure that the various international organizations involved are collaborating effectively. Failing such oversight, these organizations will expend a good deal of energy competing for turf while shirking the high risk of expensive tasks.

Neighboring states always have a profound effect, for better or worse, on the outcome of nation-building operations. These countries cannot afford to remain uninvolved: It is they that must harbor the refugees and cope with the crime, corruption, terrorism, epidemic disease, and commercial disruption that violent conflict engenders. Neighbors, therefore, can neither be safely ignored nor effectively barred from exercising their considerable influence.

When states fail, contenders for power invariably seek foreign sponsors, while neighbouring governments back one faction or another in an effort to preserve their influence. When these governments back dissident elements and collaborate with spoilers, the task of the intervening authorities is greatly complicated and, indeed, often irremediably compromised. It is wise, therefore, to find ways to engage neighbors constructively. This does not mean accepting troop contributions from adjoining states. That is almost always a bad idea, raising as it does the specter of permanent partition or border adjustments. It does mean giving neighboring governments a forum through which to express their opinions and pursue their legitimate interests in a transparent fashion.

In the mid-1990s, NATO nations recognized that they could not put Bosnia back together without the active cooperation of Serbian President Slobodan Milosevic and Croatian President Franjo Tudjman, the two men personally responsible for the genocide NATO was trying to stop. In late 2001, the United States recognized that it could not install a broadly based successor regime to the Taliban without the active support of those neighboring nations that had been tearing Afghanistan apart for several decades. The success of both these efforts depended on creating a favorable regional climate, requiring that the United States engage its adversaries as well as its friends.

In the Balkans, the United States and its allies created the Peace Implementation Council, which accorded each of Bosnia's neighbors a role in overseeing its transformation. In Afghanistan, the United Nations established the "six plus two" forum, bringing together all of that country's neighbors, along with the United States and Russia. It was this group that formally launched the process of establishing a successor regime to the Taliban. Its principal member governments all participated actively in helping choose and install that government.

When organizing a large-scale nation-building effort, it generally makes sense to create several concentric forums. At the core are the major powers contributing troops and money to the operation. The next circle widens to include all the major financial donors, whether or not they have also committed troops. The third circle includes all the neighboring states. Consensus should be sought and built from the first to the second, and finally to the third groups.

Setting Initial Priorities

All nation-building operations must move quickly to fill a security vacuum, deal with severe humanitarian distress, repair inadequate capacity for governance, and restore economic activity. Such missions require several components in addition to the military, including a police contingent to monitor existing local police and train and develop new police forces; humanitarian relief agencies; civil administrators; and experts in the fields of finance, reconstruction, development, and democratization. Ideally, all these elements should arrive at the same time, ready to operate at full strength from day one. Unfortunately, this ideal is never achieved, forcing the intervening authorities to phase in these operations as capacity becomes available.

In any society emerging from conflict, security, economic growth, and political reform are interdependent. Most programmatic objectives can be achieved only if others are as well. Yet money must be allocated, projects sequenced, and targets set, ideally against some hierarchy of objectives. With infinite personnel and money, it might be possible to launch and fully fund all desired activities simultaneously. As a practical matter, choices must be made among competing priorities. Humanitarian relief and the establishment of a secure environment are normally the intervening authorities' first priorities. Humanitarian relief is usually provided in some measure in the midst of conflict. Consequently, relief agencies are often on the ground and operating even before the first peacekeeper arrives.

Nation-building missions are not launched to make poor societies prosperous, but rather to make warring ones peaceful. Prosperity and security are linked, but the linkage is stronger in one direction than the other. Security is a prerequisite for economic growth. The economies of societies in civil conflict almost invariably contract, while also reducing the growth rates of surrounding states. Societies emerging from such conflict will usually experience positive growth even if they receive no economic assistance. Security, even in the absence of economic assistance, will thus produce some economic growth, while economic assistance in the absence of security will produce neither peace nor prosperity.

This is not to suggest that postconflict societies do not need or cannot use economic assistance. On the contrary, they are attractive candidates for development aid. Their absorptive capacity is perhaps twice as high as that of a more peaceful society at the same level of development. Further, the rate of additional growth likely to be achieved as a result of such aid is also much higher than it would be in a more settled society.

Studies do suggest a correlation between poverty and societal conflict. Economic growth is thus an important factor in forestalling a return to conflict. Nevertheless, in most conflicts, people are not killing each other because they are unemployed. Rather, they are unemployed because they are killing each other. The initial priority for any nation-building mission, therefore, is to establish a secure environment in which people, goods, and services can begin to circulate more freely. Given those conditions, economic activity will resume and incomes will rise. They will rise even faster if security is accompanied by aid and sound economic policy.

Those responsible for managing the early stages of any nation-building operation need to give priority not to the reconstruction of physical infrastructure, but to rebuilding the society's capacity to govern and secure itself. Except in unusually well-financed operations, infrastructure improvement, beyond that needed to restore basic public services, and large-scale employment-generating schemes are unlikely to yield benefits commensurate with their costs. The longer-term benefits of infrastructure improvements can ordinarily be realized through project financing from international financial institutions that exist for this purpose. Make-work schemes to generate short-term employment have little lasting impact and are generally too expensive to reach the bulk of the population.

There is an important exception to this principle: The employment of former combatants should be treated as a security task rather than an economic or developmental objective. These individuals may be among the least deserving members of society and are probably also among the least promising recipients of vocational training. But their employment should be placed among the intervening power's highest priorities, not because it contributes to economic growth, but because it bolsters security, offering former combatants an alternative to violent crime or continued resistance.

Once security has been reestablished and the population's basic human needs addressed, other aspects of the mission should receive increased emphasis, including the resumption of public services, democratization, and economic development, in more or less that order of priority. This is not to suggest that such steps need be sequential. When resources permit, they should be pursued simultaneously. Higher-priority needs should be adequately resourced, however, before lower-priority ones are funded, because when first-order objectives are not met, money spent on second-order priorities will be wasted.

On this basis, a rough hierarchy of nation-building tasks can be identified as follows:

- *Security:* peacekeeping, law enforcement, rule of law, and security-sector reform
- *Humanitarian relief:* return of refugees and response to potential epidemics, hunger, and lack of shelter
- *Governance:* resuming public services and restoring public administration

- *Economic stabilization:* establishing a stable currency and providing a legal and regulatory framework in which local and international commerce can resume
- *Democratization:* building political parties, free press, civil society, and a legal and constitutional framework for elections
- *Development:* fostering economic growth, poverty reduction, and infrastructure improvements.

Seizing the Golden Hour

The weeks immediately following the arrival of foreign peacekeepers tend to be a time of maximum possibility. The appearance of an intervening force often produces a combination of shock and relief among the local population. Resistance is unorganized, spoilers unsure of their future. The situation is, in consequence, highly malleable. But the intervening authorities' capacity to capitalize on these opportunities is inevitably limited by the absence of many components of the mission.

To take advantage of this "golden hour" that often follows the onset of "peace" and the arrival of international forces, the mission leadership will need to have at its disposal upon arrival a minimum set of assets, including troops, police, civil administrators, and humanitarian workers, followed quickly by judicial and penal experts with funded plans for police training and for the disarmament, demobilization, and reintegration of former combatants.

Nation-building missions are usually launched in circumstances in which local security forces have disintegrated or have been discredited. Whatever remains of the local police force will need to be supervised closely while new officers are trained. These jobs are best undertaken by international civilian police rather than by the military. Accordingly, an effort should be made to deploy civilian police along with soldiers in the first wave of any nation-building operation. If civilian police are lacking, a large number of military police officers (MPs) should be included in the initial peacekeeping force. Before the first boots hit the ground, plans for a police training facility should be drawn up, instructors selected, a location chosen, and the program funded.

Police cannot perform effectively without courts in which to try criminals and prisons in which to keep them. These institutions, too, will almost certainly be found to be highly defective, if not entirely absent. It is important, therefore, that programs to reform the justice and penal systems be initiated simultaneously with police training. If these three efforts do not move forward in tandem, newly trained and reformed police will have to either let those criminals they arrest go or punish them extrajudicially. Either response will quickly demoralize the best-trained police force and undermine public security.

While local police establishments need to be reformed and strengthened, local militaries need to be scaled back. Among the most urgent tasks in any intervention are separating armed adversaries and demobilizing former combatants. Putting in place, as quickly as possible, a program to register such individuals, gather personal data on them, and provide for their immediate livelihoods will contribute to security in the short term while providing the basis for longer-term decisions regarding the size and nature of the state's new security forces. Drawing up and funding a plan for disarmament, demobilization, and reintegration of former combatants should feature prominently on any preintervention checklist.

Perhaps most importantly, the intervening authorities need to arrive with a carefully thought out set of mission objectives commensurate with the resources to be committed and appropriate for the challenges to be confronted. If the population can be made to feel that its security is enhanced by the intervening presence, it will be inclined to collaborate. If potential spoilers are faced with overwhelming force and offered peaceful avenues to pursue their interests, resistance may be minimized. If neighboring states are drawn into the process of defining the mission, they will be less likely to undermine its efforts.

It has often been said that no military plan survives first contact with the enemy. Similarly, no nation-building plan can expect to survive first contact with the society being rebuilt. The function of planning is not to plot an operation from start to finish, but rather to assemble the necessary resources and establish objectives achievable within those limits. The test of any nation-building plan is not whether it accurately predicts future events, but whether it provides the nation-builder the resources and flexibility needed to meet such challenges as they develop.

CHAPTER TWO

The Military

The presence of foreign military forces is a unique feature of nation-building, distinguishing these operations from other forms of political or economic intervention. International military forces can separate contending parties, disarm and demobilize former combatants, substitute for or supplement local police, secure borders, deter external interference, and reform or create new indigenous military forces. Their primary objective should be to establish a secure environment in which people and goods can circulate freely, licit political and economic activity can take place free from intimidation, and external donors can bring financial resources and expertise to bear to promote political reform and economic growth. Most nation-building endeavors have been multinational. They have involved military coalitions formed for the purpose by an ad hoc group of nation-states, the United Nations, or regional organizations such as NATO or the African Union.

Key Challenges

Planning and Preparation. As a first step, the intervening authorities need to acquire sufficient information on potential security threats, the organizational structure of local security forces, and sociopolitical conditions within the country that may affect military operations. Key questions include the following: How many military and other security forces are necessary to establish law and order? How many of these should be international forces, and how many should be local forces? What should their primary tasks be? Much of this information will need to be gathered for the combat phase in cases in which forced entry is believed necessary.

Public Security. Providing for public security is essential to gaining any population's cooperation. Only when the local population feels safer because of the presence of international forces will citizens likely collaborate with the intervening authorities. Even when an intervention is welcomed by the great majority of the local population, the intervening military forces must anticipate the emergence of criminal and extremist elements intent on preying on the population and frustrating the objectives of the intervening authorities. It is essential that political and military steps be taken *immediately* to deter, dissuade, or prevent these criminal and extremist elements from evolving into a source of organized and violent resistance. Failure to preempt the development of overt violent resistance can result in the transformation of the stability mission into a counterinsurgency campaign.

Disarmament, Demobilization, and Reintegration. The disarmament, demobilization, and reintegration (DDR) of former combatants are important priorities. DDR programs have been developed for tribal militias in Afghanistan, the Farabundo Martí National Liberation Front in El Salvador, the Resistencia Nacional Moçambicana in Mozambique, and the Khmer Rouge in Cambodia. These programs have met with mixed success. Militias often strongly resist disarming and demobilizing. The success of such programs hinges on the consent, support, and participation of local political and military leaders, including political representatives of the warring parties. Strong international forces can, to some extent, compensate for weak consent among the parties. But under any circumstances, significant attention needs to be given to providing the parties political and economic incentives to cooperate, as well as establishing a framework for international military oversight of the process.

Intelligence, Surveillance, and Reconnaissance. According to British Colonel C. E. Callwell, a military historian,

> It is a very important feature in the preparation for, and the carrying out of, small wars that the regular forces are often working

very much in the dark. . . . What is known technically as "intel-ligence" is defective, and unavoidably so.[1]

Nation-building operations demand greater attention to civilian considerations—political, social, economic, and cultural factors in an area of operations—than do more conventional offensive and defensive operations. Military commanders must expand intelligence preparation beyond geographical and force capability considerations. Key missions are not just combating insurgent or criminal forces, but may be restoring basic services or encouraging public support. Cultural information is critical in gauging potential reactions to the operation, avoiding misunderstandings, and improving the operation's effectiveness. Changes in the behavior of the population may suggest a need to change tactics or strategy. Biographical information and leadership analysis help to improve understanding of adversaries, their methods of operation, and how they interact with their environment. Knowledge of the ethnic and religious factions in the area of operations and the historical background of the conflict is vital to mission success.

Civic Action. As Mao Tse-Tung argued, "The richest source of power to wage war lies in the masses of the people."[2] If spoilers are able to separate the population from the government and acquire its active support, they increase the likelihood of an insurgency. In the end, the exercise of political power depends on the tacit or explicit agreement of the population or, at worst, on its submissiveness.[3] Consequently, stability operations must seek to separate spoilers from their support base by helping indigenous governments provide security and essential services to the population. This often means that military forces become involved in civic action or small-scale reconstruction programs. These activities can include a wide variety of projects that range from helping

---

[1]   C. E. Callwell, *Small Wars: Their Principles and Practice*, Wakefield, UK: EP Publishing Ltd., [1906], 1976, p. 43.

[2]   Mao Zedong, *Selected Military Writings of Mao Tse-Tung*, Peking, China: Foreign Languages Press, 1963, p. 260.

[3]   Roger Trinquier, *Modern Warfare: A French View of Counterinsurgency*, Daniel Lee, trans., New York: Praeger, 1964, p. 8; David Galula, *Counterinsurgency Warfare: Theory and Practice*, New York: Praeger, 1964, pp. 7–8.

the indigenous government offer basic health care to the local population to rebuilding schools, government buildings, and hospitals.

Security-Sector Reform. Existing military and police forces will almost certainly have to be rebuilt, in some cases from scratch. At the conclusion of any conflict, the number of soldiers will usually be in excess of the society's needs, while the number of police officers is likely to be in deficit. One will have to be decreased while the other is increased. Quality and control are at least as important as numbers in reconstituting state security forces. End-state goals need to be established to provide the society adequate numbers of police officers and military personnel to meet its security needs without overburdening its fiscal resources.

Best Practices

Planning and Preparation

Key components of advanced preparation include intelligence, command-and-control arrangements, education, and training. Several types of intelligence are needed for stability operations. The first concerns the country's current and potential security threats, including an analysis of the root causes of the conflict. These causes may be a result of economic conditions, interethnic disputes, or other factors. A second type of intelligence involves information on the organization of local military and police forces and of other armed combatants. Who are they? How are they organized? How effective have they been? How does the population perceive them? A third category of intelligence relates to social, political, and cultural conditions in the country. International military forces need to be sensitive to such issues as the role of women in the local society, the importance of tribal affinities, and religious practices.

Unity of command is as desirable in a stability operation as in war. Planners should attempt to maintain unit integrity to the extent possible. Most military forces train as units and are much better able to accomplish a mission when deployed as a unit. By deploying as an existing unit, forces are able to continue to operate under established procedures, adapting these to the mission and situation as required. When personnel and elements are drawn from various units, they are less effective. It takes them more time to adjust to the requirements of the mission.

Political and other considerations often lead to divided command arrangements in stability operations. In Sierra Leone in 1999–2000, British forces operated independently in support of a UN military mission. In 2003 in the Democratic Republic of Congo, an EU force operated in support of, but independently from, a larger UN force. In Afghanistan, two separate coalitions operated in increasingly close proximity—one led by the United States and the other led by NATO. While such arrangements may maximize the capacity of national governments to control or circumscribe the activity of their troops, they increase the risk of losses through either fratricide or failure to render effective and timely support. The activities of these separate forces can be deconflicted, but only at the cost of additional command time and effort and with unnecessary friction.

The education of commissioned and noncommissioned officers is a key component of stability operations. Preparation requires different skills and a different mindset from major combat operations. Of particular importance is recognizing the need for popular support and designing a strategy that ensures public security and basic humanitarian needs for the population. Education for such operations should begin with basic leadership training and culminate at the senior service or academy level. Education on stability operations should ensure that leaders at all levels understand the objectives, principles, and characteristics of stability operations, and can plan and conduct these operations. Leader education should include discussions, lessons learned, and situational exercises, and should culminate with senior leaders performing in command or staff positions during stability operation exercises.

Training should ensure that individuals and units have the necessary skills for the mission and that the staffs can plan, control, and support the operation. Depending on the anticipated operation, predeployment training should include individual skills training; situational training exercises; field training exercises; combined arms live-fire exercises; mobility exercises; command post exercises; and simulation exercises to train commanders, staff, and units. If there is sufficient time prior to actual deployment, predeployment training for units should culminate in a joint training exercise based on the anticipated operation. The unit tasked with the operation should participate in the exercise with the supporting units with which it normally deploys, and, if possible, with the next-higher headquarters for the actual operation. Once deployed, and if the situation allows, military skills training at the individual and unit levels should continue. Training following redeployment should again focus on the unit's missions. There may not always be time to train soldiers for a specific operation, but a well-prepared force can adapt to stability operations under the leadership of commissioned and noncommissioned officers in these operations.

Public Security

International interventions are invariably launched to deal with a *security gap* that has emerged: Either a civil war is under way, public order has broken down, or a regime is abusing its own citizens or threatening its neighbors. In general, in the immediate aftermath of civil or interstate wars, a period of anarchy ensues in which groups and factions seek to arm themselves for protection. Some may also have offensive intentions and want to impose their ideology on others, seize the property of rival factions, or exploit public resources for private gain.[4] Whatever the antecedent circumstances, the intervening military force will almost always need to provide some measure of public security, either because the indigenous security institutions have disintegrated or because they have been discredited as a result of abusive behavior. A key element in filling this security gap is to quickly vet and deploy indigenous security forces. Even minimally competent, vetted indigenous forces can be extremely beneficial in quickly establishing a minimal level of order. These forces speak the local language, are familiar

---

[4]   Barry Posen, "The Security Dilemma and Ethnic Conflict," in Michael E. Brown, ed., *Ethnic Conflict and International Security*, Princeton, N.J.: Princeton University Press, 1993, pp. 103–124; Michael W. Doyle and Nicholas Sambanis, "International Peacebuilding: A Theoretical and Quantitative Analysis," *American Political Science Review*, Vol. 94, No. 4, December 2000, pp. 779–802 [p. 780]; Roland Paris, *At War's End: Building Peace After Civil Conflict*, New York: Cambridge University Press, 2004, pp. 161–163.

with the culture, and may be more trusted than international forces by the local population. The use of local security forces brings with it attendant problems of potential human rights abuses and difficulties in separating out those found to be unsuitable for a reformed police force or military. Nevertheless, it is usually preferable to rely on flawed local security forces, provided these are closely monitored, than to cede the streets to criminals and political extremists. Only an exceptionally large and well-equipped external intervention force can expect to fully substitute for such local capacity.

If the intervening authorities do not move quickly to provide for public security, the resultant vacuum will be progressively filled by criminal and extremist elements. The longer such elements are left unchallenged, the more opportunity they have to organize, gain confidence, intimidate the population, cow any remaining local security forces, and present an enduring threat to the intervening authorities. As discussed in Chapter One, international interventions can profit from a "golden hour." This is an initial period during which the shock of their arrival, the relief at the end of conventional combat, and uncertainty about the future can help secure for the intervening authorities a high degree of local cooperation, a degree of cooperation that is likely to diminish over time. To the extent that international forces arrive quickly, in sufficient numbers, and with well-conceived plans for rapidly expanding public security, this "golden hour" can become the period during which the intervening powers' authority is consolidated, and that of local and transnational spoilers is marginalized.

The contrast between the international community's experience in Bosnia and Kosovo in the late 1990s is illustrative. In the former, local police remained responsible for public security while international military forces separated combatants and enforced disarmament and demobilization. In Kosovo, by contrast, the international community was compelled to assume responsibility for law enforcement from the first day of the intervention. In Kosovo, the international community deployed a much larger number of international police officers, but the society was still plagued by disorder and high levels of violent crime. On the other hand, Kosovo has probably come further than Bosnia in creating a professional, honest, multiethnic police force because it could start from scratch. Thus, while the Kosovo approach may have its advantages, it is only feasible in relatively small societies in which the international community is ready to make a relatively large investment. Replicating the Kosovo approach in Iraq, for instance, with a population 12 times larger, would have required the deployment of 60,000 international civil police officers, a number far exceeding the total number of such police currently deployed worldwide.

Once military forces have been deployed to help fill the security gap, they conduct a range of operations: basic law enforcement, counternarcotics, counterterrorism, counterinsurgency, and miscellaneous functions such as securing elections. International forces engaged in stability operations may not have to conduct all of these tasks. But they will likely have to conduct many of them and may need to conduct all of them. Local security forces should be associated with such missions as soon as possible; leadership should be transferred to them as quickly as their capacity permits.

Intervening military forces should be prepared to conduct law enforcement operations and to support, reinstate, and establish civil authorities. Law enforcement operations should be designed to restore stability to the point at which indigenous forces and international police can effectively enforce the law and reinstate civilian authorities. Basic tasks include patrolling streets; guarding key public buildings, weapon depots, and other infrastructure such as oil facilities; and monitoring borders. Military forces may be given the authority to detain people suspected of criminal or unlawful actions. Interpreters and military police officers should be used when possible. Military forces may also be asked to capture war criminals.

Military forces should be prepared to counter drug traffickers and other organized criminal groups. Virtually all stability operations have faced serious problems with organized crime. In general, military forces may be asked to help detect, monitor, and counter the production, trafficking, and use of illegal drugs and other substances. They may also be asked to target the infrastructure—personnel, materiel, and distribution systems—of illicit entities. This may involve searching areas and apprehending personnel, confiscating contraband, or interdicting smuggling operations. Operations may be as simple as using checkpoints to search personnel and vehicles, or may involve more complex missions such as cordon and search operations. Searches, apprehensions, and seizures must be legal and in compliance with the mandate or agreement worked out at the beginning of the operation.

Terrorism may pose a significant security challenge. Combating terrorism involves both offensive and defensive operations. Offensive actions usually involve strikes and raids against terrorists and their infrastructure. They are generally conducted by special operations forces that are organized and trained for this purpose. Defensive actions should aim to reduce the vulnerability of individuals and property to terrorist acts and should include response and containment by indigenous military forces. This usually involves improving the capabilities and resources of indigenous personnel in such areas as crisis management, airport security, terrorist financing, and border control. Military commanders are responsible for planning, resourcing, training, exercising, and executing counterterrorism measures.

Military forces may assist in holding elections. This may include providing administrative support and security at polling stations and voter registration centers, as well as creating an environment that permits refugees and internally displaced persons to vote. The integrity of elections is typically the responsibility of the election commission. But military commanders should work with the appropriate international and local agencies during elections to help ensure that integrity, especially since those who stand to lose power may use violence to destabilize or discredit elections.

Finally, demining has been important in establishing security during stability operations in such countries as Afghanistan, Cambodia, El Salvador, Mozambique, and Namibia. Antipersonnel landmines cause serious injuries to civilians, including blindness, burns, destroyed limbs, and shrapnel wounds. Most of these countries already had mine-clearing programs before their respective interventions. These were run by the UN or nongovernmental organizations (NGOs). In addition to supporting demining, normally a civil function, international military forces should provide education on mine awareness and train host-nation personnel to survey and mark minefields and to clear mines. Military specialists, such as explosive ordnance disposal personnel, may be called on to destroy unexploded ordnance, such as shells and rockets.

Disarmament, Demobilization, and Reintegration

Successful DDR of former combatants hinges on the consent, support, and participation of local political and military leaders. These include the political representatives of the state and warring parties, military commanders, and warlords. Strong international forces can, to some extent, compensate for weak consent among the parties. But only a voluntary process is likely to be very effective. Consequently, the intervening authorities need to pay attention to providing the parties political and economic incentives to cooperate, as well as arranging for the nuts and bolts of this process.

Under most disarmament programs, combatants hand over weapons to international or local authorities, who are responsible for their collection, safe storage, disposal, or destruction. Disarmament generally involves three steps: (1) a weapon survey; (2) weapon collection; and (3) weapon storage, reutilization, or destruction. A weapon survey is necessary to answer vital planning questions at an early stage: Approximately how many weapons are there? Who is expected to turn them in? Who controls weapons outside the armed forces? For weapon collection programs to be successful, advice and assistance from explosive ordnance disposal and ammunition specialists is needed. Weapon collection programs should minimize the risks of loss posed by the movement, management, and storage of collected arms. Programs may involve exchanging weapons for food, goods, or money. Those running the program need to create storage areas large enough to secure, store, inspect, and possibly destroy weapons and materiel. Space must be allocated to support a security force and administration capabilities, such as accounting for materiel stored, collected, transferred, or destroyed. The program needs to maintain logs accounting for personnel or units surrendering materiel. Security and accountability are critical. Disarmament may include seizing ammunition, collecting and destroying weapons and supplies, closing weapon and ammunition factories, and preventing resupply.

Demobilization entails disbanding a formerly armed unit or reducing the number of combatants in an armed group. It can also involve disassembling—and then reassembling—the host country's armed forces. Demobilization entails registering, counting, and monitoring combatants, and then preparing them for discharge (see Figure 2.1). The process of demobilization comprises different scenarios, from individual combatants flowing through temporary centers to the collection of soldiers in camps designated for this purpose. The dwelling time in the camps should be as short as possible and should lead to a direct transition to reintegration. If the capacities of the reintegration programs are insufficient, the implementation of these measures will be delayed. Until then, the combatants should remain in the camp. Some camps are dissolved years after demobilization, since they provide reliable maintenance and take care of the ex-combatants. International forces can play an important role in demobilization in several ways:

- Provide intelligence support and overall security during demobilization.
- Provide incentives for forming, arming, and training a competent new defense force under government control.
- Support information operations.
- Provide liaison coordination teams to local commanders as a confidence-building measure.

Reintegration is the process under which combatants reenter the civilian workforce. The objective of reintegration programs is to assist ex-combatants in their social and economic reintegration into civilian society so that they do not return to banditry or violence. Programs need to incorporate into their plans the community in which the ex-combatant will settle. Matching the skills and needs of the individual to the receiving community can mean the difference between an individual who becomes a productive member of a community and an ex-combatant who resorts to violence and crime. One of the first steps of reintegration programs should be to provide training; employment; shelter; and, where appropriate, land to ex-combatants. The demand for land cannot be addressed solely within a DDR program.

Figure 2.1
Demobilization Steps

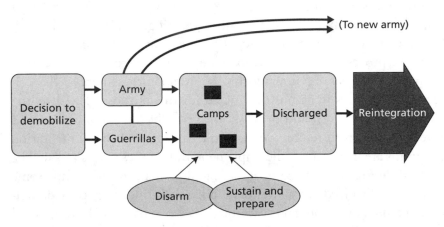

SOURCE: Adapted from Colin Gleichman, Michael Odenwald, Kees Steenken, and Adrian Wilkinson, *Disarmament, Demobilization and Reintegration: A Practical Field and Classroom Guide*, Frankfurt, Germany: Druckerei Hassmuller Graphische Betriebe, 2004.
RAND *MG557-2.1*

Reintegration programs should be linked with existing programs for agricultural training and land distribution to facilitate access to land.

The military may not be the appropriate actor to lead reintegration efforts, which are probably better handled by civilians. However, military forces have nonetheless provided temporary jobs to former combatants. In the Balkans, for example, NATO forces employed ex-combatants for such short-term jobs as painting, repairing sidewalks, repairing roads, and picking up garbage. Over the long run, however, reintegration programs need to incorporate a training component, since many ex-combatants have few marketable skills. There will be considerable differences in the social and educational profiles of ex-combatants. Target groups can be differentiated on the basis of age, sex, marital status, formal qualifications, work experience, and education. Training should improve the chances for ex-combatants to find better-paying employment. Business training and small credits may be used to support those who want to set up their own businesses.

Employment creation schemes are seldom a productive use of donor resources following a conflict. The exception to this rule is for former combatants. Finding alternative sources of livelihood for these individuals is an important security concern and should be addressed accordingly. Based on past behavior, former combatants may well be the least deserving elements of society. However, they remain the most necessary to assist if renewed conflict is to be avoided. While long-term employment of former combatants should be the goal, this may not be realistic. The minimum objective should be to detach these individuals from their former associates long enough to prevent them from easily reassembling, rearming, and again posing a threat of renewed conflict.

An alternative to demobilization is to integrate some former combatants into new or reformed local security units. These units will require careful vetting and oversight. International authorities should be careful not to build new security forces larger than the country can afford to maintain over the longer term. In most cases, the host state will not have the resources to pay for and maintain its own security forces for several years following the intervention. If the intervening authorities also fail to do so, these new units will themselves become a source of insecurity and renewed conflict.

Critical to an effective DDR program is the process of registering the former combatants and providing each some source of livelihood while the process goes forward, either in the form of a stipend, in-kind payment, or alternative employment. Once the former combatants have been registered, and have had their immediate needs cared for, the process of deciding which are to be demobilized, which are to be reformed into new units and retrained, and which are to be offered alternative civil employment or vocational training can proceed at a more deliberate pace. One does not need to begin the process knowing exactly how many former combatants will be discharged and how many retained, as long as all the former combatants are rapidly identified and assured an interim source of livelihood while their longer-term prospects are determined.

Intelligence, Surveillance, and Reconnaissance

Stability operations require multidisciplined, all-source, fused intelligence. Human intelligence (HUMINT) is usually the most useful way to gather information in stability operations. Interpreters, low-level source operations, debriefs of indigenous personnel, screening operations, and patrolling are good sources for assessing the economic and health needs, military capabilities, and political intent of adversaries. Military commanders should emphasize to all personnel the importance of being conscious of sources of intelligence and should provide basic guidelines to improve their intelligence-gathering capabilities. Medical personnel must be aware of Geneva Convention restrictions against their collecting information of intelligence value except that which is observed incidentally while accomplishing their humanitarian duties.

However, a single-source approach cannot support all requirements. Manned and unmanned aerial intelligence sensors can provide valuable information when other means of collecting intelligence are not available. Remote sensing systems can provide information on terrain, weather, and other environmental factors. Data from space systems can be used to update antiquated maps and provide up-to-date locations of facilities and obstacles. Sensors on space and aerial platforms can also monitor terrestrial force movements and assist in treaty verification. Communication systems can provide secure, reliable dissemination of intelligence and other information where there are few or no existing civilian communication systems.

Counterintelligence should support operations even if no well-defined threat exists. Adversary HUMINT efforts focus on gaining access to international military personnel and operations information by providing services such as laundry, cooking, driving, and translating. Adversaries or spoilers may also attempt to exploit other members of the local populace who interact with international forces.

Surveillance and reconnaissance may be employed to determine the disposition, activities, and intentions of civilian populations (hostile and neutral) and uniformed or irregular threats. Reconnaissance for information collection and security should continue throughout the operation. Forces conducting domestic support operations must know the legal limitations when acquiring information on civilians. In many instances, international organizations and nongovernmental humanitarian agencies have been in the area of operations long before international military forces. These organizations produce reports, have Web sites, and maintain databases. These organizations have often conducted surveys of minefields using global positioning system (GPS) data. International forces can access much of this information before deploying. Military commanders should communicate and coordinate with these organizations to become familiar with the cultures and sensitivities of the local population. This means establishing trust and good relations with international and nongovernmental organizations *before* an operation so they are willing to share information.

Civic Action

The nature of stability operations places military forces in direct contact with civilians, local and government officials, and NGOs. These relationships make humanitarian and civil-military operations critical to any stability operation. As noted previously, international and nongovernmental organizations—not military forces—should normally take the lead in providing humanitarian assistance. But military forces are often the first international personnel on the ground and have become increasingly involved in humanitarian operations. In addition to providing a security shield for early humanitarian relief and reconstruction activities, civil affairs units of the military can help provide health care, supply food and water to the population, deal with mines and hazardous materials, institute quarantine measures in the event of communicable disease outbreaks, guide the return of refugees, and perform emergency repairs of infrastructure. In Afghanistan, for example, military forces worked closely with civilian personnel in provincial reconstruction teams. Projects implemented by these teams included roads, water supply plants, irrigation systems, government administrative buildings, schools, health clinics, and micro–power-generation plants. Military forces need to include personnel with the language and background skills necessary to work effectively with a wide range of official and civilian actors in a dynamic, complex, and sometimes murky environment.

"Team Village" missions have been used effectively in some stability operations. *Team Village* refers to a group of personnel—usually a mix of civil affairs and psychological operations personnel—tasked with conducting civil-military operations within a larger campaign. Many include tactical HUMINT teams, interpreters, military police, media and public affairs personnel, medical personnel, and local forces. Health care operations can be particularly successful in winning support from the local population. International military forces may encounter lines of patients seeking treatment for everything from mild bumps and bruises to more serious injuries and illnesses. These can be treated from the back of the high-mobility multipurpose wheeled vehicles or in more secured compounds.

Security-Sector Reform

The military component of any mission usually contributes to the rebuilding of a local military, either by promoting the reform and professionalization of an existing military force or building a new military force. The military has also participated in efforts to rebuild the police in such countries as Iraq and Afghanistan, though it is usually preferable for the civil element of the mission to organize such training.

A first step in building or rebuilding a security unit is vetting those who are retained for past human rights abuses, corruption, and ability. Vetting is important in verifying that soldiers and police have not been involved in major human rights violations, are not corrupt, and have achieved at least a minimal level of competency. Individuals who successfully pass through the vetting process are likely to require retraining, new equipment, and a period during which international supervisors monitor their performance. Blanket exclusions on the basis of membership in political parties or other groups are not usually a good way of undertaking vetting. In Iraq, the decision to ban ranking Baath Party members from public-sector employment meant that large numbers of senior officers in the defense and interior ministries and security-related services were released from duty, not to mention thousands of schoolteachers and other mid-level functionaries. Some of these individuals were apolitical and had only become party members as a condition of employment. Vetting can be challenging: International and local military forces and personnel may be unable to accurately evaluate applicants because of the loss—or absence—of central government files and databases. International staff should be employed in these capacities until it is clear that indigenous personnel can execute these responsibilities effectively.

Training of indigenous forces should create skills necessary for effective operations and maintenance of equipment, assist in developing the expertise needed for effectively managing the defense establishment, and foster development of an indigenous training capability. Infantry training includes basic rifle marksmanship; platoon- and company-level tactics; use of heavy weapons; and engineering, scout, and medical skills.

There are three primary methods of training. The first includes mobile training teams, which are used when a host nation requires on-site training or needs surveys and assessments of training requirements. These teams may be single-service, joint, special operations forces, or conventional forces. But they must be tailored to the host country's needs. A second method involves technical assistance field teams deployed for extended periods to train host-nation personnel on equipment or in specific military skills. The third method includes international military education and training outside the host nation. This involves bringing local military personnel to other countries to attend training and education programs. Training abroad is often provided on an individual basis for more senior officers.

Equipment needs will vary by country. International military forces may assist host-nation militaries to design, implement, and integrate command, control, communications, and computer systems to counter likely security threats. Military commanders must consider sustainability issues when providing equipment, as well as interoperability with existing equipment. Host nations may request expensive equipment as a status symbol when improved training and professionalism among the existing force would enhance the overall strength of the military. Service support is usually integrated with equipment support. It includes any service, test, inspection, repair, training, publication, technical assistance, or other aid used to furnish military assistance. Many types of service teams exist. Quality assurance teams inspect equipment to ensure that it remains mission-capable. Technical assistance teams respond when the host nation has difficulty with imported equipment.

Institutional development also requires building the capacity of ministries of defense to support the armed forces; building command, control, and coordination capabilities; improving management, personnel, and financial processes; reforming military legal codes; and transforming the armed forces' logistical tail. Institutional development in a postconflict state must be tackled within the wider context of public administration reform. Leadership training is a critical component. The aim should be to staff defense ministries with a significant number of civilians, as well as to tie the armed forces into the civil service by adopting budgeting and management practices similar to those in other parts of the government. Sustainability is a critical element of institutional development. In the immediate postconflict phase, external involvement is likely to be significant. However, reforms will be successful only if they are embraced by the host government, ministry of defense, and armed forces.

Key Actors

With few exceptions, most post–Cold War stability missions are conducted by multinational coalitions—sometimes under the command of a lead nation, sometimes under the control of an international institution. Ad hoc coalitions offer the lead nation maximum control, in exchange for which it must also bear most of the expense and risk. Coalitions overseen by international organizations spread the burden of expense and risk more widely, but also disperse responsibility for decisionmaking. Sometimes one type of coalition can give way to the other. For example, the United States led ad hoc coalitions into Somalia in 1991, into Haiti in 1994 and again in 2004, and into Afghanistan in 2001. The first three operations were quickly turned over to the United Nations, and the last is in the process of being turned over to NATO.

Operations requiring forced entry normally call for a coalition led by single major power capable of providing most of the command, control, and enabling forces. Most such coalitions are organized specifically for a particular operation, although NATO also meets this definition. In situations in which permissive entry and some level of acquiescence among the contending parties can be anticipated, the United Nations offers the best combination of competence, legitimacy, cost-effectiveness, and burden-sharing.

Sizing

In settled societies, the ratio of military personnel to local inhabitants generally ranges from 0.2 soldiers per 1,000 inhabitants to nearly 1 per 1,000 inhabitants. Examples include the Philippines (0.8), the United States (0.2), Chile (0.2), Britain (0.3), Japan (0.5), and South Africa (0.8).[5] Postconflict societies are likely to need a higher proportion of military personnel, though probably considerably less than that under arms when the conflict ceases. Figure 2.2 shows military-to-population ratios for eight postconflict societies five years after stability operations began (or, in the case of Afghanistan, as of this writing). They ranged from a low of 0.3 in Mozambique to a high of 7.7 in Cambodia, with an average of three soldiers per 1,000 inhabitants. The highest ratios were usually in countries with high levels of violence or criminality. Afghanistan is an outlier with significant violence but few soldiers, probably because local and tribal militias are not captured in the figures.

International forces must be large enough to maintain order; capable of training indigenous forces; and have a robust intelligence, surveillance, and reconnaissance capability down to the small-unit level. Peace enforcement requires a much greater commitment of military force than do more benign types of operations, such as peacekeeping. However, entry by force is by no means the most demanding aspect of the operation. For a well-equipped Western force, the conventional

---

5 Christopher Langton, ed., *The Military Balance, 2006*, London: International Institute for Strategic Studies, 2006.

Figure 2.2
Local Military Forces Five Years After Start of Stability Operations

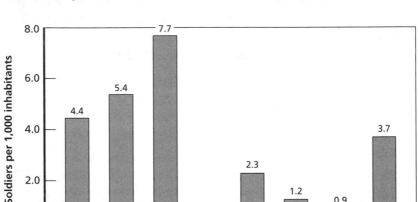

SOURCE: Data compiled from the International Institute for Strategic Studies; United
Nations, Department of Peacekeeping Operations; *Jane's Online*; U.S. Department
of State, Afghan Progress Reports and Iraq Weekly Progress Reports; and UN
Secretary-General's reports to the United Nations Security Council.
RAND MG557-2.2

battle, if any, is likely to prove the quickest and least costly aspect of the
operation. In some cases, the mere threat of force may be sufficient to
gain entry (as in Haiti in 1994); in some cases, air power may largely be
sufficient (as in Kosovo in 1999); and in other cases, air power in support of indigenous forces in addition to small numbers of international
forces may suffice (as in Bosnia in 1995 and Afghanistan in 2001).
Even where conventional ground operations prove necessary, the numbers required will probably not approach those needed to subsequently
stabilize the society.

Figure 2.3 shows peak levels of international military forces in
eight stability operations. High levels of forces have generally tended to
correlate with high levels of security and order and low levels of casualties. Failure to deploy sufficient numbers in a peace enforcement operation can lead to incipient local resistance taking organized and violent
form, as has occurred in Somalia, Afghanistan, and Iraq.

Figure 2.3
Peak Military Levels for Peace Enforcement

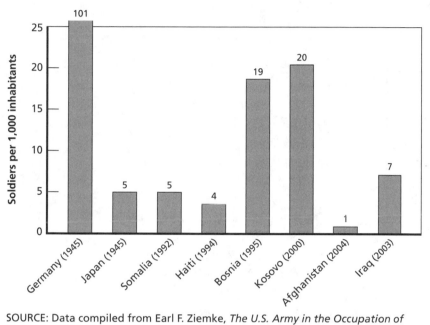

SOURCE: Data compiled from Earl F. Ziemke, *The U.S. Army in the Occupation of Germany, 1944–1946*, Washington, D.C.: U.S. Army Center of Military History, 1975; U.S. Department of the Army, *Strength of the Army*, weekly report series, STM-30, Washington, D.C., December 1, 1946; International Institute for Strategic Studies; United Nations, Department of Peacekeeping Operations; *Jane's Online*; Oliver Ramsbotham and Tom Woodhouse, *Encyclopedia of International Peacekeeping Operations*, Santa Barbara, Calif.: ABC-CLIO, 1999; United Nations, Department of Public Information. Population data, U.S. Census Bureau International Data Base.
RAND *MG557-2.3*

In situations in which the parties have ceased fighting more or less of their own accord and have been persuaded to invite in an international military mission, personnel needs can be significantly lower, on occasion fewer than one foreign soldier per 1,000 inhabitants. In these circumstances, the international authorities are not imposing, but facilitating, a settlement. The international force is not choosing sides, but attempting to maintain peace between contending factions with the cooperation, or at least the acquiescence, of each. Public security is left mostly in the hands of local forces. Figure 2.4 illustrates the peak levels of international military forces in eight UN stability operations.

Figure 2.4
Peak Military Levels for UN Operations

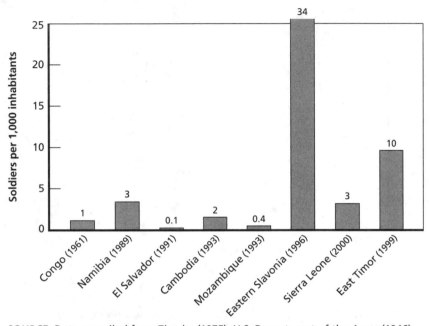

SOURCE: Data compiled from Ziemke (1975); U.S. Department of the Army (1946);
International Institute for Strategic Studies; United Nations, Department of
Peacekeeping Operations; *Jane's Online*; Ramsbotham and Woodhouse (1999);
and United Nations, Department of Public Information. Population data, U.S.
Census Bureau, International Data Base.
RAND *MG557-2.4*

Force levels in some UN operations—such as Congo, El Salvador,
and Mozambique—were significantly lower, at one or fewer soldiers
per 1,000 inhabitants. Many of the UN operations cited, including
Namibia, El Salvador, and Mozambique, were nevertheless successful
despite lower troop numbers because the contenders had exhausted
themselves and were ready to cooperate.

The size, capability, and cost of an international military force
that intervenes for the purpose of a heavy peace enforcement operation are substantially greater than in a light peacekeeping scenario,
consistent with the international community's experience with these
two types of operations. For the heavy peace enforcement scenario, we

calculated the number of soldiers using the average number of international military personnel deployed in the first year of eight peace enforcement operations.[6] For the light peacekeeping scenario, we used the average number of soldiers in the first year of six peacekeeping operations.[7] This resulted in an average of 13 soldiers per 1,000 inhabitants for peace enforcement operations, and two soldiers per 1,000 inhabitants for peacekeeping operations.

The necessary size of the international force should be determined by the scope of its mission or, alternately, the scope of its mission should be limited by the likely size of the available force. Only when large numbers of well-equipped, capable soldiers are available can the intervening authorities prudently embark on rapid and thorough reform of a nature that fundamentally redistributes power, thereby directly challenging powerful and entrenched interest groups in the society. In the majority of cases, the ratio of foreign troops to population falls well below 13 soldiers per 1,000 inhabitants, and success depends on co-opting local power brokers, reconciling contending factions, and promoting gradual reform. This will require redirecting competition for wealth and power in the society from violent into peaceful channels without threatening the complete eclipse of any important faction, community, or interest group.

Costs

Intervening powers must anticipate funding not only their own expenses, but also most of the expenses for local security forces over the first several years of an intervention. The indigenous government, if there is one, is in most cases unlikely to have sufficient revenue to equip, maintain, and pay for a professional army and police force. If

---

[6] The eight operations were East Timor, Eastern Slavonia, Japan, Somalia, Haiti, Bosnia, Kosovo, and Iraq. We excluded the two outliers—Germany on the high end and Afghanistan on the low end—from the average.

[7] The six operations were Congo (in the 1960s), Namibia, Cambodia, Mozambique, Sierra Leone, and El Salvador.

local security forces do exist, they are likely to be funding themselves through various forms of corruption and extortion, living in a symbiotic relationship with the criminal and extremist elements they are supposed to be combating. Until such links are broken, these forces will remain a source of insecurity.

The international cost burden may be borne by the following: (1) U.S. and other high-end Western forces conducting peace enforcement operations and (2) UN forces engaged in peacekeeping, not peace enforcement. We first estimate the cost of deploying peace enforcement forces based on the cost of coalition operations in Iraq and Afghanistan after the overthrow of Saddam Hussein and the Taliban regime, respectively. Using data on the force size and cost of these operations, we calculated the average cost per soldier for military and civilian personnel, personnel support, operational support, and transportation. We estimate that annual costs are approximately $200,000 per soldier per year for peace enforcement operations.[8] These costs would be somewhat lower in a more benign environment, like Bosnia or Kosovo.

Second, we estimated the cost of deploying UN soldiers for non-enforcement missions based on four operations: Haiti, Sierra Leone, Congo, and Liberia.[9] We calculated the average per-soldier cost by compiling information on personnel costs for military observers and

---

[8]   Data are from U.S. Congress, Congressional Budget Office, *Estimated Costs of Continuing Operations in Iraq and Other Operations of the Global War on Terrorism*, Washington, D.C., June 25, 2004. We thank Adam Talaber at the Congressional Budget Office for his assistance with the calculations.

[9]   Data compiled from United Nations General Assembly, "Budget for the United Nations Stabilization Mission in Haiti for the Period from 1 July 2005 to 30 June 2006 and Expenditure Report for the Period from 1 May to 30 June 2004: Report of the Secretary-General," A/59/745, 59th session, agenda item 155, March 18, 2005b; United Nations General Assembly, "Performance Report on the Budget of the United Nations Mission in Sierra Leone for the Period from 1 July 2003 to 30 June 2004: Report of the Secretary-General," A/59/635, 59th session, agenda item 136, December 21, 2004b; United Nations General Assembly, "Performance Report on the Budget of the United Nations Organization Mission in the Democratic Republic of the Congo for the Period from 1 July 2003 to 30 June 2004: Report of the Secretary-General," A/59/657, 59th session, agenda item 127, March 4, 2005a; and United Nations General Assembly, "Performance Report on the Budget of the United Nations Mission in Liberia for the Period from 1 August 2003 to 30 June 2004: Report of the Secretary-General," A/59/624, 59th session, agenda item 134, December 20, 2004a.

military contingents, as well as on what the UN calls "operational costs."[10] These include a combination of transportation, infrastructure, and other costs. We estimate a cost to the UN of roughly $45,000 per soldier per year.[11] The major difference between U.S./Western and UN costs is that UN soldiers are paid by their own governments according to their own national rank and salary scale. The contributing countries are reimbursed by the UN at a flat rate of a little over $1,000 per soldier per month. The UN also reimburses countries for equipment and other operational costs.

Costs for building and maintaining a local military force include those for personnel, equipment, facilities, operations, and oversight, including the costs of staffing a ministry of the defense. Figure 2.5 shows the total costs of fielding a national military force for 14 different countries. We express each in terms of cost per soldier as a multiple of the country's per capita GDP. To arrive at these figures, defense ministry budgets from the 14 countries were converted into U.S. dollars and divided by the number of soldiers in the military. These persoldier costs were then compared to per capita GDP in dollars converted at market exchange rates. RAND found that, on average, the cost per soldier averaged roughly seven times a country's per capita GDP at market exchange rates.

What does this analysis imply for the military component of stability operations? To illustrate, assume the that United States and European countries lead a peace enforcement mission to Macedonia, which in 2006 had a population of 2 million, to halt a hypothetical civil war in that country. Using three soldiers per 1,000 inhabitants, the average number in postconflict societies cited previously, Macedonia would ultimately need 9,000 of its own soldiers to maintain security.

---

[10] We aggregated costs for facilities and infrastructure, ground transportation, air transportation, naval transportation, communications, medical services, and special equipment. Since the UN does not disaggregate the operational costs of military personnel from civilian personnel, our estimates may slightly overstate per-soldier costs. However, military personnel account for the majority of operational costs.

[11] The per-soldier cost was approximately $32,395 for Sierra Leone, $49,692 for the Congo, $51,201 for Liberia, and $45,540 for Haiti. The average was $44,775, which we rounded to $45,000.

Figure 2.5
Cost of Fielding a Local Military Force

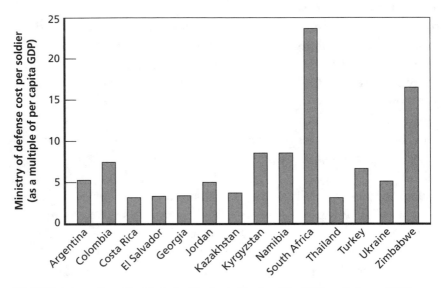

SOURCE: International Institute for Strategic Studies, *The Military Balance, 2004–2005*, London: Taylor and Francis, 2004.
RAND *MG557-2.5*

Macedonia's per capita GDP in 2006 was approximately $8,000. Multiplying $8,000 by seven, then multiplying by 9,000 soldiers, gives a projected annual budget of $500 million. This is a very rough estimate of what would be needed to operate the Macedonia defense establishment following a postconflict intervention.[12] In addition, using the average number of international soldiers (13) per 1,000 inhabitants cited earlier, Macedonia would need approximately 26,000 international force personnel. We then multiply this number by our estimate of $200,000 per soldier noted previously (assuming as we do that the international force in this case is predominantly Western), giving a total interna-

---

[12] The estimating equations for peace enforcement missions are as follows:

number of local soldiers $= 3 \times$ population $/ 1,000$
cost of running ministry of defense $=$ per capita GDP $\times 7 \times$ number of soldiers
number of international soldiers $= 13 \times$ population $/ 1,000$
cost of international military $=$ number of soldiers $\times \$200,000$.

tional military cost of $4 billion per year. Consequently, the total cost of deploying a major U.S.-led stability operation to Macedonia could approach $4.5 billion in the first year alone. Table 2.1 summarizes the results of this analysis and includes comparable estimates for a UN-led stability operation to Niger.[13] These estimates are meant to provide a first cut at estimating numbers and costs for the full range of international and local military operations in the aftermath of an external intervention.

Table 2.1
Estimates for Operations in Macedonia and Niger, Year One

Mission	Number of Local Soldiers Needed	Cost of Running Local Defense Establishment (2006 US$)	Number of Int'l Soldiers Needed	Cost of Int'l Force (2006 US$)	Total Expenditure (2006 US$)
Peace enforcement mission to Macedonia[a]	9,000	500 million	26,000	4 billion	4.5 billion
Peacekeeping mission to Niger[b]	37,500	200 million	25,000	1 billion	1.2 billion

SOURCE: RAND calculations.

[a] The calculations for Macedonia assume a population of 2 million and a per capita GDP of $8,000 (Central Intelligence Agency, The World Factbook 2006, Washington, D.C., 2006).

[b] The calculations for Niger assume a population of 12.5 million and a per capita GDP of $800 (Central Intelligence Agency, 2006).

---

[13] The estimating equations for peacekeeping missions are as follows:

number of local soldiers = 3 × population / 1,000
cost of running ministry of defense = per capita GDP × 7 × number of soldiers
number of international soldiers = 2 × population / 1,000
cost of international military = number of soldiers × $45,000.

CHAPTER THREE

The Police

Societies emerging from war face a variety of threats from extremist and criminal organizations. Indigenous capacity to meet these challenges is almost always inadequate and sometimes nonexistent. The insertion of international military forces may suffice to halt open conflict, separate combatants, and begin disarmament. However, even if these efforts achieve success rapidly, the local population will be vulnerable to criminals and extremists who seek to undermine the emerging order. Crime often rises, particularly in circumstances in which repressive regimes and abusive security establishments have been dismantled. The failure of the intervening powers to establish law and order will reduce the confidence and willingness of the population to cooperate with intervening authorities and enhance the influence of criminals and spoilers. It may contribute to overt resistance when spoilers are sufficiently emboldened to engage in terrorist or insurgent tactics.

Over the past 15 years, international police have become a standard element of stability missions, representing some 10 percent of the personnel of most current UN-led operations. International police play an important role in the oversight and training of local police forces. In cases in which the domestic security establishment has disintegrated or has been irremediably compromised, international police perform direct law enforcement roles until reliable local police units can be assembled and trained. There are three major categories of international police: military, civil, and gendarmerie (the latter shares characteristics of the first two).

In conventional combat operations, MPs expedite the forward and lateral movement of combat resources and ensure that military commanders get forces, supplies, and equipment when and where they are needed on the battlefield. MPs conduct reconnaissance and intelligence operations to obtain information on routes and terrain from which enemy forces can influence troop movement. They may take charge of prisoners of war, detainees, and dislocated civilians, registering them and providing detention facilities or shelter. MPs may also conduct law enforcement tasks, such as responding to civil disturbances, conducting raids, investigating traffic accidents, and searching vehicles.

Most international civilian police are drawn from active or retired members of national and local law enforcement agencies of contributing countries. They are usually recruited as individuals rather than units. They are more likely than military police to have substantial experience in criminal investigation, crowd control, forensics, and community policing. They include regular police and specialized units, such as special weapons and tactics (SWAT) and counternarcotics forces. They are not subject to military discipline and will typically be less heavily armed than military police—if they are armed at all. Border policing is a specialized police function normally performed by personnel specifically trained and equipped for that purpose. Border policing serves two distinct functions: border control (staffing and monitoring border crossing points in cooperation with immigration and customs authorities) and border patrol (monitoring the green space between checkpoints, often with military support). Gendarmerie or civil police should not be expected to perform duties related to border security without receiving specialized training and relevant equipment.

Gendarmerie forces are designed to function as civil police in peacetime and military police in wartime; they thus share characteristics of both types of units. When serving on stability missions, these police are typically deployed in formed, nationally distinct units that have their own command-and-control arrangements. This contrasts with civil police, who are often deployed as individuals in mixed, multinational units. Gendarmerie forces operate under military discipline; they are generally more heavily armed than civil police. They are also trained in sophisticated criminal investigative techniques. They have experience in riot control, counternarcotics, and counterterrorism. They are often employed in combating organized crime in their home countries. This makes gendarmerie units especially well suited for bridging the gap between military and civil security tasks in stability operations. However, only a few countries—such as France, Italy, Spain, and the Netherlands—have gendarmerie forces.

Civilian police are the best choice, when available in sufficient numbers, for the oversight, training, monitoring, and mentoring of local police forces. Gendarmerie units are particularly useful in circumstances in which international police are called on to exercise a direct law enforcement role, engage in crowd control, or confront large-scale organized crime. There are seldom enough gendarmerie units to meet the demand; civilian police are often in short supply as well, particularly early in an operation. Consequently, the military component of the mission is often called upon to impose public order, a task for which military police are generally better suited than are standard infantry units.

Key Challenges

Predeployment Planning. International police should be deployed in conjunction with or in the immediate aftermath of the insertion of military forces. This will require preparation even before the operation commences, and several questions will need to be addressed. What objectives and strategies should international authorities adopt? What kind of posture should be established to deal with potential insurgents, criminals, and other spoilers? How many police officers should be deployed? What rules of engagement and standard operating procedures should be adopted? What types of equipment will police need? How much will the deployment cost? Adequately answering these questions *before* the intervention is critical to preventing a security gap. Numerous operations have experienced a debilitating deployment lag, since it takes time to acquire funding, personnel, and equipment when needed. These planning steps can be extremely challenging, but are necessary to maximize the likelihood of a smooth transition from major combat to stabilization.

Law Enforcement and Public Security. The prime responsibility of any police force is to enforce the law and provide for public security. In the aftermath of conflict, these tasks may fall directly on the intervening authorities, and in particular on its police and military forces. Timing can be critical. As noted in Chapter One, the immediate aftermath of major combat is sometimes called the *golden hour*. During this period, efforts by outsiders can prevent—or trigger—a spiral of conflict that becomes an insurgency. Intervening early with overwhelming force is easier than trying to retrieve a deteriorating security situation when consent is declining and spoilers are on the offensive.

Intelligence, Surveillance, and Reconnaissance. Gathering sufficient intelligence may be extremely difficult in the early stages of stability operations. Chapter Two addressed intelligence challenges for the military; this chapter examines intelligence for police units. While there is some overlap between the two, intelligence is challenging—and important—for both. In past operations, HUMINT has provided the majority of actionable intelligence. But this requires devoting sufficient time and resources to penetrating criminal and insurgent groups, as well as building a network of informants. The police element of stability missions should contain criminal intelligence specialists, along with the funding and the authority needed to conduct such operations.

Recruiting, Vetting, and Training Police. In some instances, a new local police force will need to be recruited in its entirety, as was necessary in East Timor in the aftermath of the 1999 referendum for self-determination. In other instances, existing forces must be vetted and new recruits will need to replace those dismissed for prior abuses. In some cases, both may be done simultaneously; that is, the old force is retained and vetted as an interim measure, while an entirely new force is recruited and trained from scratch. Background checks are needed to weed out officers and applicants who have committed crimes. This is particularly important when recruits are drawn from former combatant formations that have abused the civilian population. Vetting can be extremely difficult. There is often little reliable information on the background of individuals or units. Documents may have been destroyed by the ministry of interior—or never existed to begin with. In addition, most intelligence services do not systematically collect information on mid- and lower-level police officers.

Infrastructure and Equipment. Local police forces are likely to require everything from new uniforms to transport and communication equipment. There is a strong tendency in the donor community to equate police effectiveness with the acquisition of advanced technology. A sophisticated forensic lab may be useful in some instances, but it will do little to improve criminal investigation unless there is a trained staff to run it and police have the skills to collect evidence in a timely fashion. This means that international authorities have to help build infrastructure and provide equipment that is sustainable over the long run.

Institutional Reform. Depending on the nature and state of the local police, the intervening authorities may choose to reform and rebuild the existing establishment or to dismantle what is left of it and begin anew. The former is usually easier and faster, while the latter may result in more thorough reform. Sometimes there is no choice. In Somalia, East Timor, and Kosovo, the police force had disintegrated or been withdrawn. Postconflict environments are often the most conducive to changing the system and culture of internal security bodies. They frequently provide a "window of opportunity" to rebuild internal security forces from scratch, giving policymakers the opportunity and power to make significant reforms. In virtually all major postconflict stability operations since World War II, internal security bodies—especially the police—have been partially or wholly rebuilt.

Long-Term Development. Once an initial effort to reform an existing police force or establish a new one has begun to produce results, efforts should shift to developing the skills needed to sustain professional institutions and practices. Intervening authorities should emphasize training the trainers. Lasting reform will require training and mentoring at many levels over extended periods of time. Viable reform needs to take place in an atmosphere of support from the local government, including the leadership of key ministries. Sustained and committed leadership by top policymakers in the host state, including ministry of interior officials, is critical for improving the effectiveness and accountability of police and internal security forces. Significant reform cannot be implemented from below against the indifference or hostility of senior managers. When political will for reform is lacking, international police training programs have had little or no success.

Best Practices

Predeployment Planning

One of the first decisions during the planning phase is to establish a mandate for the police—especially whether the police should be armed and have arrest authority or be unarmed and have no arrest authority. This decision is typically made by political authorities, not by mission planners. Both types of missions may have a mandate for local security reform, including the restructuring of local police institutions and retraining of local police. Recently, the UN has deployed hybrids, missions in which some police units (such as gendarmerie) are armed and have limited executive authority while others (such as general police) are unarmed and serve as monitors and trainers. In most postconflict cases, the use of armed police with executive authority is preferable, since local police are often unable or unwilling to provide police services. Executive missions can then transition to monitoring missions as local police forces become more competent. Police monitors are severely limited in their functions and, as Bosnia demonstrated, powerless if the local police refuse to cooperate. Failure to adequately empower international police will throw more of the burden of law enforcement onto the military component of the mission. When in doubt, it is preferable to plan for the more robust alternative.

Police planners also need to collect, analyze, and disseminate information on a wide variety of issues to appropriate personnel. They should collect information on all aspects of the host country's police: its historical role and functions, organizational structure, accountability, and effectiveness. They should also collect information on the specific cultural environment, contemporary political issues, and potential security threats that the police may encounter.

Another critical element during the planning phase is the placement of the police in the mission chain of command. If there cannot be unity of command, as there is in most UN missions, with both the military and police components answering to the Secretary-General's Special Representative, then there should be clear command relationships between the military and police elements in the mission. Police headquarters should be collocated with the military. Police (including gendarmerie) should participate in mission planning for operations.

Police-military cooperation is critical to the success of any stability operation, especially if several military, gendarmerie, and international and local police forces are involved in establishing security, each with its own chain of command. The civil police chain of command begins with the reporting officer up through formal first-line supervisory channels to the civilian police commissioner. This chain of command should be adhered to strictly if information is to move reliably along the lines of communication. The same should apply with regard to orders, instructions, and directives passed down from the civilian police headquarters. The civilian police commissioner should exercise final and complete control over all international civilian police personnel and their operations. The commissioner may delegate such authority as necessary to maintain the efficient operation of the civilian police component. Key subordinates may include a director of operations who controls the communication center; specialized units such as SWAT teams; an information system that tracks crimes, suspects, and convicted felons; and a director of investigations, who oversees forensics and a central criminal investigation unit. It may also include several operational layers:

- civilian police headquarters with support staff to facilitate field operations
- regions (districts or divisions), usually determined by local police administrative headquarters, supervised by an international civilian police regional commander with support staff
- police stations, which report to regional headquarters.

A critical issue that needs to be decided during the planning phase is whether police are subordinate to military or civilian command. The problem is confusing capacity with mandate and authority. In Bosnia and Kosovo, NATO multinational specialized units (composed of French gendarmerie and Italian carabinieri) were subject to military rules of engagement like other military forces. They could perform public-order functions—such as patrolling, information gathering, and riot control—but could not engage in law enforcement functions such as criminal investigations and arrests despite being fully trained and equipped to perform them. U.S. military police were part of NATO Kosovo Force (KFOR) and were subject to military rules of engagement. In Kosovo, the civilian UN specialized units (including the Spanish guardia civil and Romanian national gendarmerie) had the authority to perform both public-order and law enforcement functions. French gendarmerie served as members of embedded units in French KFOR, in the multinational specialized unit (constabulary), and in the United Nations Interim Administration Mission in Kosovo (UNMIK) police as individual officers performing civil police functions.

Gendarmerie units are capable of acting within a military or civilian command chain. If available, these units need to be assigned to one or the other element of a mission. In the early stages of an operation, when civilian assets are scarce and the military component has primary responsibility for public security, it may be desirable to place gendarmerie units under military command. As lead responsibility for law enforcement shifts from the military to the civil side of the mission, however, so should the necessary assets, including the gendarmerie units.

Law Enforcement and Public Security

International police may need to assume law enforcement responsibilities, especially when indigenous police have disintegrated during the conflict or have been discredited because of their abusive behavior. A key to law enforcement is determining which legal code to enforce. This is discussed in more detail in Chapter Four. Establishing which legal codes and laws are to be applied should occur prior to deployment. Purging and reforming existing penal codes is an early postintervention priority.

Policing tasks may include coordinating with the military to fight or deter insurgent groups, patrol borders, secure roads, investigate and break up criminal organizations, or even direct traffic. Law enforcement is particularly important in combating organized crime. In previous stability operations—such as Bosnia, Kosovo, Afghanistan, and Iraq—organized criminal enterprises began or resumed activities following the arrival of the international intervention force. Without the ability to conduct sophisticated investigations and incarcerate and try major crime figures, the international effort will fail to curb the power of key spoilers. International police forces must include officers skilled in investigating organized crime and forensics units for analyzing evidence.

In addition, international police may be required to conduct mobile patrols and provide area security in sensitive locations, such as ports, airports, bridges, and border-control points. They may provide security for election candidates and high-ranking officials, as well as polling stations during elections. They may also help oversee the movement of refugees and displaced persons and provide protection during humanitarian assistance efforts. Gendarmerie units may be necessary to respond to situations that require forces specifically trained and equipped to deal with civil disturbances, terrorism, drug trafficking, and organized crime. In contrast to most international civil police, these specialized units typically deploy with their own weapons, transport, communication, and logistical support.

Interoperability among international police units and between the police and military components of the mission is a particular challenge. The different contingents are likely to have different capabilities, equipment, doctrine, culture, language, legal and policy constraints, and command-and-control arrangements, while their home governments may have differing political objectives. Orchestrating police operations requires standardized procedures, communication capabilities, equipment, and liaison within the constraints of operations security. Coordination is the key to mission accomplishment. A civil operations center may help meet this requirement. It provides access for other agencies in need of police assistance and coordination, including NGOs, major international organizations, and host-nation authorities and agencies.

Intelligence, Surveillance, and Reconnaissance

Chapter Two discussed the importance of intelligence, surveillance, and reconnaissance operations for the military. This chapter focuses on the police. While there is inevitably some overlap between the two, intelligence, surveillance, and reconnaissance are critical for police in generating information on hostile and criminal groups in the area of operations, as well as on the environment (including weather, terrain, and civil considerations) and the performance of local police forces.

Police generally require tactical intelligence—actionable information related to civil disturbance and crime. A key challenge is often how to declassify military or other intelligence in a timely manner that does not compromise sources and methods. Police routinely collect tactical intelligence that can be useful to other parts of the international mission. Timely and accurate intelligence facilitates identifying and exploiting opportunities and depends on aggressive and continuous reconnaissance and surveillance. Cultural information is critical in gauging potential reactions to the operation, avoiding misunderstandings, and improving the effectiveness of the operation. Changes in the behavior of the population may suggest a need for change in tactics or strategy. Biographical information and leadership analysis are key to understanding potential adversaries and their methods of operation. Knowledge of the ethnic and religious factions and the historical background of the host country are important for achieving the objectives of the operation.

As with the military, the police should seek to acquire the capacity for collecting and collating intelligence by setting up an intelligence collection and analysis center—perhaps collocated with the military. Such a center poses difficulties in a multinational environment and one in which civilians and military need to operate together. Human sources are likely to provide the most useful information. Interpreters, low-level source operations, debriefs of locals, screening operations, and patrolling are the primary sources for assessing the capabilities and intentions of criminals and other security threats to the state. Police officers should emphasize to all personnel the importance of always being intelligence-conscious and should provide basic guidelines to improve their intelligence-gathering capability. Surveillance and reconnaissance may be employed to determine the disposition, activities, and intentions of civilian populations (hostile and neutral) and uniformed or irregular threats. Reconnaissance for information collection and security should continue throughout the operation. Success requires integrating all available information from civilian and other sources. However, police must also be informed and mindful of the legal limitations and those imposed by the mission leadership when acquiring information on civilians.

In many instances, international and nongovernmental organizations may have been in the area of operations long before international police. These organizations can provide valuable information through the reports, Web sites, and databases that they produce or maintain. For example, these organizations often collect GPS data on mines and unexploded ordnance. International police can access much of this information before deploying. However, these organizations and their representatives may resist being employed as a source of intelligence. Because of the nature of their work, humanitarian organizations feel that they must keep their distance from intervening authorities, especially international police or military. To the extent possible, police should foster communication and share information with these organizations. These organizations can be especially valuable in helping the international police force become more familiar with the cultures and sensitivities of the local population.

Recruiting, Vetting, and Training Police

Given the mutual suspicions and vested interests of most contending factions, intervening authorities should generally take charge of vetting—or at least closely monitor the process. Recruitment standards should be fair and transparent. Starting salaries should be adequate to attract appropriately qualified candidates, provide a decent standard of living, and thereby reduce incentives for corruption. In most countries, police salaries range from two to approximately four times the per capita GDP. Where ethnic or sectarian differences have driven past conflicts, police recruitment must reach out to marginalized communities. Efforts to recruit women and minorities will set a positive example and emphasize a break with the past.

A new force will require both basic and specialized training. An existing force will require substantial retraining to instill respect for human rights and the rule of law. It may also need to develop the skills necessary to maintain public security without recourse to more customary methods of arbitrary arrest, torture, and indefinite pretrial detention. Prior to any intervention, plans should be made and funding identified for a robust training effort. Suitable training sites should be located, a curriculum drawn up, and training staff hired. Assuming that such preparations are made, recruitment for the new or renewed police force can begin within a few weeks of the intervention. The training curriculum should include the following areas:

- basic police procedures, such as patrolling and crime-scene protection
- physical security
- corrections
- civil disturbance operations
- customs operations
- traffic control
- use of force
- special-unit training, such as counterdrug or counterterrorist operations
- human rights.

It may also be important to begin to develop an independent forensic capacity, including the ability to conduct fingerprint identification and basic evidentiary forensic testing. The construction of forensic crime labs and the training of relevant police officials in basic explosive detection, as well as in preserving evidence for prosecution, are also important.

Field training should ideally occur under the supervision of international police officers. Police academy graduates should complete a field training program that includes periods in the classroom as well as on-the-job experience. Kosovo is a useful example: The 19-week field training program included six weeks of classroom instruction after graduation from the police academy. Basic police training normally requires at least several months, followed by extensive on-the-job training, conducted under the oversight of international police experts. Pressure for rapid deployment sometimes results in more accelerated schedules. In Iraq, the most extended basic course of instruction was eight weeks, and many new police officers were fielded with considerably less training. Not surprisingly, the resulting standards of performance were unacceptably low. Even with extended basic training, new police will function poorly unless led and mentored by experienced officers. International police can play these roles to some extent, but an early start is needed to identify and develop local leadership. Candidates for such positions may be drawn from among the more capable new recruits, the existing police forces, or from individuals with legal or other relevant experience. Selecting, training, and mentoring such individuals will shape the resultant force decisively; it cannot be started too early.

Infrastructure and Equipment

Local police forces are likely to require everything from new uniforms to transport and communication equipment. Examples of appropriate nonlethal and lethal assistance include the provision of communication equipment such as radios, protective gear such as helmets and flak jackets, handcuffs, vehicles such as police cars and jeeps, and handguns. The construction and rehabilitation of police infrastructure and facilities presents a more straightforward task than achieving a change in the culture of the police force. An important guide will be in providing infrastructure and facilities through a development lens. Where police aid missions are managed by Western personnel with little development experience, the tendency has been to import state-of-the-art solutions in prison design, communication equipment, or weaponry. These may be inappropriate for the local context. After international police depart, the country may not be able to cover the cost of maintenance or replacement or may not have the technical ability to conduct repairs.

Many donors are reluctant to provide weapons for police. In some cases, international arms embargoes adopted prior to the intervention may remain in existence, as in Liberia, raising another obstacle. Weapons provided should be appropriate for local circumstances rather than dictated purely by availability or the most common weapons in use in the donor country. If the intervening military and international police units have prepared themselves to provide for public security for some extended period, it may be feasible and desirable to phase in weaponry for a new local police force gradually. On the other hand, if local police are to be the first line of defense against criminal and extremist elements in the society, it makes little sense to arm them less well than their adversaries.

Institutional Reform

Institutional reform includes either reforming the current police and ministry of interior or building a new institution largely from scratch. There are three factors that should be considered. First, is there enough left of the old police organization to provide a basis for rebuilding? Second, how discredited and unpopular is the current police force with the local population? Third, how likely is it that the intervening powers will dispose of enough military and police resources to provide for public security during the lengthy time needed to build a new police force?

Even the most incompetent and corrupt local police force will normally be regarded by an intervening power as better than nothing. Assuming that such a force exists, the decision is then whether to rebuild a new force on the foundation of the old or to rebuild a completely new force while retaining the old for an interim period. In El Salvador, UN civilian police oversaw the elimination of the military-controlled national police force over a 24-month period and supervised the construction of a new national civil police force under civilian command. UN police were also responsible for overseeing the abolishment of several other branches of the police, such as the national guard, treasury police, and national intelligence directorate, which operated under military command. A similar process was undertaken in Haiti in the mid-1990s, where the old police force, an element of the Haitian

Army, was disbanded slowly over a two-year period during which an entirely new force was trained and deployed.

In most instances, the choice has been to build upon the foundations of the old police force rather than to start anew. This is less disruptive and requires less initial investment on the part of the intervening authorities. To the extent that the old police force has been even moderately successful in dealing with common crime, this approach may also minimize the increase in violent crime that often accompanies the reform of abusive security establishments. On the other hand, building reformed institutions on the foundations of existing ones is less likely to ensure a thorough break with patterns of corruption and abuse or to provide the public with an image of a new start.

However abusive or incompetent the old security establishment may be, intervening authorities cannot afford to disband it unless something is immediately available to take its place. Thus, where international police are not likely to be available in sufficient numbers, disbanding the local police force is not going to be a viable option, however desirable such a step may be in principle.

There is no universally accepted template for structuring national and local police forces. Some countries, such as the United States and India, have a decentralized policing structure with independence of command at the state and local levels. Other countries, such as France, maintain a more centralized police establishment with a single center of control. Both approaches can produce effective, democratic policing. Intervening authorities need, therefore, to devise solutions that deliver order and accountability in the particular social, cultural, and political setting in which they are needed. Structural questions that need to be tackled include the degree of national centralization over the police force and the decision whether to create a gendarmerie that is functionally and organizationally distinct from the police and military. It is generally better to define solutions responsive to local needs and expectations than to try to replicate the intervening power's domestic arrangements.

Long-Term Development

Once an initial effort to organize the new police force has begun to produce results, the focus of training should shift to developing long-term skills needed to sustain professional institutions and practices. Intervening authorities should emphasize training the trainers. Field training programs, long-term mentoring, continuous professional education, and management and specialist training are key to institutionalizing reformed practices, attitudes, and new skills among the local police. At least as important is ensuring that the ongoing training drives a change in culture among local police. One way to achieve this result is to encourage local police officials to observe practices in democratic states and consider the adaptability of such practices to their country. This may be a better option than encouraging international advisors to import systems and procedures wholesale from their home jurisdictions.

Responsiveness and accountability are critical aspects of institutional development. Responsiveness is the ability of the police to take its cues from individual members of the public, not simply from the government. The most obvious example of responsiveness is the implementation of a 911-type emergency system like that used in the United States. Such a system demonstrates the power of the individual to summon police assistance regardless of social and political standing. Responsiveness brings two advantages. It shows that police are accountable to diverse interests, including those from minority ethnic groups. It also shows that the authority of the state will be used in the interest of the people.

Accountability is measured by the police authority's submission to and acceptance of outside supervision. Courts, legislatures, the media, ombudsmen, and complaint processes are all outlets of accountability. Accountability is critical because it demonstrates that police are ultimately responsible to laws, not simply to the government of the moment. Law enforcement must be held accountable to an independent and effective judiciary. The police must not enjoy immunity from prosecution. They should be required to obtain warrants from a judge before conducting activities like searches or wiretapping. To hold police accountable for their actions, it is also important to develop policy documents and operational manuals that are grounded in national law and international standards and to ensure that these procedures and standards are fully integrated into all aspects of police training.

Sustainability is the final element of institutional development. In the immediate postconflict phase, external involvement is likely to be significant. But reforms will take root only if there is a transition to local responsibility. This can occur only if the force created can become fiscally sustainable. It makes little sense to use international aid to build a large police force and buy expensive equipment if the host state has to slash the budget and police numbers within a few years when the aid dries up. It is also important to encourage the development of local support for the reforms being introduced. Measures such as civic education and transparency programs may help citizens come to expect effective, honest, and impartial service from the police. If the political process allows citizens to articulate these expectations, there is a greater likelihood that the reform program will be sustainable in the long term.

Corruption will reduce the effectiveness of the police. It can be as much a problem for international personnel as it is for local governments. Steps need to be taken to increase transparency in awarding international and local contracts, monitoring financial transactions, and holding accountable those who are guilty of crimes, including local and international police officials.

Key Actors

Two international organizations are structured to deploy international police: the United Nations and the European Union. The UN currently deploys over 6,000 international civil police officers to multiple operations and has extensive experience in the field. The EU organized an international police mission to Macedonia and took over UN police operations in Bosnia. Neither the UN nor the EU has a standing police force. Rather, they manage police missions, and police are made available for international missions by individual countries. Several other international organizations have also been involved in the police component of stability operations. For example, the Organization for Security and Cooperation in Europe (OSCE) organized a successful police training establishment in Kosovo.

The United States organized a civilian police component of the 1994 operation in Haiti. In Bosnia and Kosovo, the United Nations organized the civilian police component while NATO supplied the military component of the mission. The U.S. Department of State funded and managed the U.S. police deployments to Haiti, Bosnia, and Kosovo, employing a contractor, DynCorp, to recruit and pay the individual U.S. police officers. The officers involved were either active or retired members of state or local police forces.

The U.S. government has not sought in any systematic way to tap federal law enforcement agencies for recruits for such missions. Neither has it made provisions to compensate state and local law enforcement agencies for personnel released for such duty. As a result, the United States has developed little capacity to deploy civil police officers in formed, cohesive units; is unable to recruit individual police officers in sufficient numbers; and must rely on other nations or its own military to perform functions such as SWAT, riot control, counterterrorism, and counternarcotics where such capabilities are needed. U.S. difficulty in deploying civilian police is also caused by the absence of a systematic effort to reach out to the many thousands of law enforcement personnel throughout the country. Those who do volunteer for such operations tend to become involved informally, through word of mouth, leading many potential sources of personnel untapped. The decentralization of the U.S. law enforcement system makes this a significant challenge. The inability to mobilize civilian police for stability missions has negatively affected the performance of U.S.-led missions in Afghanistan and Iraq.

In the 1994 intervention in Haiti, the United States organized an international police element of over 1,000 officers from among a coalition of the willing, before turning these functions over to the United Nations six months later. In Bosnia and Kosovo, the UN provided the police elements of the international mission, about 2,000 strong in the former and 5,000 in the latter. In Afghanistan and Iraq, the burden of ensuring public security and organizing a reformed Iraqi police establishment has fallen almost exclusively on U.S. military police and other U.S. military units even less prepared for such responsibilities. This solution has had mixed success; in both countries, there has been a dramatic increase in common crime. In Afghanistan, organized crime, in the form of drug production, may account for up to 40 percent of the country's GDP.

Throughout the 1990s, foreign police training was done by the U.S. Department of Justice International Criminal Investigative Training Assistance Program, under the oversight of the U.S. Department of State Bureau of International Narcotics and Law Enforcement. Historically, the U.S. military has provided limited police training in the context of stability operations, despite legislative prohibitions that make clear that the Congress is not comfortable with the U.S. military having such a role. In Afghanistan and Iraq, the U.S. military has greatly increased its responsibilities for police training. Other nations have established substantial police training missions, including Germany in Afghanistan, Italy in Albania, and Britain and France in a number of their former colonies. The United States runs a regional police training establishment in Budapest, the International Law Enforcement Academy.

International police are drawn from countries with a wide variety of policing techniques, skill sets, positions on human rights and democratic policing practices, cultures, and approaches to hierarchy and rank. Before deployment, they should undergo testing and orientation, including physical training, psychological testing, firearms and defensive tactics training, and a variety of short modules covering peace operations and regional politics and history. Before deployment, civilian police personnel should be made familiar with international standards that apply to a broad range of public security and human rights functions. They should have some understanding of the general differences among legal systems based on the Napoleonic code, English common law, and sharia, as they may relate to the mission at hand. They should also be trained in techniques for effective monitoring and mentoring. Based on UN practices, at a minimum, police officers should receive the following specialized training:

- basic individual and collective crowd-control techniques and procedures, with special attention given to weapon training, maneuverability, and negotiation
- basic individual and collective training related to other special police functions, including hard entry, vehicle checkpoints, building security, VIP protection, and escorts
- basic map reading, use of GPS, truck driving, and radio procedures
- competency in the language of the mission, usually English or French
- mine awareness.

Sizing

In most societies, the ratio of police to total population ranges from 150 to 300 police officers per 100,000 inhabitants, with an average of 225. Examples include the Philippines (148), the United States (244), Chile (195), Britain (234), Japan (182), Turkey (254), and South Africa (287).[1] Postconflict societies tend to suffer from high levels of social conflict and common criminality, suggesting a need for police numbering in the higher end of this range. More urbanized societies also require higher levels of policing. Figure 3.1 highlights the police-to-population ratios in 11 postconflict societies five years after stability operations began. In over half the cases, there were more than 200 police officers per 100,000 inhabitants. The highest levels occurred in countries with significant violence or criminality, including Cambodia at 582, Bosnia at 429, and Iraq at 366. The low number in Haiti reflects

---

[1]   United Nations Office on Drugs and Crime, *The Eighth United Nations Survey on Crime Trends and the Operations of Criminal Justice Systems*, Vienna, 2002.

Figure 3.1
Local Police Levels Five Years After Stability Operations

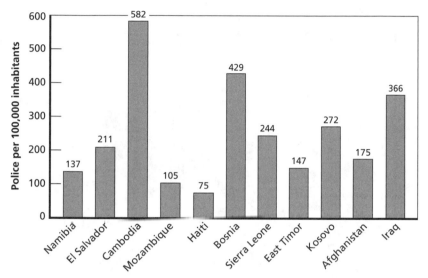

SOURCE: Data compiled from International Institute for Strategic Studies; United Nations, Department of Peacekeeping Operations; *Jane's Online*; U.S. Department of State, Country Reports on Human Rights Practices, Afghan Progress Reports, and Iraq Weekly Status Reports; and UN Secretary-General's reports to the United Nations Security Council. Police levels are after two years for Iraq and after three years for Afghanistan.
RAND *MG557-3.1*

that country's inability to fund a more substantial force, combined with a decline in international assistance for police. This dearth of police in Haiti contributed to the breakdown in security that occasioned another international intervention in 2004.

In cases in which local police do not exist or are hopelessly compromised, international police and military forces may need to carry the burden for public security. In Kosovo, the United Nations deployed nearly 5,000 international civil police personnel, 250 per 100,000 inhabitants, while NATO also deployed a significant number of military police. Figure 3.2 illustrates the range of international police deployments. In such cases as Kosovo and East Timor, there were no indigenous police available. In El Salvador and Cambodia, local police undertook most public-order functions. In cases such as Afghanistan

Figure 3.2
Peak International Civil Police Levels

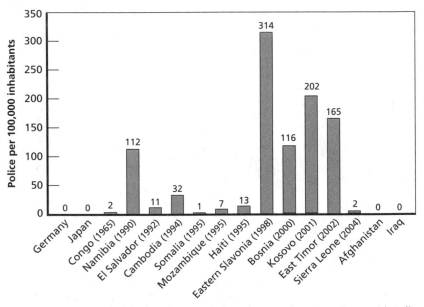

SOURCE: Data compiled from Robert M. Perito, *The American Experience with Police in Peace Operations*, Clementsport, Canada: Canadian Peacekeeping Press, 2002; International Institute for Strategic Studies; United Nations, Department of Peacekeeping Operations; *Jane's Online*; Ramsbotham and Woodhouse (1999); United Nations, Department of Public Information; Robert B. Oakley, Michael J. Dziedzic, and Eliot M. Goldberg, eds., *Policing in the New World Disorder: Peace Operations and Public Security*, Washington, D.C.: National Defense University, 1998. Population data, U.S. Census Bureau, International Data Base.
RAND *MG557-3.2*

and Iraq, the absence of both local and international police prevented the establishment of a secure environment, despite significant military deployments. Figure 3.3 illustrates the ratio of international police to military personnel in 16 different operations. UN-led operations such as those in Namibia, Cambodia, Mozambique, and East Timor have had the highest ratios of police to soldiers; U.S.-led operations in Germany, Japan, Afghanistan, and Iraq have had the lowest. The United States has generally used military police and regular troops to perform the functions that civilian police perform in UN-led operations.

Figure 3.3
Police-to-Military Ratio

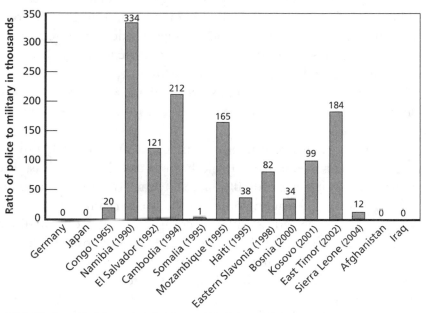

SOURCE: Compiled from data in Figures 2.3, 2.4, and 3.2.
RAND *MG557-3.3*

International civilian police deployment can be divided into two types for sizing and costing purposes. The first are comprised of unarmed police, whose activities are limited to advising, training, monitoring, and mentoring.[2] The second includes armed police with arrest authority.[3] The average deployment of the first, more limited type has been 23 police officers for every 100,000 inhabitants. The average deployment of the second type has been 161 officers for every 100,000 inhabitants.

---

[2] The cases include Congo (in the 1960s), Namibia, El Salvador, Cambodia, Somalia, Mozambique, Haiti, and Sierra Leone.

[3] The average was 161 per 100,000 inhabitants. Afghanistan, Germany, and Japan were excluded from the average because no civilian international police were deployed to these three countries.

Costs

Intervening powers must anticipate funding much or all of the costs for public security in the first several years of any intervention. The local government is unlikely to have the revenues needed to perform such functions, even assuming that it has the competence to do so. Local security forces that do exist are likely to be funding themselves through various forms of corruption and extortion, living in a symbiotic relationship with the criminal and extremist elements they are supposed to be combating.

In situations in which international police are assuming a direct law enforcement role, a general rule has been to deploy at least 100 international police per 100,000 inhabitants. The precise number varies significantly depending on the security environment in the host country, strategic objectives, rules of engagement, and the condition of the existing police force. There are several types of costs for deploying international police: personnel, procurement, and operation and maintenance costs. The personnel costs for international police vary depending on the country of origin. Currently, the United States pays between $80,000 and $100,000 per police officer per year—roughly $90,000 on average—as part of most UN or other stability missions. These costs include a base salary plus completion bonuses and hazardous duty pay. In addition to personnel costs, the UN also budgets approximately $65,000 per person for procurement, operations and maintenance, and other related expenses for civilian police missions.[4] We thus estimated the cost of deploying a well-trained international police officer as roughly $155,000 per year.

Costs for building and maintaining a local police force include those for personnel, equipment, facilities, operations, and oversight, including the cost of staffing a ministry of interior. Figure 3.4 shows the total costs of fielding a national police force in 15 different countries, expressed as the cost per police officer, as a multiple of each country's per capita GDP. To arrive at these figures, interior ministry budgets

---

[4]   Statistics provided in an interview with a member of the Civilian Police Division, Department of Peacekeeping Operations, United Nations, New York, October 7, 2005.

Figure 3.4
Cost of Fielding a Local Police Force

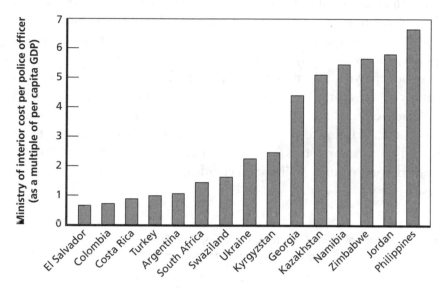

SOURCE: Data courtesy of each country's ministry of interior in response to RAND requests.
RAND *MG557-3.4*

from the 15 countries were converted into U.S. dollars and divided by the number of police officers in the national force. These per–police officer costs were then compared to per capita GDP in U.S. dollars converted at market exchange rates. We found that, on average, the cost per police officer of running a ministry of interior is roughly 3.2 times a country's per capita GDP at market exchange rates.

What does this analysis imply for postconflict nation-building operations? To illustrate, assume that the international community intervenes in Macedonia. It had a 2006 population of 2 million. Using the average number of police officers (225) per 100,000 inhabitants, cited earlier, Macedonia would need 4,500 police officers. Macedonia has a per capita GDP of $7,800. Multiplying $7,800 by the ratio 3.2, and then by 4,500 police officers, gives a projected annual budget of approximately $100 million needed to operate the police and ministry of interior following an intervention. Were local policing capabilities to have collapsed to the point at which international police were needed to conduct law enforcement operations, intervening authorities might deploy international civilian police. Using the estimate of 161 armed international police officers per 100,000 inhabitants cited previously, Macedonia might need approximately 3,200 international police officers. Multiplying this number by $155,000—our estimated cost of deploying an international police officer for one year—gives a total cost for an international police presence of approximately $500 million per year. For a smaller force of unarmed international police to conduct training and mentoring, approximately 460 police officers would be necessary. This works out to approximately $70 million per year for international civilian police officers. Table 3.1 summarizes the results.[5]

Table 3.1
Estimates for an Operation in Macedonia, Year One

Operation Type	Number of Local Police	Cost of Running Ministry of Interior (2002 US$)	Number of Int'l Police	Cost of Int'l Police Force (2002 US$)	Total Expenditure (2002 US$)
Peace enforcement operation to Macedonia	4,500	100 million	3,200	500 million	600 million
Peacekeeping operation to Macedonia	4,500	100 million	460	70 million	170 million

SOURCE: RAND calculations.

NOTE: Data for Macedonia are from Central Intelligence Agency (2006).

---

[5] The estimating equations for police missions are as follows:

number of local police $= 225 \times$ population $/ 100,000$
cost of running ministry of interior $=$ per capita GDP $\times 3.2 \times$ number of police
number of international police (peace enforcement) $= 161 \times$ population $/ 100,000$
number of international police (peacekeeping) $= 23 \times$ population $/ 100,000$
cost of international police $=$ number of police $\times \$155,000$.

CHAPTER FOUR

Rule of Law

The rule-of-law sector includes the courts, ministry of justice, correctional system, legal statutes, and other institutions that ensure, in Aristotle's words, "a government of laws, not men."[1] It also includes the police, addressed in the preceding chapter. *Rule of law* refers to an ideal that ensures fairness, justice, and equality before the law. Rule of law also implies preventing official arbitrariness.[2] Almost by definition, rule of law will have broken down in any postconflict society, which is often characterized by nonfunctioning courts, substandard prisons, inadequate salaries for judges and other personnel, insufficient operating budgets, and poor training.

Protecting private property and enforcing contracts are critical to the operation of a market economy. Ideally, under the rule of law, regulations are intelligible; there are effective dispute-resolution mechanisms and a predictable legal framework in which commercial disagreements can be resolved and property protected. Key legal provisions include procedures for setting up limited-liability companies, contracts, and mechanisms for resolving commercial disputes. Security also requires

---

[1] This chapter does not examine the international legal framework regarding the decision to intervene in a country, such as acquiring international legal authority for an intervention from the United Nations Security Council. While an important topic, the primary focus of this chapter is on building rule of law once major combat has ended.

[2] On definitions of the rule of law, see Richard H. Fallon, Jr., "'The Rule of Law' as a Concept in Constitutional Discourse," *Columbia Law Review*, Vol. 97, No. 1, January 1997, pp. 1–56; and Friedrich A. Hayek, *Law, Legislation, and Liberty, Volume 1: Rules and Order*, Chicago: University of Chicago Press, 1973.

a functioning justice system that is able to prosecute criminals and determine innocence or guilt on the basis of objective rules of evidence. Better policing will not sustain a secure environment if the judiciary is incompetent or corrupt, sentencing is arbitrary or politicized, or prison conditions are inhumane. Failure to establish a viable justice system has plagued many efforts to reconstruct police and security forces. The rule of law improves human rights conditions by ensuring due process, equality before the law, and judicial checks on executive power. Without the rule of law, arrests and detentions are arbitrary, there is no effective mechanism for preventing torture or extrajudicial execution, individuals or groups may be free to take the law into their own hands, and abuses may go unpunished.

Key Challenges

Preconflict Legal Planning. There is often a paucity of information on the status of a postconflict society's justice system. Personnel working for NGOs who have spent significant time in the country may provide useful advice. What are the characteristics of the legal system? How effective has it been? What are the key challenges? How should the international community prioritize and sequence efforts to rebuild rule of law?

Establishing Applicable Law. What law should apply? If the society has long been in conflict, there may be competing codes. As Figure 4.1 indicates, a wide range of legal sources may be used. Societies may rely predominantly on formal law, informal or tribal law, or some combination of the two. In many postconflict settings, such as Afghanistan and Somalia, village councils and tribal elders have played the primary role in resolving disputes and meting out justice—especially in rural areas. The formal justice system may be weak, lack legitimacy, or serve only a small portion of the population. Customary law is used widely in many parts of the world. It often survives conflicts more intact than the formal courts. Customary law may play a

Figure 4.1
Types of Rule of Law

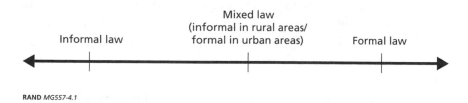

RAND *MG557-4.1*

complementary role in providing justice and a nonviolent means for resolving disputes during the postconflict phase. International actors have often tended to ignore customary law in administering postconflict justice, as it may be controversial and contrary to international standards.

Recruiting, Vetting, and Training Judges and Lawyers. A frequent difficulty in recruiting, vetting, and appointing legal personnel is identifying candidates who have the necessary professional experience and are politically acceptable to the general public. Ethnic, tribal, or religious cleavages may create a significant challenge to choosing judges because communities may not give their consent to the process unless they have adequate representation.

Building Infrastructure and Providing Equipment. Most states emerging from conflict have suffered damage to their rule-of-law infrastructure. As one lawyer involved in efforts to reconstruct the justice system in East Timor argued,

> The pre-existing judicial infrastructure in East Timor was almost entirely destroyed. Most court buildings were burned and looted, all court office equipment, registers, records and archives, and— indispensable to the practice of the legal profession—law books, case files and other legal resources were dislocated or burned.[3]

These all need to be restored.

---

[3] Hansjörg Strohmeyer, "Building a New Judiciary for East Timor: Challenges of a Fledgling Nation," *Criminal Law Forum*, Vol. 11, No. 3, September 2000, pp. 259–285 [p. 268].

Improving the Corrections System. In postconflict settings, pretrial detention facilities and prisons are often in poor condition. Compounding this problem, donor states may be reluctant to become involved in rebuilding a system with a reputation for significant human rights violations. Following the overthrow of the Taliban regime, the Afghan prison system collapsed. Prisons were physically crumbling after years of neglect and lacked trained, qualified staff. Prison staff struggled to hold thousands of people, many for long periods, in poor conditions. These conditions violated international standards relating to the treatment of detainees. Detention facilities in Kosovo were also poor. Most prewar prisons were damaged by bombs or arson; some detainees ended up in police holding cells or in NATO tents behind barbed wire. Few were held in facilities that were built for long-term detention.

Establishing a Rule-of-Law Culture. Many justice systems are characterized by the absence of judicial independence, political elites who use the judiciary to serve their own interests, and entrenched corruption. The executive and judicial branches often compete for management of the judicial system, with the ministry of justice and the supreme court vying for control. Training judges and other legal personnel, providing technical assistance, and helping rebuild infrastructure are unlikely on their own to fix a system debilitated by corruption and political interference.

Supporting Transitional Justice. Virtually all conflicts involve human rights abuses. In many cases, these abuses are widespread and systematic. Transitional justice incorporates a range of approaches that societies undertake to deal with legacies of abuse as they move from a period of violent conflict or oppression toward peace and respect for individual and collective rights. In making such a transition, societies may have to confront the painful legacy of the past to achieve a sense of justice for all citizens, establish or renew civic trust, reconcile people and communities, and prevent future abuses. However, war crime trials, truth commissions, and other types of transitional justice can also trigger nationalist backlashes and revive tensions.

Best Practices

Preconflict Legal Planning

Planning should begin with a comprehensive needs assessment. Capable individuals and organizations should be identified to quickly draft new legislation in accordance with internationally recognized standards and with the country's tradition. To facilitate this effort, international actors should develop standby arrangements with partner agencies such as the United Nations, the World Bank, universities, and NGOs. These agencies may be asked to help prepare drafts of initial needs assessments that would be finalized by international actors in concert with lawyers from the host country.

A body of legislation related to basic law enforcement may need to be developed as part of a quick-start package. Readily applicable criminal procedures and criminal codes, as well as a code regulating the activities of the police, have been essential to civilian police activities during the early phases of stability operations. Civilian police, including international police, need to have a well-defined legal framework in which to act. They need clearly spelled-out legal provisions to carry out their daily law enforcement activities effectively and without fear of breaching the law. They also need a clear legal framework under which the future local police force will be trained. Newly appointed judges, prosecutors, and lawyers must be educated on the applicable law to execute their functions. An indispensable initial step is for international actors to draft and put in place interim laws governing criminal procedures and other core areas of police activity. Examples include arrest and detention and searches and seizures.

Several critical enablers can, if put in place in advance of an operation, facilitate the rapid imposition of law and order. These include rosters of trained judicial specialists and penal officers available for rapid deployment, advanced training in various justice and reconciliation tasks, standard operating procedures and contingency plans, standing capacities for material and private-sector support, and memorandums of understanding among key international actors.

Planners need to be aware of common and civil law traditions in the countries in which they will be operating. Common law systems are developed from custom and began before there were any written laws. The courts continue to adjudicate based on common law. Civil law developed in Rome out of Justinian's corpus juris civilis. Today, the difference between civil and common law lies less in codification and more in the approach to codes and statutes. In civil law countries, legislation is seen as the primary source of law. By default, courts base their judgments on codes and statutes. Courts thus have to reason on the basis of the general rules and principles of the code, drawing analogies from statutory provisions to fill lacunae and to achieve coherence. In common law countries, rulings from past cases are a primary source of law.

Establishing Applicable Law

There is often little or no functioning justice system in the immediate postconflict phase. Uncertainty about applicable law causes great confusion. For instance, what laws should govern the apprehension and trial of criminal suspects? How should disputed property claims be resolved? A vacuum in the rule of law should be avoided by establishing at least interim judicial provisions concerning the detention and hearings of individuals apprehended on criminal charges. One key element of applicable law is the establishment of a viable constitution.

Past operations, such as those in East Timor and Kosovo, demonstrate that, where the justice sector has completely broken down, rapid deployment of military lawyers can help fill the vacuum until civilian authorities are available to take over. The advantage of such an arrangement is that military lawyers can be deployed with the troops. Military lawyers would have to be in a position to execute legal functions immediately, including authorizing arrest, detention, prosecution, and initial adjudication, without engaging in the time-consuming task of assembling and familiarizing themselves with local laws. Such military arrangements should remain in place only for a limited and clearly defined period of time, until responsibility can be handed over to an adequately functioning civilian body. Any such arrangements will have to accord strictly with internationally recognized human rights and other relevant legal standards. The role for the military as an emergency provider of law enforcement includes the construction of emergency detention facilities.

The most immediate task is to choose an applicable system of law at least for the near term. Judicial appointments; legal training; and the performance of judicial, prosecutorial, and other legal functions depend on the existence of a clear body of applicable law. In the absence of a clear body of applicable law, international actors may have to draft regulations indicating which previously existing laws still apply or set forth entirely new laws. International lawyers may be required to engage in interpreting the penal code or the criminal procedure code through the lens of international human rights. This means applying provisions that meet international standards while eliminating those that do not. Obtaining all the legislation that constitutes the applicable body of law and translating it so that international experts can assist their local colleagues are also major challenges.

There is often a temptation to use the applicable law in place during and before the war, *mutatis mutandis*. This generally means ensuring that existing laws conform to internationally recognized human rights standards and do not conflict with the international actors' mandate. It also involves reconciling regulations promulgated by the mission with existing law. Using the current applicable law may be sensible in most conditions. In East Timor, UN personnel decided that Indonesian laws would remain applicable. After a review of existing legislation, UN personnel abrogated several laws, such as those governing antisubversion and capital punishment. The most pressing need was for a mechanism to review the arrests and detentions that had been carried out by the Australian-led International Force East Timor (INTERFET). However, the UN civil police force was facing a growing number of ordinary crimes, including violent assault, rape, and murder. INTERFET had established a temporary arrest and detention system that was run by military personnel but was neither mandated nor equipped to try, convict, or sentence criminal offenders. The United

Nations Transitional Administration in East Timor (UNTAET), the UN-led successor mission, needed to install a civilian mechanism that would provide the minimum judicial functions required upon arrest and detention.

Using the applicable law in place during and before the war may not be practical in all situations, especially in cases of interethnic conflict. Kosovo offers a useful lesson. After the 1999 NATO-led military intervention, UNMIK faced the challenge of governing 1.8 million people in a devastated region with no functioning courts, prisons, or police and a legacy of ethnic bitterness between the Serbs and Kosovar Albanians. UNMIK decided to resolve the problem of applicable law by making it the same as the law that was applicable before the NATO air campaign began. UNMIK Regulation 1999/1 stated, "The laws applicable in the territory of Kosovo prior to 24 March 1999 shall continue to apply in Kosovo," insofar as those laws did not conflict with internationally recognized human rights standards or other UNMIK regulations.[4] This approach led to serious problems. For Kosovo's Albanian majority, the applicable laws before the bombing campaign were "Serb laws," a symbol of Serbian oppression of Albanians. A crisis ensued as Albanians protested the decision and Albanian judges refused to apply these laws. Six months after issuing Regulation 1999/1, UNMIK declared that the new applicable law in Kosovo would be the law in force on March 22, 1989, immediately before Serbian President Slobodan Milosevic put an end to Kosovo's autonomous status.

In Afghanistan, the legal system put in place after the collapse of the Taliban regime was derived from the 1964 constitution and was amended by the Bonn Agreement of December 2001. In addition to the set of laws based on the 1964 constitution, applicable law in Afghanistan included a mix of customary law and sharia-based law that had evolved over the previous 120 years. The three bodies of law—state law, sharia law, and customary law—overlapped and provided implementation challenges. The Afghan case demonstrates that international and local actors may have to be flexible in creating

---

4   United Nations Interim Administration Mission in Kosovo, Regulation No. 1999/1, "On the Authority of the Interim Administration in Kosovo," July 25, 1999.

applicable law. As such, key areas in which to establish formal legislation include the following:

- public administration
- civil procedural law
- trafficking, organized crime, and counternarcotics
- corruption
- corrections
- property ownership
- juvenile offenders and child protection
- immigration and nationality
- vehicular traffic
- commercial codes for partnerships, corporations, recognition of foreign entities, bankruptcy, contracts, and antitrust
- civil service.

A related issue is what to do about informal or customary systems. How should international actors design rule-of-law programs for countries that rely on customary law? There is no single answer. Legal reform should include limiting the authority of informal law mechanisms in some areas, especially criminal justice, because it can be subverted and manipulated by local power-holders. Connections between the formal and informal systems may need to be designed, perhaps by crafting procedures for courts to confirm the results of dispute settlements of using customary means of justice. In the short term, fostering the informal system makes more sense than trying to expand the formal system to remote regions. Disputes among neighbors—such as over water rights and livestock ownership—may be left to traditional law, at least temporarily. Criminal disputes—especially those involving violent crime—usually need to be adjudicated through the official system of justice. A number of postconflict law programs have first focused on standing up the legal system in major urban areas, then expanding it to rural areas. Citizens also need to be educated about their rights under the constitution and the use of courts. Table 4.1 explains several key differences between formal and informal systems.

Table 4.1
A Comparison of Formal and Informal Systems

Area	Formal System	Informal or Customary System
System	Could be based on common or civil law	Often council of tribal elders
Source of law	Secular law, or perhaps Islamic jurisprudence	Tribal tradition
Decisionmakers	Judges render a decision that can be appealed to the court of appeals	Local elders consider the case but result often must be consensual; proceedings frequently continue until consensus is reached
Geographic reach	Sometimes limited to major urban areas	Varies, but often in rural areas
Objective	Resolve the immediate dispute between the parties	Focus of the dispute may be the family, clan, or tribe rather than the individual; object is often to restore relationship between parties who must continue to live together
Civil versus criminal cases	*Criminal:* Prosecuted by government prosecutor; action for compensation of the victim is part of the same case and is pursued by prosecutor *Civil:* Local justice officer may be the gatekeeper; assists plaintiff in paperwork and may reject case; may be some linkage with customary sector	Often no distinction between civil and criminal cases; any wrong is a disruption of the social fabric; imbalance can sometimes be rectified by the transgressor transferring something of value to the wronged party

Recruiting, Vetting, and Training Judges and Lawyers

In view of the practical and symbolic significance of recruiting and appointing judges and lawyers in a postconflict environment, it is essential to proceed in a transparent manner to ensure legitimacy. Capable candidates have to be identified at all levels. Vetting and appointment have to be made in accordance with objective, verifiable criteria and merit, while also ensuring political or ethnic balance. This frequently involves having international jurists assist local personnel in cataloging the qualifications of judges and lawyers. Experienced jurists interview potential judges and lawyers and assess their competency and qualifications. The absence of trained legal professionals in past postconflict environments suggests that outside expertise would be beneficial. The process has to transparent and based on a sound legislative framework. In Kosovo, East Timor, and Afghanistan, the establishment of independent judicial commissions was the primary mechanism for the selection of judges and prosecutors. It served as an important safeguard for appointing the judiciary. The commissions were designed as autonomous bodies. They collected applications from candidates, with a law degree as a minimum requirement. The commission then selected candidates for judicial or prosecutorial office on the basis of merit and made recommendations on appointments.

In some cases, the intervening authorities may need to establish a judiciary whose composition reflects the various ethnic communities. No reconciliation effort, including the prosecution and trial of individuals charged with human rights violations, can succeed without an independent, impartial judiciary that enjoys the confidence of the population. A lack of trained individuals can present a major challenge, as illustrated by the case of East Timor. During Indonesia's occupation, no East Timorese lawyers were appointed judges or prosecutors. The UN established the Transitional Judicial Service, comprised of three East Timorese and two international experts. Because of the lack of telephone, radio, and other forms of communication, the UN resorted to leaflet drops by airplanes and word of mouth to search for qualified lawyers. Within two months, several dozen qualified East Timorese with law degrees were found. From this group, 60 applied for positions.

The first eight Timorese judges and two prosecutors were sworn in on January 7, 2000.

The intervening authorities need to meet standards for due process and fair trial. They should help recruit, appoint, and ensure the provision of adequate legal counsel to the detainees. This is of particular importance when those arrested belong to specific ethnic or political groups or are suspected of grave human rights violations and whose cases could become politically sensitive. In Kosovo, UNMIK identified lawyers from different ethnic backgrounds who were qualified and willing to serve as defense counsel in such cases. UNMIK provided each detainee with a list of names from which the detainee could choose. The number of detainees far exceeded the number of available lawyers, however. In East Timor, Section 27 of UNTAET Regulation 2000/11 expressly recognized the right to legal representation and the obligation to ensure effective and equal access to lawyers.[5] UNTAET set up the nucleus of a donor-financed public-defender system.

There has been wide variation in the training and capacity of judges and other legal personnel in past stability operations. A dearth of experienced judges and lawyers places a burden on international actors to ensure that adequate legal and judicial training programs are put in place. The objective should be to ensure that the few available judges and lawyers are prepared as soon as possible to perform their functions. Donors should set up quick-impact training and mentoring programs in core issues such as pretrial standards, the conduct of hearings, and the drafting of detention orders. Expert advice on drafting laws, including information on models from other countries, should be provided to revise existing laws, criminal codes, and regulations, as well as to write new ones. Historically, donor programs to revise the legal code have targeted the commercial code—banking regulation, taxation, antitrust, bankruptcy, and foreign investment—as part of economic reform programs. These programs are of less immediate importance following a conflict. Aid providers can help improve the legal profession by strengthening bar associations to become active advocates for

---

5   United Nations Transitional Administration in East Timor, Regulation No. 2000/1, "On the Organization of Courts in East Timor," March 6, 2000.

judicial reform and stricter ethical and professional standards for lawyers. Legal training can be provided in the following ways:

- Conduct a series of short, compulsory, quick-impact training courses for judges, prosecutors, and public defenders prior to their appointment. These courses can range from one to several weeks in duration.
- Provide mandatory, ongoing training for judges, prosecutors, and public defenders upon their appointment to office. This training should present and review relevant substantive law, procedural law, and courtroom management.
- Establish a mentoring scheme in which a pool of experienced international legal practitioners familiar with civil law systems serves as "shadow" judges, prosecutors, and public defenders without actually exercising judicial power.
- Establish a judicial training center that functions independently of the government and helps define the legal curriculum.
- Provide training for prosecutors and investigators and establish national special units for crimes such as money laundering and asset forfeiture, drug trafficking, corruption, and human rights abuses.

Professional legal training extends beyond technical assistance. It should focus not only on conveying legal and practical skills but also, equally important, on fostering an appreciation of the role of the judiciary in society and the benefits of a culture of law. In societies in which there is little respect for the formal rule of law and in which the law is widely perceived as yet another instrument for wielding control over the population, the importance of independence and impartiality of the judiciary has to be taught.

Building Infrastructure and Providing Equipment

An important step in establishing rule of law is the construction and refurbishment of court buildings and offices. A preliminary task should be to inventory and assess courts, law schools, legal libraries, and bar associations. Assistance should target the following key infrastructure:

- buildings housing the supreme court, ministry of justice, and attorney general's office
- court buildings at the provincial and local levels
- judicial training academies
- offices for justice personnel.

In addition, furniture, computers, legal texts, stationery, filing cabinets, and office supplies and equipment may also be in short supply. Basic laws should be printed and distributed to all courts and prosecutors, the ministry of justice, NGOs, and the police. They should also be available on CD-ROM and posted on the ministry of justice Web site for citizens.

The judicial system needs to be rebuilt at both the national and local levels. At the national level, the permanent institutions of justice may be in serious need of both reform and resources. The intervening authorities need to ensure that the courts adopt common procedures, ensure merit-based advancement, and provide oversight. The highest level of the judiciary should be reappointed and approved by a parliamentary committee to ensure that basic standards are met. At the local level, assistance should focus on establishing "pockets of competence"—judicial institutions in key provincial and district centers that function properly. This limited number of locations should be resourced with proven staff, buildings, and communications. Once functioning, these pockets would be perceived as legitimate and attract cases and citizens from other districts. They could also liaise with tribal or customary legal systems to ensure that disputes resolved in those forums protect individual rights. Eventually, the number of pockets should increase as both demand and resources rise. In countries in which judges and prosecutors need to handle cases involving terrorism, drug trafficking, or organized crime, they will need protection from threats of violence and assassination.

Improving the Corrections System

The corrections system is an important—though often overlooked—area. Intervening authorities or the host-country government need to provide pretrial detention facilities, prisons, and corrections personnel. Most civilian police and military deployed as part of the intervening force are not generally trained or equipped to work as prison wardens. Corrections personnel have to be recruited, vetted, and trained according to internationally accepted standards.

Constructing prisons needs to be a priority. A functioning correctional system is necessary if law enforcement is to be effective. Despite the reluctance of many donors to finance prisons, correctional facilities generally need to be built or reconstructed. Intervening authorities must make a concerted effort to convince donor countries to provide funds for this task. The intervening authorities should provide for a sufficient number of professional international prison guards and wardens in mission planning and budgeting. Juveniles should be accorded special rights according to international standards, such as the United Nations Standard Minimum Rules for the Administration of Juvenile Justice (often referred to as the Beijing Rules),[6] which require giving juveniles special protection and holding them in separate facilities from adult defendants. Accused juveniles should accordingly be separated from adults and their cases brought to the court for adjudication as speedily as possible. Women should be provided with separate pretrial detention centers and prisons from men.

Establishing a Rule-of-Law Culture

Training judges and other legal personnel, building infrastructure, and assisting with institutional reform are necessary aspects of rebuilding rule-of-law systems. But these alone are not sufficient. Rule-of-law assistance to Latin America, Eastern Europe, Africa, and Asia over the last several decades has not been as effective as hoped. Assistance programs

---

[6] The Beijing Rules, adopted by the United Nations in 1985, provide guidance to states for the protection of children's rights and respect for their needs in the development of separate and specialized systems of juvenile justice. See United Nations General Assembly, "United Nations Standard Minimum Rules for the Administration of Juvenile Justice ('The Beijing Rules')," A/RES/40/33, 96th plenary meeting, November 29, 1985.

have generally not been followed by host-government initiatives in pursuit of deeper and more comprehensive reforms.[7] Rule-of-law programs in Bosnia, Kosovo, East Timor, Sierra Leone, Afghanistan, and Iraq focused on judicial training, rewriting constitutions and key legislation, and providing other forms of structural and technical assistance. These programs have not worked particularly well. Proposed changes often encounter deep resistance from local actors.

Promoting the rule of law involves creating new norms and changing culture as much as it does creating new institutions and legal codes. Without a widely shared cultural commitment to the idea of rule of law, courts are just buildings, judges just public employees, and constitutions just pieces of paper. In most postconflict societies, the tradition of using the law to equitably resolve disputes is weak or does not exist. In such societies, well-intentioned efforts by outsiders to establish rule of law solely by creating formal structures and rewriting constitutions and statutes often have little or no long-term effect.

Key challenges include the power of the executive or other power brokers over the justice system, corruption, and fear of violence because trials involve terrorists or organized criminal gangs. In El Salvador, UN and other international officials ran into deep resistance to reforming the rule-of-law system from the supreme court, which retained a decisive voice in selecting or removing lower-court judges. For many judges who have spent their careers in dysfunctional systems, the possibility of a reformed judiciary may not be appealing. Judges, no longer able to rule their courts as personal fiefdoms, may have to stop receiving bribes, sit through training sessions, face the potential for dismissal, and sever close-knit political ties. These judges often drag their feet when implementing reforms. Afghanistan has lacked practical experience with judicial independence and the political ethos to support it.

---

[7]   Thomas Carothers, ed., *Promoting the Rule of Law Abroad: In Search of Knowledge*, Washington, D.C.: Carnegie Endowment for International Peace, 2006; Jane Stromseth, David Wippman, and Rosa Brooks, *Can Might Make Rights? The Rule of Law After Military Interventions*, New York: Cambridge University Press, 2006; Thomas Carothers, *Aiding Democracy Abroad: The Learning Curve*, Washington, D.C.: Carnegie Endowment for International Peace, 1999.

Combating corruption is a critical part of rebuilding the judiciary and establishing a culture of rule of law. Corruption undermines democratic institutions, retards economic development, and contributes to political instability. Corruption attacks the foundation of democratic institutions by distorting electoral processes and perverting the rule of law. Economic development is stunted because investors are discouraged. Entrepreneurs are discouraged from starting small businesses because they find it difficult to overcome the "start-up costs" imposed by corruption. Corruption is facilitated by low salaries for judges, laws that permit corrupt behavior, significant executive influence over the judiciary, and poor security protection of judges, especially from terrorists or organized criminal gangs. Measures to mitigate corruption include

- increasing judges' salaries
- training programs for judges and lawyers held on a regular basis
- enacting anticorruption legislation
- imposing legal constraints on unjustifiable variations in criminal sentences in similar cases, including the creation of judicial handbooks containing sentencing standards and principles and the collection of statistics on sentencing patterns
- ensuring that government contracts for goods and services are awarded through open competitive bidding; the contracting authority must provide all bidders and the general public with easy access to information about tender opportunities, selection criteria, the evaluation process, the terms and conditions of the contract and its amendments, and the implementation of the contract and the role of intermediaries and agents
- ensuring that judicial officers take responsibility for minimizing delays in the conduct and conclusion of court proceedings and for discouraging activities of the legal profession that cause undue delay; judicial officers should institute transparent procedures so that the judiciary, the legal profession, and litigants can find out the status of court proceedings

- ensuring the protection of judges and lawyers involved in the trials of terrorists or major criminals, as well as establishing a witness protection program.

Reform cannot include only top-down initiatives, but bottom-up as well. This includes drawing in public-interest law groups, human rights organizations, and NGOs engaged in judicial reform. It may also include sponsoring training for the media and other citizen-oriented projects. Most traditional rule-of-law programs focus on political and economic elites: Judges, lawyers, and politicians are targeted for training programs. But for rule of law to exist, the law's "consumers"— ordinary people—need to be convinced of the value of legal institutions and educated in what it can do. In many troubled societies, only a tiny slice of society uses formal legal institutions. In Sierra Leone, courthouses existed only in major cities. Most disputes, especially in the countryside, were handled informally by tribal elders. Changes to the formal legal code had little relevance to most people's lives. Several types of programs may be effective in reaching beyond cities and elites where informal law predominates. Some of these programs, such as building a strong civil society, can play an important role by keeping government officials accountable. Strengthening and informing the media, NGOs, and other civil institutions is often seen as a distinct task from rule-of-law promotion, but it is deeply intertwined. The following are several programs that have been effective in the past:

- *Access:* Implement programs that seek to educate non-elites about the law and legal institutions and give people access to these institutions to resolve problems. Such programs include legal aid offices that offer free or low-cost legal advice and representation; pro se projects that train people to represent themselves; and paralegal-based projects that train and employ people with some legal training, but who are not lawyers, to serve as advocates and mediators.
- *Mediation:* Offer services to help resolve conflicts through mediation to enable people to resolve disputes without using formal legal institutions.

- *Media:* Strengthen responsible and independent media, thereby helping to discourage corruption and abuse. Programs that focus on training journalists in investigative techniques may be particularly helpful.
- *NGOs:* Provide fledging NGOs with the resources and training necessary to begin functioning. NGOs can help foster the rule of law by serving as monitors and advocates, as well as by helping to ensure an educated and engaged citizenry.
- *Youth population:* Provide assistance to university programs that will shape the next generation of legal professionals. Law schools and law clinics can play a particularly important role in inculcating the value of rule of law into emerging professionals.
- *Outreach:* Innovative outreach programs can help create a sense of shared ownership if they solicit ideas for new laws and institutions across society. A successful example involved efforts made by South Africa's first postapartheid government to involve ordinary people in designing the nation's new constitution. Billboards, pop songs, and cartoons explained the process by which the constitution was being written and urged people to write or call special toll-free numbers with their thoughts on what the constitution should say.
- *Women and minorities:* Programs that seek to empower women can have spillover effects on economic development and peace-related activities. Ethnic and religious minorities should be a prime focus of rule-of-law programs. Like young people, actual or perceived marginalization drives minority groups into the role of spoilers. Focusing on minorities in rule-of-law programs helps give them the tools to protect themselves in ways that do not undermine social stability.

Supporting Transitional Justice

In postconflict settings, international and local leaders face difficult tradeoffs between the need for reconciliation among contending parties and the desire to impose accountability for large-scale crimes committed in the course of that conflict. At one end of the spectrum, the emphasis can be put on retributive justice through the device of war crime tribunals. At the other end, the emphasis may be put upon reconciliation, in the hope either that time will heal the wounds created by earlier atrocities, or alternatively, that in time the nation will become strong enough, and cohesive enough, to face its past and itself impose accountability for those crimes. Between the extremes of judicial punishment, on the one hand, and full impunity, on the other, lie a couple of other options. One is lustration, a nonjudicial means of depriving some segment of the population access to power. A second is a truth commission, a nonjudicial effort to fix responsibility without attendant punishment.

War Crime Trials. War crime tribunals are established by courts of law to try individuals accused of war crimes and crimes against humanity. They aim to bring major perpetrators to justice. Table 4.2 lists all major international war crime trials since World War I. Proponents argue that war crime trials help establish long-term peace in several ways:

- purging threatening leaders
- deterring war criminals
- rehabilitating countries and governments
- placing the blame for atrocities on individuals rather than on whole ethnic or other groups
- establishing the facts about wartime atrocities.

Proponents of war crime trials argue that a country can never be stable while dangerous leaders are still at large and not held accountable. For public attitudes to shift, this line of argument runs, criminal leaders must be tried, their aura of mystery shattered by showing their weaknesses, and their prestige deflated by the humiliation of going on trial. Second, proponents believe that war crime trials can help deter potential criminals. In 1944, near the end of World War II, the War Refugee Board's John Pehle wrote, "The failure to punish the criminals

Table 4.2
International War Crime Tribunals

Country	Year Established
Germany	1919
Turkey	1919
Germany	1945
Japan	1945
Yugoslavia	1993
Rwanda	1994
East Timor	1999
Sierra Leone	2000

of World War I may well have removed a deterrent to the commission of brutalities against civilian populations in this war, including the mass murder of the Jews."[8] Third, some argue that trials can help rehabilitate renegade states. The rehabilitation of Germany after World War II was one of the great political successes of the century, turning a fascist enemy into a democratic ally. The Nuremberg trials are believed to have made an important contribution to this success. Fourth, trials also allow individuals to be blamed for crimes, not whole ethnic or religious groups. The wounds opened by war may heal faster if collective guilt for atrocities is expunged and individual responsibility is assigned. Fifth, trials may also help establish the facts about what happened. A well-established historical record makes it difficult to deny that atrocities ever happened.

The evidence for these claims is mixed. Purging threatening leaders can be an important part of reforming a conquered country, but it may require a serious security commitment to ride out a possible nationalist backlash. This is especially true since international tribunals may be viewed as foreign-imposed justice. Although some regimes and

---

[8]   Pehle to Edward R. Stettinius, Jr., August 28, 1944, in Bradley F. Smith, ed., *The American Road to Nuremberg: The Documentary Record, 1944–1945*, Stanford, Calif.: Hoover Institution Press, 1982, p. 22.

individuals may be deterred by the threat that they may be prosecuted for war crimes, others bent on mass slaughter have shrugged off those warnings. Trials may help rehabilitate a defeated country, but only as one element in a broader program of national reconstruction. Even in postwar Germany, Nuremberg was only one element in a broader allied program of denazification, reeducation, and reconstruction. International tribunals have not been able to prosecute more than a handful of guilty individuals, so trials do not always succeed in putting the blame where it belongs. After a war, large numbers of war criminals may overwhelm the capacity of war crime tribunals to try these cases. War crime tribunals almost always help establish the facts about atrocities, and a fundamental part of all forms of justice is official acknowledgment of what happened. A well-established historical record does make it more difficult to deny that atrocities occurred, but this objective can also be achieved by nonjudicial means.

A recent trend in transitional justice is to move away from international tribunals toward hybrid courts with national participation, located in the affected countries. Hybrid courts are often considered more legitimate by domestic audiences, have greater potential for domestic capacity-building by involving local jurists directly in the work of the court, may be better able to demonstrate the importance of accountability and fair justice to local populations, and can be much less expensive to operate. Domestic prosecutions, if they are conducted in a manner widely viewed as legitimate and fair, can help demonstrate accountability in a direct way to domestic audiences. Alternatively, the International Criminal Court may be used. It was established in 2002 and is a permanent, treaty-based, international criminal court intended to promote rule of law and ensure that the gravest international crimes do not go unpunished. It has jurisdiction over individuals accused of genocide, crimes against humanity, or war crimes if states with jurisdiction are unable or unwilling to investigate or prosecute these cases themselves.

Lustration. An alternative or addition to judicially imposed penalties for past behavior is the administrative step of barring a whole class of individuals from public employment, political participation, and the enjoyment of other civil rights. Denazification in Germany, demilitarization in Japan, and debaathification in Iraq are examples of this form of sanction. Compared to judicial action, it is simpler to administer, since no proof of wrongdoing is required and no evidence beyond that of membership in a proscribed organization is necessary. To the extent that there is any avenue for redress, the burden of proof rests with the petitioner.

On the other hand, the process is arbitrary by design. Any effort to ameliorate this effect by providing a path for rehabilitation requires an administrative apparatus capable of adjudicating the resultant claims in an impartial and reasonably expeditious manner. The United States established such processes in Germany and Japan but failed to do so in Iraq. In cases in which the class to be proscribed has been thoroughly defeated, totally discredited, and deprived of any possibility for resistance, lustration may be an effective means of ensuring that those in question are not able to regain their former influence over time. In cases in which the affected individuals retain influence and are strongly rooted in the society, their exclusion is likely to occasion significant resistance.

Truth Commissions. Truth commissions are bodies set up to investigate a past history of human rights violations. They focus on the past. The events may have occurred in the recent past, but a truth commission is not an ongoing body akin to a human rights commission. Truth commissions normally investigate a pattern of abuse over a set period of time rather than a specific event. According to their mandate, truth commissions are usually given parameters of investigation in terms of (1) the time period covered and (2) the type of human rights violations to be investigated. Truth commissions are temporary bodies, usually operating from six months to two years. When a truth commission completes its work, it submits a report. Its parameters are established at the time it is formed. Truth commissions are officially sanctioned, authorized, or empowered by the state. This, in principle, allows the commission to have greater access to information, greater security, and greater assurance that its findings will be given serious consideration. Table 4.3 provides a list of past truth commissions.

Table 4.3
Truth Commissions

Country	Dates of Operation	Period Covered
Uganda	1974	1971–1974
Bolivia	1982–1984	1967–1982
Argentina	1983–1984	1976–1983
Uruguay	1985	1973–1982
Zimbabwe	1985	1983
Uganda	1986–1995	1962–1986
Philippines	1986	1972–1986
Nepal	1990–1991	1961–1990
Chile	1990–1991	1973–1990
Chad	1991–1992	1982–1990
Germany	1992–1994	1949–1989
El Salvador	1992–1993	1980–1991
Rwanda	1992–1993	1990–1992
Sri Lanka	1994–1997	1988–1994
Haiti	1995–1996	1991–1994
Burundi	1995–1996	1993–1995
South Africa	1995–2000	1960–1994
Ecuador	1996–1997	1979–1996
Guatemala	1997–1999	1962–1996
Nigeria	1999–2001	1966–1999
Peru	2000–2002	1980–2000
Uruguay	2000–2001	1973–1985
Panama	2001–2002	1968–1989
Yugoslavia	2002	1991–2001
East Timor	2002	1974–1999
Sierra Leone	2002	1991–1999
Ghana	2002	1966–2001

Truth commissions can be helpful in compiling a comprehensive account that addresses the broader context of the conflict and the factors that contributed to atrocities. They usually offer an opportunity for direct participation by a large number of victims. They may seek to promote the reintegration of lesser perpetrators into the community through reconciliation agreements. The goal of such efforts is not to prosecute or punish, but to disclose the facts about abuses. Truth commissions have frequently led to conditional amnesties. Amnesties can vary with respect to timing as well as conditions. An amnesty can be declared prior to the establishment of a commission or passed after it has finished its work. It can be unconditional and extend to all ranks or conditional upon cooperation. Without some form of amnesty, the commission will likely encounter widespread, serious opposition from political and former military leaders.

Truth commissions have several potential drawbacks. Most do not include prosecution. A sense of incompletion is likely to prevail without prosecution of the perpetrators identified by a truth commission. Amnesties often lead to popular resentment, since they benefit perpetrators of atrocities. This is especially true when a sweeping a priori amnesty is granted, in which case the commission may be seen as a fig leaf with no punitive, and little restorative, power. Governments do not always agree with the findings of truth commissions, undercutting the credibility of their results. In El Salvador in 1993, the government dismissed the truth commission. Members of the supreme court denounced it, and Defense Minister Rene Emilio Ponce referred to it as "insolent." Less than a week after the truth commission report was released, the Salvadoran National Assembly approved blanket amnesty for all abuses committed during the civil war.

Effective truth commissions should involve the following:

- *Sponsorship:* The credibility of truth commissions is affected by the choice of sponsorship, by the timing of its establishment, and by the groups involved in its creation and design. The legitimacy of sponsorship depends on the name under which the commission is established and how civil society is involved in creating or sponsoring the commission.

- *Mandate:* The mandate of a truth commission defines its purpose, powers, and limitations. Key components of the design of a truth commission are the scope of the investigation, the time horizon, legal powers of investigation, whether it will identify names, access to state and military files, and the purpose and scope of its recommendations.
- *Composition:* The commissioners appointed are highly visible and often seen as representing the seriousness of the effort to face past human right abuses. Their reputations are a crucial factor in the effectiveness of a truth commission. In some cases, the inclusion of instrumental members may enhance the commission's credibility and perceived impartiality. Key choices in selecting commissioners include the number, professional background, gender, and ethnic diversity of its members.
- *Resources:* The material and human resources of a commission are important prerequisites for the effectiveness of its operations. The number, qualification, and reputation of a commission's staff, as well as the money, equipment, and time allocated for its work will affect how many cases will be investigated, the depth of these investigations, and the geographic scope of the investigations.
- *Proceedings:* The proceedings are determined by the mandate and resources allocated. Key aspects of a commission's proceedings are assessments of communities' and victims' needs, cooperation with civil society, the visibility of the hearings, the risks of participating in hearings, the number of cases presented to the commission, and media coverage.
- *Dissemination of findings:* At the end of a commission's tenure, it issues and disseminates its findings and recommendations. In some cases, the commission's cumulative knowledge has been shared only with the leader of the country. In most cases, the findings have been published. One way to share the commission's insights is to publish a report that documents key findings.

Choosing Among Options. There are several factors to be considered in determining where along the spectrum from "forgive and forget" to "try and punish" intervening authorities may wish to position their efforts to promote reconciliation and justice. In cases in which the conflict was civil in nature, the intervening authorities have an opportunity to judge the temper of the population, which may be hungry for justice, or which may, on the contrary, be so war-weary as to prefer overwhelmingly to put the past behind it.

Another critical calculation is the level of commitment the intervening authorities are prepared to make to carry out their chosen policy. International tribunals are extremely expensive, with the trial of a single individual often costing millions of dollars. Beyond the direct cost of mounting such a process, there is also the implied cost of its enforcement. The more intervening authorities commit themselves to rapid and far-reaching reform, the more resistance their efforts are likely to engender. War crime tribunals can be viewed as the ultimate form of enforced transformation, one in which members of the previous ruling elite are deprived not just of their power and property, but of their freedom or even their lives. Any such effort is likely to encounter resistance not just from the individuals concerned, but from their families, associates, and supporters. In cases in which the ratio of intervening force to local population is very high, war crime tribunals may be an effective means of both providing exemplary justice and promoting long-term social change. Even in such circumstances, however, the opportunity costs need to be considered, given the many other claims on available economic and personnel resources.

Too often, war crime tribunals are employed not as an adjunct to effective peace enforcement but as an alternative. In Bosnia, Rwanda, and more recently in Darfur, the international community has pursued war crime prosecutions not in the aftermath of an intervention in an effort to halt the abuses in question, but as alternative to such intervention. This has allowed the international community to respond to public pressures to do something about a mounting tragedy without actually committing the troops and money needed to halt it. To the extent that such palliatives actually succeed in deflecting public opinion and reducing pressures for more forceful action, the result may be the exact opposite of that ostensibly intended, awarding the perpetrators further time to carry forward their abusive projects. For those reasons, we recommend that they resort to international tribunals only in situations in which the intervening authorities are prepared to enforce the results in an enduring and conclusive fashion.

Many of these considerations apply equally to any process of lustration. Assessing collective rather than individual guilt is obviously cheaper and easier to administer, but, to the extent that the category of individuals affected is larger, it may actually stimulate even greater resistance requiring commensurately greater efforts to counter. In Japan, the United States purged 0.29 percent of the population. In Germany it purged almost nine times more, 2.5 percent of the population. The United States also had a soldier-to-population ratio in Germany five times higher than in Japan. In Japan, most of those purged were rehabilitated within a few years, and the entire program was countermanded as soon as Japan regained its sovereignty in 1952. In Germany, the effect both on the individuals concerned and on the society as a whole was more lasting. In Iraq, the original U.S. debaathification decree was too sweeping, as its authors now acknowledge, while the United States never put in place an effective process for review and rehabilitation. These early decisions almost certainly contributed to a level of resistance that the U.S.-led coalition was unprepared to counter.

Whatever option is chosen, unless norms of accountability are institutionalized domestically by strengthening national legal institutions, the long-term impact of transitional justice proceedings will be limited. In some cases, such as Rwanda, war crime trials have had little impact on efforts to strengthen rule of law. Donors provided resources to investigate and try individuals accused of war crimes, but did not provide additional resources to improve judicial capacity. One of the downsides of the international criminal tribunals in Yugoslavia and Rwanda has been their failure to contribute to building domestic judicial capacity on which the money committed to those tribunals might well have been better spent. Major donors, international organizations, and NGOs all have important roles to play in promoting rule of law. Individual donors may take responsibility for supporting the development of certain sectors. The U.S. Department of Justice, for instance, has units that specialize in building both police and judicial establishments in postconflict countries.

Key Actors

There are at least three types of international actors that should be involved in rule-of-law efforts. The first are donor states. They are able to provide greater resources than are NGOs and major international organizations to encourage the development of rule of law. But their goals and policies may be strongly influenced by political and geostrategic considerations, which can conflict with best practices. In some countries, such as the United States, several government entities are involved in training individuals involved in rule-of-law activities: the U.S. Department of Justice (including the Office of Overseas Prosecutorial Development, Assistance, and Training), the U.S. Agency for International Development, the U.S. Department of State (including the Bureau for International Narcotics and Law Enforcement Affairs), and the Federal Bureau of Prisons. In some stability operations, donor states have agreed on a "lead nation" setup for rule-of-law efforts. Italy played this role in Afghanistan. Italy was supposed to provide financial assistance, coordinate external assistance, and oversee reconstruction efforts in the rule-of-law sector to improve efficiency and coordination. In practice, this approach did not work well. Italy simply lacked the expertise, resources, interest, and influence needed to succeed in such an undertaking. Large international organizations, such as the United Nations and the World Bank, have significant expertise and experience in fostering the development of rule of law. The United Nations Office on Drugs and Crime has been involved in efforts to advance counternarcotics through improvement in the criminal justice system. The United Nations Development Programme (UNDP) has been involved in a variety of programs to build rule of law during nation-building operations, offering training in such areas as international standards on human rights and criminal law, humanitarian law, gender justice, child protection, and codes of conduct. The World Bank promoted efforts to improve governance and investment codes.

Many NGOs specialize in the rule of law, providing training, helping to draft legal codes, building courts, or providing equipment. On the other hand, the rising number of NGOs has led to coordination problems in rebuilding the rule of law. NGOs may also have a wide range of goals and approaches that differ from those of the host government, major international organizations, or donor states. These challenges create a strong impetus to design institutional arrangements that increase efficiency and help overcome coordination and collaboration problems.

Sizing

Regarding international personnel, we recommend the provision of one advisor for every 10 judges, one mentor for every 30 prosecutors, and one advisor for every prison. These are meant to be rough estimates. They were determined by assessing and balancing cost constraints, the availability of international justice advisors, and the need for mentoring in past nation-building operations.

To estimate the number of local judges, prosecutors, and corrections personnel needed for a well-functioning justice sector, we compared data from nearly a dozen countries. We chose these countries so as to include wide variation in geographic location, type of justice system, population size, and economic conditions. As Figure 4.2 illustrates, numbers of judges vary widely, from 25 judges per 100,000 inhabitants in Germany to 0.15 in Ethiopia, with an average of six per 100,000 inhabitants across the group. The variation is a function of several factors, such as the capacity and strength of the central government; the number of criminals and others moving through the justice system; and whether the country uses a formal, informal, or mixed legal system. The number of prosecutors also varies, from a high of nearly 12 per 100,000 in Albania to 0.23 in Ethiopia. The average number is six prosecutors per 100,000 inhabitants.

As Figure 4.3 illustrates, the number of corrections personnel also varies significantly across countries. The data include numbers of staff working in adult and juvenile prisons, penal institutions, and correctional institutions. Numbers range from 12 corrections personnel per 100,000 inhabitants in Japan to 76 in the United Kingdom, with an average of 42 per 100,000 inhabitants. Not shown in the figure, the ratio of corrections personnel to prisoners ranges from roughly one

Figure 4.2
Number of Judges and Prosecutors per 100,000 Inhabitants

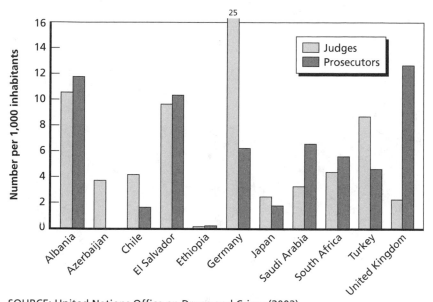

SOURCE: United Nations Office on Drugs and Crime (2002).
RAND *MG557-4.2*

corrections staff member for every two prisoners in Germany and the United Kingdom to one staff member for every eight prisoners in El Salvador and South Africa.[9] As a general rule, the higher the number of prisoners per capita, the wider the disparity in the ratio of corrections personnel to prisoners. Figure 4.4 shows comparative data on the numbers of adult and juvenile prisons, penal institutions, and other correctional institutions. Total numbers range from approximately 0.14 correctional institutions per 100,000 inhabitants in Japan to a high of 0.78 in Azerbaijan. These numbers can vary depending on the amount of international assistance, capacity of the indigenous government, the use of formal law, and the number of individuals moving through—and convicted by—the court system.

---

[9]   United Nations Office on Drugs and Crime (2002).

Figure 4.3
Number of Corrections Personnel

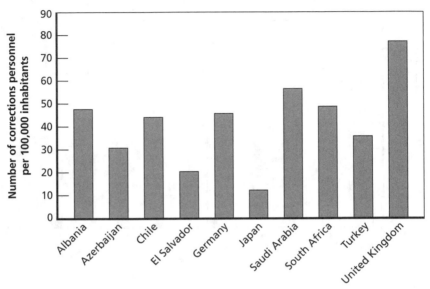

SOURCE: United Nations Office on Drugs and Crime (2002).
RAND *MG557-4.3*

Costs

Intervening powers need to anticipate funding some or most of the expenses of the justice sector over the first several years following an intervention. The indigenous government, if there is one, is likely to lack sufficient revenue to pay judges, prosecutors, and corrections personnel; to build and maintain physical infrastructure; or to run the legal system.

We estimated the costs of international personnel by evaluating the costs of deploying justice and other civilian personnel during four stability operations: in Haiti, Sierra Leone, Congo, and Liberia.[10] We

---

[10] Data are compiled from United Nations General Assembly (2004a, 2005a, 2004b, 2005a).

Figure 4.4
Number of Correctional Institutions

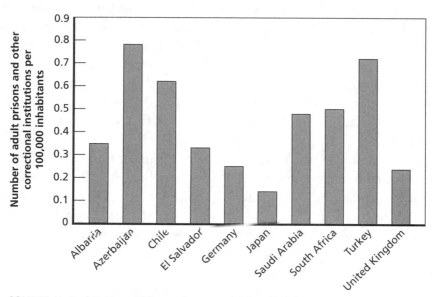

SOURCE: United Nations Office on Drugs and Crime (2002).
RAND *MG557-4.4*

calculated the average cost per person by compiling information on personnel and operational costs. The latter includes a combination of transportation, infrastructure, and other costs.[11] We estimate that it costs roughly $185,000 per person to deploy international personnel engaged in establishing rule of law, including personnel and operational costs.[12] We estimated domestic costs by noting that, on average, countries spend approximately 0.26 percent of their GDPs on their jus-

---

[11] We aggregated costs for facilities and infrastructure; ground, air, and naval transportation; communications, medical services, and special equipment. Since the UN does not disaggregate the operational costs of military personnel from those of civilian personnel, our estimates may slightly overstate per soldier costs. However, military personnel account for most operational costs.

[12] The costs per person were approximately $154,195 for Congo, $292,285 for Haiti, $163,486 for Liberia, and $122,680 for Sierra Leone. This averaged out to $183,162; we rounded to $185,000.

tice sectors, exclusive of police.[13] We use this average of 0.26 percent of GDP to estimate the cost of running a typical national justice system.

What does this analysis imply for the rule-of-law component of stability operations? To illustrate, we evaluated the cost of a hypothetical intervention in Mozambique. In 2006, that country has a population of approximately 20 million. Using the average number of judges (6), prosecutors (6), and corrections staff (42) per 100,000 inhabitants, we estimate that Mozambique would need a total of 1,200 judges, 1,200 prosecutors, and 8,400 corrections staff. Using the average of four correctional institutions per million inhabitants, we estimate that Mozambique would need a total of 80 major correctional institutions. Mozambique had a GDP of $26 billion in 2006. Assuming that Mozambique should spend 0.26 percent of its GDP on the justice sector, Mozambique's ministry of justice would need approximately $68 million annually to function effectively. Mozambique would also need an average of one international mentor for every 10 judges, one mentor per corrections facility, and one mentor for every 30 prosecutors. This translates to a total of 240 international justice personnel.

Since we estimate that each justice official costs approximately $185,000, this translates to a total international cost of nearly $45 million. These estimates are meant to provide a first cut at estimating numbers and costs for the full range of international and local employees engaged in the justice sector in the aftermath of an external intervention. Tables 4.4 and 4.5 show these results.

---

[13] There was a substantial range in spending among the 17 countries we analyzed. The standard deviation was 0.22. Countries included Argentina, Colombia, Costa Rica, El Salvador, Georgia, Ghana, India, Jordan, Namibia, Nepal, Nigeria, Philippines, South Africa, Thailand, Turkey, Ukraine, and Zimbabwe. We chose these countries to ensure variation in geographic location, type of justice system, population size, and economic conditions.

Table 4.4
Estimated Numbers of Justice Personnel for Mozambique, Year One

Personnel or Institution	Number
Local judges	1,200
Local prosecutors	1,200
Local corrections staff	8,400
Local correctional institutions	80
International advisors	240

SOURCE: RAND calculations.

Table 4.5
Estimated Costs of Restoring Judicial Services in Mozambique, Year One

Division of Costs	Justice Share of GDP	GDP (2006 US$)	Total Expenditure (2006 US$)
Indigenous costs	0.26	26 billion	68 million
International costs	—	—	45 million

SOURCE: RAND calculations.
NOTE: Amounts may not sum due to rounding.

CHAPTER FIVE

Humanitarian Relief

The humanitarian component of stability operations involves preventing large-scale loss of life by providing emergency food, shelter, clothing, and medical services to the local population. In most instances, relief agencies have already been on the ground and were providing humanitarian assistance throughout the conflict. The broad objective of humanitarian efforts should be to save lives, alleviate human suffering, and minimize displacement. In most postconflict situations, large numbers of people have been displaced. The challenge for the international community is in providing for existing and newly displaced people, then beginning the process of encouraging people to return home or find new, permanent places in which to settle. Most major humanitarian relief agencies are professionally staffed and comparatively well resourced. Funding for nation-building is always in short supply, but humanitarian relief is one area that donors are most inclined to fund. As a result, virtually no nation-building operation has been compromised by inadequacies in humanitarian relief. But there are numerous examples in which the intervening authorities' failure to establish a modicum of public security has made it impossible for humanitarian agencies to complete their mission or even to sustain their assistance to threatened populations.

Key Challenges

Conducting Preintervention Planning. Humanitarian missions usually take place under extreme time constraints, with little time and few opportunities to think strategically about planning once operations begin. This makes it important to establish plans in advance, if possible. Key challenges include gathering systematic and actionable information on humanitarian conditions prior to an intervention, coordinating plans across a wide range of governmental and nongovernmental organizations, and ensuring the preintervention mobilization of postconflict humanitarian resources. Since there is not always sufficient time to conduct planning activities, pre-positioning supplies and developing established systems are critical to effective relief operations.

Responding to Crises. Intervening authorities may have to deal with at least five types of acute humanitarian challenges. First, war can increase the likelihood of communicable diseases, which may reach epidemic proportions if not treated quickly. Diseases such as cholera and dysentery have been particularly prevalent in postconflict settings. Second, famine and drought can present significant and dire challenges. In Somalia, U.S. and UN officials had to provide sufficient food and water to much of the population in a country in which the water system had collapsed and much of the agricultural infrastructure—such as irrigation pumps and food processing plants— had been destroyed by looting. Third, war usually displaces large populations. As discussed later, international and indigenous relief workers need to quickly provide food, shelter, and other assistance to refugees and internally displaced persons. Fourth, combat destroys roads, hospitals, public buildings, and other infrastructure needed to distribute food and provide medical care. During the course of war, the electric power system is often seriously damaged. As electricity is needed to pump water, operate sewage plants, refrigerate medicines, and operate clinics, the collapse of the electric power system creates serious and acute health problems. Transportation infrastructure, such as bridges, roads, ports, and railway systems, may be heavily damaged. Finally, intervening authorities may have to deal with traumatic injuries from land mines, unexploded ordnance, and weapons.

Establishing Coordination Arrangements. Coordinating donor states, international organizations, and NGOs involved in humanitarian relief efforts is challenging. As one World Bank study notes, virtually all humanitarian relief efforts suffer from "a lack of an overarching nationally-driven plan to which all donors agree, resulting in fragmentation, gaps or duplication in aid-financed programs."[1] Poor coordination can have serious consequences by scattering assistance among a greater number of projects so that relief workers fail to tackle key priorities.

Assisting Refugees and Internally Displaced Persons. Refugees and internally displaced persons are often the greatest humanitarian challenge facing intervening authorities in postconflict societies. High concentrations of displaced people are breeding grounds for epidemics, and they face the prospect of starvation if food cannot be provided to them. Large numbers of destitute people create frictions with their hosts. Residents of surrounding areas have sometimes attacked refugees and refugee camps, forcing the intervening authorities to provide security as well as food and shelter. In some cases, people are displaced not because they were civilians fleeing the scene of the battle between two armed groups, but because they are themselves the objects of attack, either for the purpose of extermination or to cause them to flee, so as to cleanse an area ethnically. Organized military or paramilitary forces may terrorize the target population to induce them to move. The combatants may have forcibly deported groups, evicting people at gunpoint. In other cases, populations may flee because the security environment has deteriorated so much that they believe it is safer to leave than stay. Violence is not always overt. Large numbers of people fled regions of Afghanistan, Angola, Mozambique, and Cambodia because of land mines. Mines also discourage people from returning home after the fighting ceases.

Making the Transition from Relief. The humanitarian relief effort usually ends within several months following a conflict. By that time, many of the displaced have gone home or found new homes. Refugee camps are closed. International humanitarian organizations have begun to pack their bags. At this point, intervening authorities are

---

[1]   United Nations Development Group and World Bank, *An Operational Note on Transitional Results Matrices: Using Results-Based Frameworks in Fragile States*, New York, January 2005, p. 2. See also Olga Bornemisza and Egbert Sondorp, *Health Policy Formulation in Complex Political Emergencies and Post-Conflict Countries: A Literature Review*, London: London School of Hygiene and Tropical Medicine, November 7, 2002.

faced with the challenge of moving from emergency relief efforts to providing government services on a sustained basis. It is important to shift as quickly as possible into longer-term transition and development. However, this shift is rarely a linear one. Rather, it is usually a process of going backward and forward as dictated by levels of stability—often differing geographically within a country—or by waves of renewed conflict.

Creating Measures of Effectiveness. Policymakers and practitioners need to measure the effectiveness of humanitarian efforts. If they cannot measure performance, they cannot assess success or failure, making midcourse corrections difficult. One of the most significant challenges in measuring effectiveness is identifying appropriate—and inappropriate—quantitative and qualitative metrics.

Best Practices

Conducting Preintervention Planning

Humanitarian operations often take place under tight time constraints. If those in charge of the operation have not planned carefully beforehand, once it commences, there are few opportunities and little time to think strategically about the operation, making it important to plan in advance. The intervening authorities should set key objectives, tasks, and timelines, and compile relevant information on past and current living conditions of the population. This should include assembling necessary material and equipment, such as medical kits, water, tents, blankets, and food, as well as making logistical arrangements to transport material and equipment to target areas. Table 5.1 offers a sample planning matrix for humanitarian missions. Key steps include reaching a consensus on objectives, establishing a coordination unit that includes a lead actor, preparing cost estimates, and training humanitarian teams. In many cases, agencies are already on the ground when nation-building operations begin and have been there throughout the conflict. Consequently, one of the key challenges is coordinating among humanitarian agencies and collating the assessment data collected by them.

Table 5.1
Sample Humanitarian Planning Process

Summary	Description
Preparatory phase	Take a variety of preparatory steps, such as conducting an initial needs assessment. As with all subsequent steps, local leaders should be involved as much as possible in planning and implementation. This should also include pre-positioning blankets, water, medicine, and other humanitarian supplies.
Key objectives and scope	Outline the key objectives of the humanitarian effort.
Coordination	Establish at least an interim institutional arrangement for coordinating assistance, including the appointment of a lead actor.
Planning document	Establish a coherent planning document detailing what should be achieved in each sector and how this can be done. Such a planning framework is best derived by way of an outcome-based approach. It should provide a comprehensive definition of the principal objectives, vision, and scope of the effort, as well as the priority sectors.
Assess impact of cross-cutting factors	Conduct an analysis of security, political, economic, and other factors that may impact humanitarian efforts. For example, who will provide security for humanitarian agencies?
Timelines	Establish deadlines for completion of key humanitarian activities, taking into consideration that the time required may vary depending on the data, materials available, assessments already completed, and initial conditions.
Cost estimates	Develop realistic and comprehensive cost estimates.
Funding arrangements	Establish institutional arrangements for the quick disbursal of funds, and establish statutory grant-making authority to humanitarian response teams, if necessary.
Prioritization and sequencing	Prioritize key sectors in line with the initial needs assessment and sequence steps. This may include identifying key issues that cut across health and other areas (such as gender, environmental, and HIV/AIDS issues).
Staffing	Form a primary group of experts who collect data and analyze the humanitarian needs of the country and who are responsible for developing and extrapolating sectoral analyses, planning frameworks, and technical reports.

Table 5.1—Continued

Summary	Description
Logistics	Make logistical arrangements to transport material and equipment to target areas, hire contractors to support and implement humanitarian efforts, and pre-position material and equipment for quicker disbursal. This may also include making arrangements to ensure the quick disbursal of funds.
Implementation and assessments	Implement plans and programs, monitor performance, and make necessary corrections. This may include assembling necessary material and equipment, such as medical kits, water, and food.
Lessons learned	Compile major insights and lessons learned.

SOURCE: Uwe Kievelitz et al., *Practical Guide to Multilateral Needs Assessments in Post-Conflict Situations*, New York: United Nations Development Programme, World Bank, and United Nations Development Group, August 2004.

Nation-building operations take place in countries with a wide range of cultural and social conditions. International personnel must be aware of these conditions and find ways to balance them with humanitarian concerns. In Afghanistan, traditional beliefs about medicine, nutrition, and hygiene led to erroneous conclusions about what constituted safe health practices. Some Afghans believed that any moving water was clean and liquids should be withheld from children with diarrhea. The propensity to marry girls off at a young age, a reluctance to spend money and resources on health care for daughters and wives, inequitable distribution of food within the family, frequent physical violence toward women and children, and a reluctance to educate girls and women also added to the complexity of moving from relief to development. Contextual knowledge is critical to ensuring that inappropriate assistance, such as small shelters to extended families, is not provided. In Haiti and Somalia, the international community was strongly criticized for having an incomplete grasp of social and cultural realities and for attempting to impose a Western health system. The majority of Haitians and Somalis, particularly in rural areas, received their health care from traditional practitioners and healers—not from formal health care systems.[2]

In virtually all nation-building operations, some international institutions and NGOs are likely to have been involved in humanitarian efforts before and during the conflict. Through experience, these organizations and personnel have developed a good understanding of the humanitarian challenges within the country. Since reliable statistical information on humanitarian conditions is often unavailable, prior knowledge is crucial for developing programs. Bilateral donors, international institutions, and NGOs should recruit actors with in-country experience to assist in planning and developing assistance programs.

Pre-positioning material and supplies facilitates rapid delivery and saves lives. Purchasing and pre-positioning personal hygiene kits and emergency health kits helps prevent the spread of disease. Identifying the types and quantities of materials requires an assessment of local health clinics and hospitals, the availability of pharmaceuticals, and immunization rates. Water and sanitation supplies, including potable water, water jugs, and water treatment units, have to be readied. A successful emergency response requires adequate supplies of water, as well as sanitary waste disposal and wastewater removal. Pre-positioning requires an assessment of water and sanitation facilities that reach all major populations centers and of supplies of potable water. Food has to be made available to satisfy the nutritional needs of the population. Emergency shelter and supplies have to be provided to vulnerable populations. Planners need to estimate the potential numbers and movements of refugees and internally displaced persons. They must then procure sufficient plastic sheeting, tents, blankets, and other emergency shelter material. In general, pre-positioning should be done well in advance of a humanitarian emergency. Standard supplies can be warehoused at central locations and then drawn down as needed.

---

[2] Seth G. Jones, Lee H. Hilborne, et al., *Securing Health: Lessons from Nation-Building Missions*, Santa Monica, Calif.: RAND Corporation, MG-321-RC, 2006.

Responding to Crises

Once humanitarian assistance efforts begin, the immediate focus should be on dealing with at least five issues: communicable disease outbreaks, famine and drought, major flows of refugees and internally displaced persons, building key infrastructure such as the electric power system, and weapons (including WMD). Priority should be given to these areas because a failure to manage them effectively may severely affect the health and welfare of the population, and numerous other humanitarian efforts will fail if these elements are not addressed first.

The first step for humanitarian workers is to respond to the outbreak—or potential outbreak—of communicable diseases quickly to forestall epidemics of cholera, typhoid fever, dysentery, hepatitis, measles, giardiasis, and brucellosis. Children under five and pregnant women are particularly vulnerable. In Iraq, the country experienced increased rates of infectious diseases in the immediate aftermath of the 2003 conflict. The World Health Organization reported the first outbreak of cholera in al Basrah on May 15, 2003. There was also widespread reporting of pertussis and diphtheria—especially in the south. The possibility of outbreaks of communicable disease makes it important to establish a disease surveillance system that allows public health agencies to monitor disease incidence and plan responses. Surveillance systems collect and monitor data on disease trends and outbreaks so that public health personnel can protect the population's health.

Second, famine and drought require an immediate response. Humanitarian organization personnel need to assess the most vulnerable and affected areas, then rapidly disburse emergency food and water to the affected populations. In some cases, humanitarian workers may have to recreate food distribution systems. In Iraq in 2003, for example, 60 percent of Iraqis depended on the rations provided by the oil-for-food program. U.S. planners attempted to disrupt the system as little as possible during the war and to reestablish it as quickly as possible after the conclusion of hostilities. Security is required to protect relief workers, since food and water may be tempting targets for warlords and other spoilers. Aid agencies usually seek ambient security, rather than convoy security, to maximize impartiality. In Somalia, the lack of security halted relief efforts in 1991. Many of the international relief agencies withdrew their personnel. By 1991, only the International Committee of the Red Cross and a small number of NGOs remained in Somalia to provide food and medical assistance in response to the emerging humanitarian crisis. Conditions improved somewhat over the next few years, when the United Nations and the United States deployed forces to protect aid workers. After unsuccessful attempts to stabilize the security environment and negotiate with warlords, the United Nations finally determined that sustaining an effective humanitarian relief and peacekeeping operation was impossible. United Nations Operation in Somalia II (UNSOM II) forces departed the country in March 1995.

Third, humanitarian workers strive to minimize refugee flows and numbers of internally displaced persons. Once a person is displaced, he or she becomes much more vulnerable to disease and violence. Population displacements are affected by the manner and duration of the war and the extent to which the fighting produces internal political upheaval. International organizations, NGOs, and states need to put in place mechanisms and resources to respond to worst-case scenarios. Examples include the stockpiling of adequate food, water, medical supplies, and clothing, as well as plans for distributing these items. Contingency planning should also include dealing with neighboring countries that may try to close their borders and tighten policies against refugees. Without communicating with all actors involved in responding to population displacements, the humanitarian assistance effort risks delays in mobilizing and pre-positioning critical materials for displaced people. Without prior coordination, the intervening authorities also risk conducting redundant and irrelevant planning and operations, as well as encouraging counterproductive competition and turf battles.

Fourth, some infrastructure may have to be built or refurbished quickly to prevent a humanitarian crisis. The objective at this stage should not be a long-term and thorough reconstruction of the transportation, power, water, and sanitation systems. Rather, it should be to focus on areas that must be fixed *immediately* to prevent a significant deterioration in conditions. For example, the electrical network may be in poor condition, making it virtually impossible for hospitals, water treatment facilities, and sanitation systems to function. Critical transportation infrastructure, such as roads, railways, ports, and bridges, may have been destroyed. The lack of some of these may impede the delivery of potable water, medicine, and other supplies. Humanitarian and relief workers need to focus on fixing infrastructure that directly affects humanitarian efforts.

Finally, humanitarian workers need to focus on treating traumatic injuries and responding to the use of weapons. A significant portion of the population may need to be treated for traumatic injuries from such events as land mine explosions. The use of WMD presents a particular set of challenges. In the event of chemical or biological attacks, rapid response is critical, since deaths and injuries can escalate quickly. Response efforts should mirror what is sometimes called *consequence management* by emergency responders. In short, preventing an acute humanitarian crisis usually requires the following items:

- food
- medicine and medical supplies to treat injuries and disease outbreaks and to prevent the further spread of communicable diseases
- water treatment equipment and supplies, including chemicals
- sanitation materials, including latrines and hygiene kits
- emergency shelters, blankets, cooking utensils, and infant-care kits.

Security, basic infrastructure, education, governance, and economic stabilization all affect the extent of humanitarian crises. Nobel prize–winning economist Amartya Sen argues that the links among these sectors are empirical and causal:

[T]here is strong evidence that economic and political freedoms help to reinforce one another. . . . Similarly, social opportunities of education and health care, which may require public action, complement individual opportunities of economic and political participation and also help to foster our own initiatives in over-coming our respective deprivations.[3]

Humanitarian efforts are particularly sensitive to security through *direct effects*, such as the inability of patients to visit doctors, and through *indirect effects*, such as the inability of health care facilities to function properly. The absence of security can impede progress in the reconstruction of water treatment plants and hospitals, slow immunization campaigns, restrict delivery of needed supplies to health care facilities, and affect the labor force by not protecting health care providers from intimidation. Fear of attack by looters prevented health care professionals and patients in Iraq from going to health care facilities. Looters stole equipment and destroyed medical records, and facilities became overburdened by the flow of patients. The work of NGOs, international organizations, and contractors was slowed or, in some cases, halted. In Afghanistan, NGOs frequently suspended, cancelled, postponed, or downsized humanitarian programs as a result of security issues. In 2004, Médecins Sans Frontières (Doctors Without Borders) closed all of its medical programs in Afghanistan following a fatal attack on one of its vehicles in Badghis province. The converse is also true: The establishment of security can facilitate humanitarian efforts.

In short, response efforts to acute humanitarian crises—such as communicable disease outbreaks, famine and drought, population displacement, destruction of critical infrastructure, and use of WMD—may be closely linked with other developments. International organizations, NGOs, and states may need to spend time and resources refurbishing hospitals and clinics, training staff, and providing equipment. But unreliable power or unstable security conditions can undermine these efforts. In addition, there is often a short window available for stabilization after the fighting stops. In Iraq, for example, there were only a few months during which key actors could move about freely and work with affected communities.

---

[3] Amartya Sen, *Development as Freedom*, New York: Anchor Books, 2000, p. xii.

Establishing Coordination Arrangements

The coordination of humanitarian efforts is a challenge. In some ways, coordination and planning were simpler in Germany and Japan following World War II because there were fewer actors. In Germany, the U.S. military government had to coordinate efforts only with those local German authorities they had empowered and a few NGOs, such as CARE, the International Committee of the Red Cross, and the United Nations Relief and Rehabilitation Administration. The number of actors involved in humanitarian efforts has increased greatly since the end of the Cold War. The greater the number of actors, the more difficult coordination becomes—what is sometimes called the *collective action problem*.[4] In Iraq, 80 NGOs registered with the United Nations Humanitarian Information Center database; they were engaged in over 300 projects. However, only a small percentage of NGOs are usually able to stay beyond the initial provision of acute assistance and operate in severely compromised environments.

Coordination is needed between the civilian and military authorities, among international actors, and between international and domestic actors. The United Nations Office for the Coordination of Humanitarian Affairs (OCHA) has a mandate to coordinate, though this often proves difficult on the ground.

Civil-Military Coordination. International and nongovernmental organizations—not military forces—should ordinarily take the lead in providing humanitarian assistance. They are better trained and equipped for humanitarian efforts and are generally viewed as more impartial than military forces. Traditionally, there has been a distinction between the military and civilian domains, built on the international law distinction between combatants and noncombatants. However, militaries have increasingly become involved in humanitarian operations, leading to tension between militaries and NGOs. In Afghanistan, NGOs objected to the provision of humanitarian aid by U.S. military forces and objected even more strongly when those mili-

---

[4]   Mancur Olson, *The Logic of Collective Action: Public Goods and the Theory of Groups*, Cambridge, Mass.: Harvard University Press, 1971, p. 2.

tary personnel conducted operations out of uniform, creating confusion between civilian and military actors.[5]

NGOs have traditionally raised at least two broad objections to military forces participating in humanitarian relief.[6] First, they argue that such activities transgress the principle that relief should be provided by impartial parties. As the code of conduct for the International Red Cross and Red Crescent Movement states, nongovernmental humanitarian agencies are "agencies which act independently from governments." It continues,

> We will never knowingly—or through negligence—allow ourselves, or our employees, to be used to gather information of a political, military or economically sensitive nature for governments or their bodies that may serve purposes other than those which are strictly humanitarian.[7]

Some relief agencies argue that blurring the line between relief workers and soldiers places their personnel at greater risk from attacks by warring parties.

Relief agencies also note that military forces are not experts in humanitarian relief and have different priorities. They often use assistance for "hearts and minds" operations, prioritizing the delivery of aid based on criteria other than need. Substantial military involvement in the delivery of humanitarian (and reconstruction) assistance can become particularly problematic during the transition phases, during which the groundwork is laid for longer-term recovery. In some instances, military efforts may create more harm than good, jeopardiz-

---

[5] Olga Oliker et al., *Aid During Conflict: Interaction Between Military and Civilian Assistance Providers in Afghanistan, September 2001–June 2002*, Santa Monica, Calif.: RAND Corporation, MG-212-OSD, 2004.

[6] See, for example, Jane Barry and Anna Jefferys, "A Bridge Too Far: Aid Agencies and the Military in Humanitarian Response," Network Paper No. 37, London: Humanitarian Practice Network, January 2002.

[7] International Federation of Red Cross and Red Crescent Societies, "Code of Conduct for the International Red Cross and Red Crescent Movement and NGOs in Disaster Relief," Geneva, Switzerland, 1994.

ing long-term development projects and relationships with the local people. Relief efforts may distract the military from its primary mission and responsibility of providing security.

All these objections have some merit, and military involvement in the delivery of humanitarian relief always needs to be considered carefully. However, the military may have engineering and medical capabilities that can be of real use in a relief effort. Further, there may be situations in which security is so bad that only the military can deliver assistance. Such situations are, however, prima facie evidence that the military component of the mission has failed in its primary role, the establishment of a secure environment.

Ideally, the military and the humanitarian agencies should both focus on their primary responsibilities, providing security and providing relief, respectively. Further, both sides need to work together to establish guidelines that protect as much as possible the impartiality of NGOs. Thus,

- NGOs should not serve as implementing partners of the military in conducting relief activities.
- Military personnel should not wear civilian clothing when conducting humanitarian operations.
- NGO personnel should not travel in military vehicles.
- Militaries and NGOs should not locate their facilities together.
- NGO personnel should not go to military bases for recreation or other activities not associated with the mission. They are likely to be seen by local residents if they fraternize with military personnel.
- Military forces should concentrate on their highest-priority mission, which should be public security. To the extent that they succeed, humanitarian agencies and NGOs will subsequently be capable of meeting the population's emergency needs.

Some types of civil-military coordination do not compromise the impartiality of NGOs. For example, NGO personnel can participate in security briefings conducted by the military, though a common concern is that the bulk of military information is classified and not able to be shared with NGOs. If this barrier can be overcome, both sides can share information on security conditions, operational sites, the locations of mines and unexploded ordnance, humanitarian activities, and population movements. This information sharing should be for the purpose of facilitating humanitarian operations. Often, NGOs establish liaison arrangements with military officials before and during military operations to ensure that humanitarian installations and personnel are protected. One example is the stationing of InterAction (an umbrella humanitarian NGO association) representation at U.S. Central Command during Operation Enduring Freedom in Afghanistan. Military forces may provide protection for convoys (although usually only in extreme cases), assist in delivery, and provide evacuation assistance for medical treatment or for withdrawal from a hostile environment. The military often has the capability to help to secure areas in which humanitarian organizations are working. They may also have the means to assist in delivering aid, such as rapid deployment of large numbers of personnel, equipment, logistics, and supplies.

Coordination Among International Actors. Because of the proliferation of international organizations and local, national, and international NGOs involved in humanitarian efforts, coordination among civilian agencies is essential. A lead actor should be put in charge of coordinating humanitarian activity. This actor could be the local government, a donor state, or an international or nongovernmental organization. As noted earlier, OCHA has a mandate to coordinate such efforts. In Kosovo, the United Nations High Commissioner for Refugees (UNHCR) was assigned this responsibility. The lead actor approach is usually the most efficient option, since it creates a unified command-and-control structure. However, it can be difficult to agree on a lead actor, since donor states, international institutions, and NGOs generally have different advantages, priorities, and interests. If there is no agreement on a lead actor, international and local actors can establish a coordinating body involving the main national and international actors and the principal NGOs. This body's role should be to coordinate and oversee joint assessments, establish key objectives and strategies, prioritize steps, oversee implementation, establish joint offices, and simplify procedures such as setting common reporting and financial requirements.

Humanitarian workers should share lessons learned and best practices in coordinating mission activities. International actors should coordinate with those institutions and NGOs that were involved in humanitarian relief before and during the conflict. Such experience provides an invaluable understanding of the ways in which people procure food, shelter, water, and health care; the condition of the population; and the major humanitarian challenges facing the country. International and local actors should avoid pitfalls that have complicated past humanitarian efforts. They should minimize personnel changes. Frequent changes in UN personnel, humanitarian coordinators, and military and relief personnel increase the problems of coordination. Failure to agree on common objectives is another problem. Major discrepancies in the objectives of states, international organizations, and NGOs can make it difficult for donor states and international organizations to determine which NGOs are most effective and worthy of support.

Coordination Between International and Domestic Actors. International and domestic actors may wish to form an advisory council composed of representatives from both parties to guide the overall humanitarian strategy and facilitate coordination. This council could establish functional committees from key humanitarian sectors, such as those addressing the needs of refugees, which would be responsible for sharing information and creating partnerships.

Assisting Refugees and Internally Displaced Persons

A primary goal of nation-building operations should be the return of refugees and internally displaced persons. Indeed, some nation-building operations have been organized principally for that purpose. The number of refugees in past nation-building operations has varied widely. In East Timor, the violence that followed the September 1999 referendum displaced close to 80 percent of the territory's population. Approximately 265,000 East Timorese became refugees; another 500,000 escaped to the interior of the country. In Kosovo, more than half the population was displaced, and a quarter fled or were driven out of the country in 1999. In Iraq, few people left their homes despite predictions of a humanitarian crisis.[8] As fighting escalated in Iraq, however, displacement eventually occurred. U.S. Agency for International Development (USAID) Disaster Assistance Response Teams were deployed to Iraq, but, since significant humanitarian assistance was unnecessary, they focused on assessing needs, working with military civil affairs personnel, and granting funds for community projects.

Civilian relief agencies should take the lead in returning refugees and internally displaced persons. International militaries can help provide a secure environment in which those civilian and international agencies can do their work. They also may provide limited relief and assistance when these agencies do not have the presence or capability to act on their own, such as during the early phases of a war. However, once combat operations wind down, relief agencies are usually capable of operating on their own. Civilian agencies should abide by the principle of *non-refoulement*. No refugee should be sent to a country in which his or her life or freedom would be threatened because of race, religion, nationality, membership in a particular social group, or political opinion.

Figure 5.1 shows the percentage of refugees who returned to their country within five years following the end of conflict in 13 nation-building operations. A low level of refugee return is often a sign of continued conflict, as in Somalia, Iraq, Haiti, and Afghanistan.

Assisting refugees and internally displaced persons involves several steps. First, humanitarian workers need to assess the nature of the challenge. Before the intervention, key tasks include identifying the factors that are likely to increase or decrease the number of displaced people, affect their choice of destination, and affect the conditions in which they live. Second, humanitarian workers should assemble and train humanitarian response teams. These teams should assess the immediate humanitarian needs of displaced people, coordinate the provision of relief efforts, and allocate local grants for relief projects. Third, agencies need to pre-position and stockpile supplies in the region. Critical materials include water, pharmaceuticals, shelter, blankets, and

---

[8] Dobbins, Jones, et al. (2005).

Figure 5.1
Percentage of Refugees Returning Five Years After Conflict Ceases

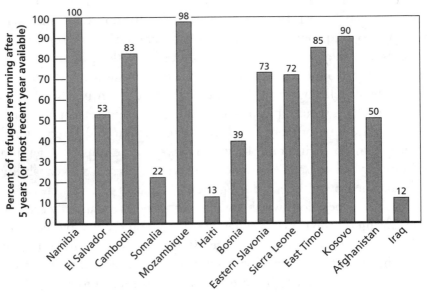

SOURCE: Data compiled from U.S. Department of State, *Occupation of Germany: Policy and Progress, 1945–1946*, Washington, D.C.: U.S. Government Printing Office, 1947; UNHCR statistical yearbooks; Federal Statistical Office, Yugoslavia, *Statistical Yearbook of Yugoslavia 1997*, Belgrade, 1997; and U.S. Committee for Refugees refugee surveys.
RAND *MG557-5.1*

food. Fourth, humanitarian agencies can help international forces involved in combat to design military campaigns to minimize displacement. International forces coordinated with humanitarian agencies in Bosnia, Kosovo, and Afghanistan. Humanitarian "mapping programs" can be a key element of this process. They involve military outreach to humanitarian organizations to identify important facilities, such as hospitals and cultural and historical sites. Militaries can also provide international and nongovernmental organizations with a phone number or the address of a Web site through which to nominate targets to be placed on a "no-strike" list.

Most humanitarian agencies have adopted a common set of standards for assisting refugees and displaced persons—as well as for other humanitarian activities such as water, sanitation, hygiene, nutrition, and food aid. These standards, which are often referred to as *Sphere standards*, are designed for use in disaster response and are applicable in a range of situations in which relief is required. They are designed to be used in slow- and rapid-onset situations, rural and urban environments, and developing and developed countries.[9]

Shelter and site planning often pose specific problems. Refugees or internally displaced persons arriving in an area settle down in various locations. In some cases, they take an unoccupied site and create a camp. In others, they spread out over a wide area and establish rural settlements or are hosted by local communities. A poorly planned camp or settlement can easily become a pathogenic environment. Overcrowding and poor hygiene are major factors in the transmission of epidemic diseases. Lack of adequate shelter deprives the population of privacy and exposes them to rain, cold, heat, and wind. Camps usually present a higher risk than refugee settlements, since they tend to become overcrowded and it is less likely that basic facilities—such as water and health care services—will be available when people arrive. To reduce health risks, site planning and organization should take place as early as possible to minimize overcrowding and maximize the provision of relief. Shelters must be set up as rapidly as possible to protect refugees from the elements and facilities installed for sanitation and food. These activities must be initiated within the first week of the intervention. Relief agencies are usually faced with either a displaced population that has spontaneously settled in a camp prior to the arrival of relief agencies or an empty site that can be set up prior to the arrival of displaced people. Whichever is the case, prompt action must be taken to improve the site and its facilities. Poor organization in the early stages may lead to a chaotic, overcrowded camp that creates substantial health risks. An ideal site is rarely available. The choice is generally limited, since the best sites will already be inhabited by local communities. Table 5.2 highlights key issues to consider.

The preferred way to end displacement is for people to return to their original homes or, if these have been destroyed, to their communities voluntarily. This is usually possible once conflict ends. The

---

[9]   See, for example, Sphere Project, *The Sphere Handbook*, Geneva, Switzerland, 2004.

Table 5.2
Shelter and Site Planning

Issue	Explanation
Security and protection	The settlement must be in a safe area (e.g., one free of mines) and away from any war zones.
Water	Water must be available either on the site or close by.
Space	The area must be large enough to ensure sufficient personal space and to minimize disease conditions. Thirty square meters per person is considered satisfactory.
Accessibility	Access to the site by trucks and other vehicles must be possible during all seasons.
Environmental health risks	Health workers should avoid camps or settlements close to breeding sites for mosquitoes and other carriers of serious diseases. Where such areas cannot be avoided, pests should be eliminated through spraying or other means.
Local population	Every effort should be made to avoid tensions between local and displaced communities.
Terrain	The terrain should slope to provide natural drainage for rainwater and sewage from the site.

first movements are often spontaneous, led by a single member of the family. The rest of the household may follow later. Families usually need help with transportation and require food and basic tools to restart their lives. If they find their houses burned, fields destroyed, or land occupied by others, humanitarian agencies should work to ensure that returning refugees and displaced persons—as well as their communities—receive proper assistance. Particular attention should be devoted to preventing and dealing with ethnic conflict, as well as assisting vulnerable groups such as widows, orphans, and the disabled.

Making the Transition from Relief

The goal of humanitarian efforts is to provide for the immediate needs of the population. Once these have been satisfied, the humanitarian effort should be wound down. This progression from relief to development is usually not linear or uniform and requires flexibility. From the earliest stages of relief assistance, programs are most effective when beneficiaries are involved in the design, management, and implementation of the assistance program. This approach becomes particularly critical when transitioning to longer-term development approaches. Ideally, transition programs strengthen the local community's voice while enabling local and central governments to assume substantial responsibility. Indeed, a key objective of postconflict nation-building should be to reach a "tipping point." This is the point at which the national and local governments begin to assume substantial responsibility for providing government services.

After World War II, it took Germany approximately two and a half years to reach the tipping point. By January 1948, German authorities had taken over full responsibility for the provision of local services, including health services, from the U.S. Office of Military Government. But U.S. advisors continued to observe, inspect, advise, and report on health activities. Haiti has never reached the tipping point. The United States largely withdrew in 1997 after three years, and the UN a couple of years later. The Haitian government never developed the capacity to effectively provide government services. There was no functioning ministry of health or administrative personnel within the ministry who could receive donor support, oversee financial administration, and ensure effective implementation. Haiti lacked trained health care workers and civil servants in the public sector. Many Haitian professionals had left the country, and the remaining personnel were often poorly trained and had little experience in administration or government. Aid organizations and donor states frequently funneled resources through the NGO community. Training indigenous personnel is a critical aspect of the handoff. Otherwise, the programs "neither reflect favorably on the host government nor will they remain effective after withdrawal of outside forces."[10]

Governance is important for long-term sustainability. In countries with a strong governance capacity, long-term reconstruction may be more rapid. Since national contributions and ownership are likely to be high, planning can be oriented beyond the short term (0 to 18 months) to include medium-term (18 to 36 months) recovery and development

---

[10] Robert J. Wilensky, *Military Medicine to Win Hearts and Minds: Aid to Civilians in the Vietnam War*, Lubbock, Tex.: Texas Tech University Press, 2004, p. 132.

needs. In countries with weak capacity, national and private humanitarian and development institutions usually do not have the ability to provide services effectively. In Somalia, for example, warlords did not support relief efforts and attacked, looted, and extorted payments from relief convoys. Humanitarian assistance had the perverse effect of exacerbating tensions among rival groups within the country that were competing for control of scarce resources. In Afghanistan, most of the country has historically been controlled by tribes and local warlords, and since its establishment in late 2001, the Karzai government has made only limited progress in delivering public services, including security, to much of the country.

Creating Measures of Effectiveness

Program management entails tracking inputs, outputs, and outcomes. Inputs are the resources utilized, such as the amount of financial assistance provided, the number of international personnel deployed, and the amount and type of equipment and material supplied. Outputs are the results generated by the program. Examples include the number of doctors and nurses trained, as well as the number of hospitals and health centers built or refurbished. Outcomes are measures of the efficacy of the program.[11] Outcome measures include the percentage of displaced people who return home, death rate, infant mortality rate, infectious disease rate, and the percentage of the population suffering from malnutrition. Are these rates improving, deteriorating, or remaining constant as humanitarian assistance is being provided? Since these outcome measures may not always be readily available, tactical, short-term measures serve to give policymakers some indication of performance. Examples include the percentage of children under one year of age who have been immunized; the percentage of births with skilled attendance; percentage of the population with access to basic health services within two hours; and the percentage of health facilities that report "stock outs" of essential drugs. Building such assessments into

---

[11] See Harry P. Hatry, *Performance Measurement: Getting Results*, Washington, D.C.: Urban Institute Press, 1999; and William T. Gormley, Jr., and David L. Weimer, *Organizational Report Cards*, Cambridge, Mass.: Harvard University Press, 1999.

humanitarian assistance programs makes it possible for donors to design assistance programs better. The most basic measures in acute emergencies are simple mortality and morbidity indicators—including the avoidance of significant infectious disease outbreaks.

Figure 5.2 shows a performance matrix that nation-building missions could create. It lists key inputs, outputs, and outcomes over time. Any competent performance matrix should include information that has been gathered on baseline conditions. It can be used to track performance over the course of humanitarian assistance to monitor whether conditions are improving or deteriorating.

There are six major steps to compiling performance metrics for humanitarian assistance programs.[12] First, inputs and outputs need to be tied to outcomes. Second, good indicators are simple. They must come in a clear format and be easy for all stakeholders to interpret. This is especially true in fragile states, where national capacities are very limited, communications between stakeholders are usually difficult, and the political dynamics may create fractures through which complex information could be lost or misused. Third, performance indicators should be selective. There must be a limited number of focused

Figure 5.2
Example of Performance Matrix

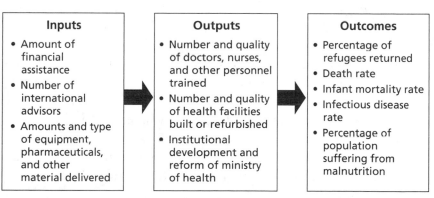

---

[12] See, for example, United Nations Development Group and World Bank (2005).

targets, and they must be prioritized to offer sequenced strategic direction. Fourth, performance metrics should guide policy actions and donor interventions across all areas where lack of progress carries the risk of reversing recovery—from political and security issues to the economy and health. Fifth, indicators should get sufficient donor buy-in to translate promises into financial commitments, disbursements, and priority technical assistance. This type of buy-in may help to avoid the fragmentation of donor assistance and its associated inefficiencies.

Key Actors

At least three major groups of actors should be involved in humanitarian efforts: major international organizations, NGOs, and donor states.

The first group includes large international organizations, especially those within the United Nations' family of agencies. The United Nations has a number of a organizations that play critical roles in humanitarian assistance: UNICEF (United Nations Children's Fund), UNHCR, the World Health Organization, the World Food Programme, and the Office of the Coordinator for Humanitarian Affairs. Some tackle specific problems, such as the distribution of food or other provisions for refugees. Others, like UNICEF, focus on a specific group, in this case children. In Kosovo, all humanitarian activities were put under the direction of a Deputy Special Representative of the UN Secretary-General who was nominated by UNHCR. This individual was able to bring to bear the resources of his own organization and had the authority to coordinate the efforts of other UN, national, and nongovernmental agencies. This model worked well and should be emulated where possible.

Many NGOs specialize in specific areas of humanitarian relief, such as providing emergency medical care, delivering food or water, or setting up camps. NGOs range from large international organizations, such as the International Federation of Red Cross and Red Crescent Societies, to much smaller organizations. NGOs often have very specific knowledge about the country or region of concern. At the same time, NGOs can also pose challenges. The rising number of NGOs has created coordination problems. As noted earlier, these problems create a strong impetus to establish institutional arrangements that increase efficiency and help overcome coordination and collaboration problems. NGOs may also have a wide range of goals and approaches that differ from those of the local government, major international organizations, other NGOs, and donors. Most highly experienced NGOs are part of networks, such as InterAction, an alliance of U.S.-based NGOs, or the International Council for Volunteer Agencies. Membership is often overlapping, and these networks comprise the primary actors in any emergency. They have established standards and membership criteria and have been the drivers in many of the key performance initiatives.

Several U.S. government entities are involved in humanitarian efforts, including USAID; the Bureau of Population, Refugees, and Migration at the U.S. Department of State; and Department of Defense forces involved in humanitarian assistance and stabilization efforts. Donor states' goals and policies may be driven by political and geostrategic considerations rather than strictly by considerations of need. The pursuit of these goals may sometimes result in programs at variance with best practices viewed from a purely humanitarian perspective.

Costs

To assess humanitarian costs, we examined the per capita relief costs in the first year of four nation-building operations: Afghanistan, Sierra Leone, Haiti, and Liberia. The data come from OCHA's Financial Tracking Service.[13] We compiled the total amount of humanitarian

---

[13] United Nations Office for Coordination of Humanitarian Affairs, Financial Tracking Service, Web-based, global humanitarian aid database, updated daily. The Financial Tracking Service is a global, real-time database that collects all reported international humanitarian aid (including that for NGOs and the International Red Cross and Red Crescent Movement, bilateral aid, in-kind aid, and private donations). It breaks down humanitarian costs into a variety of sectors: food, multisector, health, coordination and support services, human rights, agriculture, economic recovery, water and sanitation, shelter and nonfood items, education, and mine action and other security.

assistance and divided this by the population of each country, yielding an average figure of $34 per person.[14] This suggests that, on average, nation-building operations require a commitment of $34 per person to respond to a range of humanitarian challenges affected such needs as food, health, water, sanitation, and shelter. The actual figure for an operation would, of course, depend on specific conditions within the country and the extent of the humanitarian disaster. But this estimate offers a useful first cut. To illustrate, we evaluated the cost of a hypothetical intervention to Mozambique, which in 2006 had a population of 19,686,505. Using the average cost of $34 per capita, we estimate that Mozambique would require approximately $700 million in humanitarian assistance in the first year of the stability operation. We also evaluated the cost of an intervention to Macedonia, which had a population of 2,050,554 in 2006. Using the average cost of $34 per capita, we estimate that Macedonia would require approximately $70 million in humanitarian assistance in the first year of the operation. Table 5.3 highlights the results.

Table 5.3
Estimates for Operations in Macedonia and Mozambique, Year One

Hypothetical Intervention	Population (2006)	Estimated Humanitarian Expenditures (2006 US$)
Peace enforcement mission to Macedonia	2,050,554	70 million
UN-led mission to Mozambique	19,686,505	700 million

SOURCE: United Nations Office for Coordination of Humanitarian Affairs, Financial Tracking Service. Population data, Central Intelligence Agency (2006).

NOTE: Based on an average cost of $34 per capita. Amounts may not sum due to rounding.

---

[14] The amounts included $61 per person for assistance in Afghanistan, $12 in Sierra Leone, $9 in Haiti, and $52 in Liberia.

CHAPTER SIX

Governance

Societies emerging from conflict may be able to wait for democracy, but they need a government immediately to provide law enforcement, education, and public health care. Electricity, telecommunications, water, and other utilities also require a government to regulate them, and, in some instances, to provide the service. Sometimes the intervening authorities initially serve as the government. However, they will never be in a position to deliver these services without relying on host-country nationals and local institutions to provide attendant government services. The intervening authorities provide funding, guidance, and oversight and select people and organizations to provide services, but teachers, health workers, and the police force must be drawn from among host-country nationals. By their selection, these individuals and organizations acquire funds and power. The intervening authorities need to ensure that their choices do not exacerbate existing discontents, especially among those groups that were party to the conflict. The intervening authorities need to choose partners carefully with a view to creating a government and distribution of power that will survive their departure.

Key Challenges

Establishing a Transitional Administration. If an acceptable government is already in place at the time of the intervention, the intervening authorities may be able to focus on strengthening and reforming it rather than creating a new government. However, if the state has failed or has been overthrown, the intervening authorities may have to govern the country in its stead. Alternatively, the intervening authorities may choose to immediately constitute an interim government through a mechanism other than election—by co-option, appointment, or consultation. The first approach is the most common, but the latter two approaches have also been used frequently. In all instances, this first government is transitional, a makeshift arrangement designed to prepare the way for a more legitimate and more capable successor.

Restoring Public Services. In all societies, even the poorest, governments are expected to provide basic public services: security, state-run education, public health care, and the construction and maintenance of roads. During conflict, the provision of these services is disrupted and, in some cases, ceases. By opening and operating schools and public health clinics, the intervening authorities not only restart the provision of important services, they also send a signal that times have changed: The country is becoming more stable. Wages paid to teachers, health care workers, and other government employees put money into the local economy, as these individuals purchase food and other locally produced goods and services and provide financial support to friends and relatives. Paying the wages of teachers and health care professionals supports respected leaders who are often voices for moderation. Reopening schools has the additional advantage of getting children off the streets.

Most nation-building missions are short of personnel and other resources at the beginning of the intervention. They are poorly equipped to satisfy demands for public services. A lack of administrative capacity severely constrains the ability of the intervening authorities and the host government to organize, pay for, and deliver government services. In an environment of scarce funds and administrative ability, donors and governments have to prioritize expenditures, focusing on those services that have the greatest effect on quality of life and those that can be delivered most effectively.

Setting Up Local Governments. In many countries, outlying regions are difficult to access. Citizens in these regions prefer to have local or regional governments provide services and address their concerns because they are more accessible or may be more representative of the ethnic or religious composition of the area. But local govern-ments may have collapsed during the conflict. The intervening authori-ties, usually located in the capital city, are often too far away or too focused on rebuilding the central government to pay adequate atten-tion to reconstituting local governments. Because smaller towns are often inaccessible, lack amenities for international civil servants, or do not present immediate challenges, they are neglected. Yet, creating capable, representative local governments may be key to preventing a return to conflict.

Best Practices

Establishing a Transitional Administration

Conduct Predeployment Assessments. To create or bolster an existing transitional administration, the intervening authorities need to assess how the past and current governments operated. The United States often deploys assessment teams under the auspices of USAID through its Disaster Assistance Response Teams to evaluate the capa-bilities of host governments. Other countries and international organi-zations do the same. These assessments are usually conducted based on the type of assistance needed. One team analyzes humanitarian needs while another assesses the logistical requirements for transporting relief supplies into the country. Combining these assessments into an overall evaluation of the capabilities of the host government is a major chal-lenge. Multidisciplinary teams, augmented by teams of financial audi-tors to gather and assess financial information, are needed to conduct assessments shortly after the intervening authorities enter the country so that an effective strategy to set up or bolster an interim administra-tion can be devised.

Assessments should include factors such as the key motivations of the conflict. The assessments must evaluate the weaknesses of the existing government institutions to combat illicit economic activity, especially activities that finance spoilers. The assessment must evalu-ate how warlords, militias, and other spoilers might be integrated into legitimate institutions, marginalized, or eliminated from positions of power. These groups must also be progressively separated from illicit sources of financial support and military power. The following key factors should be taken into consideration:

- size of the country and its demographics
- situation in the country prior to the intervention
- nature of the conflict that led to the intervention
- impact of the conflict on the population, especially in areas such as health, population displacement, and employment
- condition of key infrastructure
- presence and capacity of government institutions
- political traditions
- availability of human capital in the country
- preexisting laws
- state of law and order
- degree of corruption in society, especially within government institutions
- type and scale of legal and illegal financial resources
- presence of militias, warlords, criminal organizations, and other spoilers
- type, amount, and location of natural resources
- ethnic, tribal, religious, and other potential fissures in the country.

Writing the Mandate. Most nation-building missions, including those undertaken by coalitions of the willing, operate under a mandate from the United Nations Security Council. In cases in which the United Nations is leading the operation, that mandate tends to be rather detailed, carefully setting out the mission's objectives and authority. Mandates should spring from an honest assessment of which institutions need to be created and which indigenous and international actors should contribute. Those chosen to lead international missions should play an important role in developing the mandate. A UN mandate can be beneficial in setting up new government institutions. It signals that the international community has agreed that the operation is legal and morally justified. The absence of an explicit mandate and, in particular, an explicit UN mandate, increases the likelihood that locals will view the nation-building mission as illegitimate.

The contrast between strong and weak mandates is illustrated by the missions in East Timor and Haiti in 2004. In East Timor, UN Security Council Resolution 1272 established a clear mandate in 1999 that gave the United Nations significant power to build government institutions:

> [The UN Security Council] decides to establish, in accordance with the report of the Secretary-General, a United Nations Transitional Administration in East Timor (UNTAET), which will be endowed with overall responsibility for the administration of East Timor and will be empowered to exercise all legislative and executive authority, including the administration of justice.[1]

All powers were concentrated in the hands of Sergio Vieira de Mello, the transitional administrator. UNTAET had the authority to do everything from sign treaties to stamp passports at the Dili airport. It was treated as a de facto government by countries and international organizations, with the power to negotiate projects, disburse funds, and make reporting arrangements. The UN Security Council resolution also gave the UN mission the power to provide security, establish an effective administration, assist in the development of civil and social services, and ensure coordination and delivery of humanitarian assistance. To accomplish these activities, the UN Security Council established a governance and public administration component, a humanitarian assistance and emergency rehabilitation component, and a military component of the mission.

By contrast, the United Nations adopted a much weaker mandate for Haiti in 2004 through UN Security Council Resolution 1542. The resolution stated that the United Nations would support the constitutional and political process under way in Haiti; assist the transitional Haitian government in its efforts to bring about a process of national dialogue and reconciliation; assist the government in its efforts to orga-

---

[1]   United Nations Security Council, Resolution 1272, on the situation in East Timor, 4,057th meeting, October 25, 1999.

nize, monitor, and carry out free and fair elections; and assist the government in extending the state's authority throughout Haiti and in supporting good government locally as well as nationally.[2]

These disparate mandates reflect more the differing levels of commitment of the international community than the needs of the societies in question. In 1999, the UN membership was ready to pour large resources into the small receptacle of East Timor. In 2004, it was not ready to do the same for Haiti, a larger but perhaps even needier society. Regrettable as this may seem, experience suggests that it is better to match the mandate to the anticipated level of commitment than to the needs of the recipient state. Providing a broad mandate without the resources needed to fulfill it inflates expectations and increases the probability of failure.

Coordination Among International Actors. A key task for any mission is to address the challenge of coordinating among international actors by establishing umbrella structures; regular consultative processes among key institutions; and centralized, transparent reporting mechanisms to monitor the disbursement of aid and the results of programs. Over the past 15 years, intervening authorities have used a variety of arrangements to combine unity of purpose, while also promoting broad international participation.

Coordination Between International and Local Leaders. Mechanisms should be set up between the mission and the host-country authorities. These mechanisms will differ depending on whether there is an interim indigenous government or an international administration with indigenous "advisors." The head of the mission needs to consult with key donor states, the Secretary-General of the United Nations, and local leaders to arrive at acceptable mechanisms.

In cases in which the intervening authorities exercise sovereign functions, the leader of the mission may create an advisory council composed of local leaders. As the central advisory body of the mission, the council can help guide the overall strategy for political cooperation between the mission and the various political leaders. To ensure

---

2   United Nations Security Council, Resolution 1542, on the question concerning Haiti, 4,961st meeting, April 30, 2004.

cooperation from the former contending militaries, the international force commander may establish a joint military committee with the top military commander of each force. This committee focuses on the execution of key military tasks and problems involved in sharing information and coordination. To assist in civil administration, UN missions often set up joint functional committees for education, health care, transportation, and other sectors. These committees enable local actors to participate in decisionmaking and implementation.

In East Timor, for example, the UN mission established the National Consultative Council, a political body consisting of 11 East Timorese and four international members, during the transition period to independence. The National Consultative Council agreed on a series of regulations required to establish effective administration in the territory, including setting up a legal system, establishing a judiciary, adopting a national currency, putting in place border controls, setting up a tax system, and creating a consolidated budget for East Timor. The National Consultative Council then adopted a regulation establishing a transitional cabinet composed of four East Timorese and four international representatives.

In Kosovo, indigenous leaders and UNMIK created the Joint Interim Administrative Structure. The UN appointed local counterparts to UNMIK administrators in Kosovo, ensuring that there was adequate representation among Kosovo's ethnic communities. The Joint Interim Administrative Structure was composed of three elements: the Office of the Special Representative of the Secretary-General; the Kosovo-wide oversight and advisory bodies representing Kosovo's institutions and political groupings; and the Pristina-based departments responsible for administration, service delivery, and revenue collection. The careful cultivation and integration of the Albanian Kosovar and Serb moderates helped abate interethnic tensions. The Joint Interim Administrative Structure became operational about nine months into the mission, with offices, organizations, and staff. In the later stages of the mission, in the aftermath of general elections, the Provincial Institutions of Self-Government were established, which took over administrative functions previously conducted by UNMIK.

Building Mission Staff. One of the most difficult tasks facing any intervening authority is to deploy sufficient numbers of competent staff. Experienced personnel are critical for effective governance. In Kosovo, as in most nation-building operations, finding enough personnel to reach "mission strength" was a long, arduous process. The United States suffered even more acutely from such shortages and delays in seeking to staff the Coalition Provisional Authority in Iraq. While intervening authorities may be able to identify qualified personnel, the most difficult challenge is often in convincing them to go and then to stay once there.

Restoring Public Services

Resuming the provision of government services is a key step toward restarting growth. Security, which is provided by the legal system (e.g., police, prisons, prosecutors, courts); public health; and primary and secondary education are the most important such services.

In most postconflict situations, the restoration of government services starts at the top and bottom simultaneously; filling in the middle is less urgent. Starting at the top, the intervening authorities are often involved in selecting and appointing ministers and department heads. Where possible, host-country nationals should be appointed. Foreign nationals do not know the host-country bureaucracy (to the extent that it still exists) and usually do not speak the local language. Therefore, the bureaucracy can more easily ignore their decisions. In some instances, in East Timor, Kosovo, and Iraq, for example, the intervening authorities gave executive authority to foreign nationals. The use of foreign advisors was dictated by the absence of a cadre of locals with the requisite experience, as was the case of East Timor and Kosovo, or who were not trusted by the intervening authority, as was the case in Iraq. Political sensitivities, especially where one ethnic group has dominated past governments, also may dictate an interim period during which expatriate staff has executive authority. This is especially important in societies in which one ethnic group, sometimes a minority, has dominated other groups, monopolizing key positions in the bureaucracy and channeling resources to its compatriots. The intervening authorities can help break this pattern through the use of foreign advisors or staff and the introduction of more meritocratic hiring conditions.

One of the more successful options for staffing ministries has been to recruit nationals who have international work experience. Finance ministers in Afghanistan, Iraq, and Liberia have had previous experience in international banking. The current finance minister of Liberia (as well as the president) worked at the World Bank. These individuals, if they do not have too much political baggage, are often able to communicate effectively with host-country nationals, elites, and the populace, while maintaining open lines of communication with the international donor community. They have to contend with charges of "carpetbagging," returning to their country of origin to enrich themselves in the postconflict environment, but by introducing transparent contracting procedures and payments and improving government services, these charges can be dampened.

The choice of ministers, expatriate or local, is a choice about who is to make decisions. When a host-country government exists or can be set up quickly, it, not the intervening authorities, needs to make decisions on the provision of government services. If host-country nationals do not make and are not responsible for decisions, they can and are likely to overturn them in the future. Policy reversals waste time and disrupt government operations. A lack of local control results in a lack of local responsibility: Implementation of decisions made by foreign nationals may lag or not take place at all. Kosovo and Bosnia's indigenous leaders have successfully derailed efforts to restructure their electric power utilities, in part because they did not ever make the decision their own. It is often better to take more time up front to gain consensus and create an acceptable permanent solution to a problem, even in the immediate aftermath of a conflict, than to use stopgap measures that may never be fully implemented and are eventually overturned.

Where the intervening authorities believe that foreign nationals are necessary to run government operations, locals need to be recruited and mentoring relationships need to be established as soon as possible. In these instances, clear lines of responsibility and a clear timetable based on the performance of local appointees need to be established early on, laying out when and how authority will be transferred to the emerging host government and its ministers. In East Timor, a more aggressive mentoring program and a more rapid transfer of authority to host-country nationals might have made the transition to local control more successful. Mentoring programs, provided that the advisors and ministers establish a good rapport, are useful, especially in core ministries (ministries of security, justice, finance, education, and health, and the central bank). Good advisors provide counsel on best-practice policies and management procedures, often from their own experience, and act as liaisons with the intervening authorities.

Because of the potential influence these individuals can wield, care needs to be taken to recruit the best possible advisors. Because experienced individuals may be unable or unwilling to make multiyear commitments, it is sometimes useful to designate a donor country or international institution as the lead agency responsible for each core ministry. The lead country or institution is responsible for recruiting and funding the senior advisor as well as for coordinating international assistance to the ministry. This designation provides institutional continuity when personal continuity is not practicable. However, the senior advisors should report to the intervening authorities. The intervening authorities should have the right to request that the lead country or institution dismiss an advisor, and such a request should be honored.

Utilities. The intervening authorities face the immediate problem of turning on the lights and water in the aftermath of a conflict. Garbage collection, electrical power, water, sewage, and public transportation are also important. Rudimentary service levels can often be restored by locating and working with key employees. When those individuals cannot be found, expatriate staff will need to be brought in until local replacements can be trained. In all cases, utility experts should arrive with the first contingent of the intervening authorities.

Once a skeletal staff has been assembled, it needs to ascertain which components of the system are operable (e.g., garbage trucks, generators, transformers, pumps) and the availability of fuel and other supplies. The intervening authorities may need to jump-start the provision of power and water by supplying funds and assisting the utility in procuring and installing vital missing parts. In some instances, the intervening authorities will need to import portable generators or bring in clean water to provide interim services. These activities are usually provided as humanitarian assistance rather than administered as programs to rebuild government.

Utilities tend to be capital-intensive; purchasing or repairing equipment tends to be expensive. Although donors may be able to restore some services almost immediately, improving the reliability and geographical coverage of these services is a long-term problem of development and cannot be solved in the first postconflict stage.

Resuscitation of payment systems for utilities should be high on the list of priorities. It is not the job of the intervening authorities to provide levels of service common to developed countries, but rather to restart the provision of power and water and to support the system so that supplies are provided at sustained preconflict levels. As soon as the lights are turned on and water begins to flow, the utility needs to bill and collect compensation for the provision of services. Otherwise, service will once again deteriorate. In Kosovo, blackouts remain common seven years after the intervention because the utility fails to receive full payment for service.

Collection is not an easy task: Theft of power and water are standard practices in many developing countries and utility tariffs are contentious political issues. But by setting up billing and collection services in conjunction with the renewal of the power and water supplies and cutting off consumers who fail to pay, the intervening authorities lay the foundations for increasingly comprehensive payment systems further down the road.

In many postconflict countries, preconflict service levels were very low. Liberia has not had electric power or water service for over 15 years. Service in Afghanistan is very spotty. By implementing rational pricing schemes and ensuring collection, the intervening authorities will provide the resources to ensure fewer future interruptions in supplies of electricity and water. Continuity of supply is more important than cost for facilitating economic growth. For example, it is better for a dairy to pay more for electricity and have continuous access to refrigeration than to pay less and suffer the losses caused by the abrupt loss of refrigeration due to fluctuating power supplies.

To restart the operation of utilities, the intervening authorities may need to hire new managers with international expertise or outside consultants to serve as mentors to current managers. Although extensive reorganization often needs to wait until a later date, these individuals can initiate some organizational changes, including setting up separate units in charge of distribution to final customers. These distribution units are responsible for collecting funds to pay for power or water from the larger utility. If insufficient funds are raised, the utility can cut off service to the unit, providing motivation for collection and payment by customers. Without this discipline, provision of electric power, water, and other such services will be slow to improve.

Education. In most postconflict societies, the education system has deteriorated. Educated elites, including teachers, have emigrated. Children have attended school sporadically, if at all, resulting in large gaps in their education. School buildings have been damaged. Schoolbooks and supplies have disappeared. Some children have taken part in the conflict with all the terrible psychological consequences that entails.

To create a functional educational system, first and foremost, competent teachers have to be hired and motivated to teach. Providing teachers with competitive salaries is the most effective way of attracting educated individuals to the profession. Although salaries need to be commensurate with the resources of the country, by paying teachers at least as much as educated civil servants in other departments, the host country should be able to attract high-caliber teachers to schools. In those instances in which educated individuals are in short supply, the intervening authorities can assist the host government to set up "crash programs" for training high school graduates or talented grammar school graduates in the basics of teaching. Donors should fund teacher salaries and teacher-training programs and, where needed, support the renovation of damaged schools and the construction of new schools. The first reconstruction programs should be concentrated in areas that have suffered most during the conflict. New or refurbished schools send a powerful signal that the times have changed. This said, not every dilapidated school should be renovated. In depopulated areas, some damaged schools should be abandoned.

Most educational systems function better with curriculum guidelines and national testing rather than a rigid national curriculum. Local conditions and student preparation may vary dramatically across economic, ethnic, and social groups. Teachers need to have some flexibility in addressing these different populations. In countries with more than one ethnic group, courses on history, language, and literature will need to be tailored to the various groups, and curricula will need to be developed in the various languages.

Along with attractive salaries, teachers need to be held accountable for performance, especially in postconflict environments where hiring standards may need to be looser. National tests to measure educational performance are useful for measuring student progress and teacher performance. Tests are especially important in secondary school, where examination results should be used for providing graduates with credentials.

Although national testing and suggested national curricula help ensure that minimal standards are met or exceeded, local involvement and control have also been shown to improve educational results. The education ministry needs to set clear qualifications for principals, consonant with the availability of applicants, and establish transparent competitions for positions. However, the local community should interview candidates and be given the authority to select principals from a group of qualified candidates. Parents should be encouraged to meet with teachers and extend their compliments and criticisms to the principal. Principals need to exercise financial and operational control over their schools. Providing schools with payments per attending pupil is a useful way of directing money to successful schools. State audits and monitoring are necessary to ensure that funds are expended appropriately and that enrollment and attendance records are accurate.

In many postconflict societies, remedial education programs are needed for individuals whose education was interrupted by the conflict, as well as for adults who have lacked opportunities to improve their skills. Remedial education programs can be especially important for former combatants or older students whose education has been disrupted. Limited tuition grants can be useful in adult education. Under these programs, students enroll in a course, often taught privately. The government pays part or all of the student's tuition, but full payment is predicated on the student completing the course satisfactorily. Programs in which the student has to make partial payment are likely to be more successful than programs in which the state pays the entire cost, as students tend to make a greater investment of time and effort when they use their own funds. They also shop harder to find courses that provide the highest value for their investment. This holds true even in very poor societies.

Governments face difficult choices concerning tertiary educational institutions in postconflict societies. Reviving a national university or opening a university for an ethnic minority that was party to the conflict make important political statements. In Macedonia, government support for an Albanian language university was key to fostering support for conciliation. But universities are expensive to operate. Faculties have usually dispersed and facilities have been damaged. In societies in which education levels are low, the social benefits of money spent on primary or secondary education are frequently higher than those from comparable expenditures on university education. Globally, there is considerable capacity in tertiary education. Most postconflict societies would be better off concentrating resources on primary and secondary schools than on state-run universities, at least until economic growth has created a stronger tax and funding base.

Donors and the host-country government have several options for encouraging post-secondary school study other than the expansion of state-run universities. Donors may choose to provide scholarships to study abroad for high-scoring secondary school graduates, especially in areas such as science and engineering, for which expensive laboratories and facilities are needed. Such a division of labor permits the host government to concentrate its resources on teacher training or business education, if those skills are in short supply. The state may also wish to encourage the use of private educational institutions for post-secondary training. Private or public, schools at all levels need to be subject to standards. Testing and school inspections are two means of ensuring minimal standards; demanding that schools go through independent accreditation programs is also helpful.

Health Care. Following a conflict, systems of public health and health care delivery are often in shambles. Employees have gone unpaid; many have left their jobs. Facilities have been damaged or destroyed. The government has lacked funds to purchase pharmaceuticals and other supplies, and distribution channels have been disrupted. Vaccinations and programs for expectant mothers and infants have been stopped.

Even where public delivery and finance systems function effectively, a considerable share of health care services are procured and paid for privately. Because health care can be so expensive, the host-country government, in conjunction with the intervening authorities, needs to carefully plan and decide what the role of the government should be in financing and providing health care. Systems need to be designed such that they can be sustained when assistance declines.

In postconflict countries, especially lower-income ones, the initial focus should be on primary health care. Goals for primary health care should be immunization, treatment of injuries and infectious diseases, maternal and infant health care, the provision of vitamins and other nutritional supplements, and management of chronic illnesses such as diabetes and heart disease. To deliver these services, the intervening authorities, host government, and ministry of health need to establish or reconstruct clinics throughout the country. In the early stages, choices of sites are likely to be dictated by existing facilities, even if they are damaged. However, the intervening authorities and the host government need to create a planning mechanism for siting clinics based on population, access, and ethnic divisions. In regions of conflict, setting up separate clinics serving the different groups may reduce tensions, especially if languages differ.

Clinics, even if funded by the government, are often better run by private providers, including NGOs and private doctors. In Afghanistan, the health ministry subcontracts clinic operations to the private sector;[3] NGOs were considered better able to run these clinics than was

---

[3] Alistair J. McKechnie, "Humanitarian Assistance, Reconstruction and Development in Afghanistan: A Practitioners' View," CPR Working Paper No. 3, Washington, D.C.: World Bank, March 2003, p. 11.

the nascent Afghan government. Directors should be given responsibility for budgets and personnel. Regulated copayments are often useful for curbing overuse of health services. Payments from the national government to the clinics should be based on the number of clients served and the types of illnesses treated. Hiring decisions should be made on a competitive basis. In the likely event that qualified applicants are in short supply, provisional qualification standards can be applied. In many postconflict societies, the intervening authorities will turn to foreign candidates to fill the need for doctors, other trained personnel, and clinic directors. Donor funding can be utilized to set up in-country training courses coupled with on-the-job training to remedy some of the shortages of qualified health care professionals.

The intervening authorities should reopen some acute care facilities to provide general hospital services. Specialized mental and physical rehabilitation services are necessary to help the population overcome traumas stemming from the conflict. National planning for health care delivery is of even greater importance for secondary and tertiary health care than for primary care because of the cost of hospitals and more sophisticated clinics. The capital costs of these facilities are large; operating costs are even larger over the life of the facility. The host government needs to make sure that facilities are properly sized and located and that health care delivery modes other than through hospitals are utilized so as to create an efficient, fiscally sustainable health care system. As with clinics, government payments should be made based on services rendered, not on a facility's budget. Donors often need to play a role in providing technical assistance to help make these difficult decisions. However, the final decisions need to be made locally and presented as such.

Outpatient delivery systems are generally more cost-effective than hospitals for many types of health problems. However, cases that might be handled in outpatient clinics in wealthier societies require overnight hospital stays in postconflict countries. Patients are unlikely to have suitable transport home following treatments. Their homes may lack sewage service and clean water. One option for postprocedure care is to set up sanitary hostels adjacent to clinics or hospitals, as an alternative to keeping patients overnight in acute care hospitals. These facilities can be designed such that family members can nurse patients, easing pressures on staff and improving quality of care.

Tertiary care facilities, which have advanced operating rooms and use more sophisticated medical techniques, are expensive to build and operate. Following a conflict, many countries lack the personnel, equipment, supplies, and funds to run such facilities. Among the cases we have analyzed, only the southeastern European countries and Iraq had much capacity to provide tertiary care.

In light of all the other demands for resources in postconflict societies, investing heavily in tertiary care facilities is often a poor use of resources. It is better to set aside funds to help individuals travel to and receive care from facilities in other countries. The quality of care is likely to be higher and the number of patients that can be treated per dollar spent is likely to be higher. In Iraq, the Coalition Provisional Authority proposed to construct a children's hospital in al Basrah. If constructed, this one hospital would absorb the entire construction budget of the ministry of health and a very appreciable share of the ministry's total operating budget. A small portion of the funds needed to build and operate such a hospital could be used to send a comparable number of children to nearby Persian Gulf states where several modern hospitals already exist.

Focusing Assistance. Traditional approaches to development are poorly adapted to restarting government services in postconflict societies. Traditional assistance projects often entail creating prototype projects that, if successful, would be replicated elsewhere in the country. These types of projects are expensive in terms of management time: Host-government officials are expected to run the current system while observing, tweaking, and ultimately introducing successful prototype projects throughout their areas of responsibility.

Management time and resources are so scarce in postconflict situations that it is often better to resuscitate a poorly functioning existing system than to try to set up a new program. For example, the first order of business after the invasion of Iraq was to ensure that the food-rationing system was up and running, despite its many faults. When old systems are so broken that they cannot be repaired, the host-country government and intervening authorities need to plan carefully for the transformation of the current system into a new system and then methodically replace the old with the new, giving civil servants adequate training and the tools necessary to undertake their new jobs. Half-completed projects have even more pernicious consequences in postconflict situations than in the normal course of events.

In planning such projects, less is often more. Donors often fund too many projects. In a society that is recovering from war, almost any project would improve the lives of the people of the country. But each additional project comes with costs: project design, consultants who set up and run the project, project oversight, audits, and supervision. In the immediate aftermath of a conflict, assistance needs to be focused on restoring security by getting the legal system up and running; reopening primary and secondary schools; ensuring that public health institutions are operating; and seeing to it that the new government is putting in place systems that will enable it to operate efficiently, effectively, and transparently. At this stage, projects to reform pension systems, create a stock market, or develop higher education tend to distract from rather than contribute to the effective provision of government services. It is better to carefully plan the comprehensive transformation or improvement of a current system (giving everyone new textbooks, for example) than start dozens of prototype projects that cannot be fully implemented in the near future. A substantial amount of resources could be saved by focusing on a few major tasks and sticking with them until completion rather than letting a hundred flowers bloom.

Setting Up Local Governments

Because they are frequently more honest, more efficient, and better able to communicate with international donors than are representatives of national or local governments, international NGOs are often the intermediaries of choice to distribute postconflict assistance. NGOs are more likely to ensure that assistance goes directly to those most in need, not into the pockets of government officials. Despite these advantages, to the extent possible, assistance should be channeled through the government, national or local. The key task of postconflict reconstruction is to create functional governments. Although NGOs may serve as intermediaries with nascent local governments and mentor and monitor local officials, they cannot replace government.

Involving local governments in reconstruction is an important means through which officials gain experience in budgeting, contracting, and overseeing projects. In most postconflict situations, aid budgets are the primary sources of money for investment projects run by local governments. In Afghanistan and Sierra Leone, they have been almost the only source. Local government authorities should manage operational and capital budgets as soon as appropriate controls are introduced. Contracting should be handled through or in conjunction with local governments rather than directly with NGOs. Better to use assistance funds to set up systems, train, and provide incentives for government operations to improve than to channel funds to NGOs that will eventually be superseded by these same governments.

In some instances, most notably in Iraq, intervening authorities have been reticent to devolve authority to local governments because of fears of setting political precedents in periods when new constitutions are being written. Even in the absence of a constitutional framework, devolving budget and management authority to local governments is generally a good idea. It leads to better provision of services and the development of a cadre of local leaders, provides local experience with management, and teaches political leaders how to respond to local constituents. It also can assist in creating a better foundation for the resolution of grievances that contributed to the conflict. Regionally based insurgencies, such as in Sudan and Congo, are driven in part by perceptions that a distant, venal, incompetent central government is exploiting the region. By fostering the development of local governments that recognize the sovereignty of the national government but are responsive to local interests, some of the drivers of the conflict may be dissipated. The decentralized structure that has emerged in Afghanistan appears to have helped dampen some potential conflicts in that country. Local government can also serve to make antagonistic groups work together. In Eastern Slavonia, committees comprised of representatives of all ethnic groups were charged with managing government services. By providing incentives to representatives of these different groups to work with each other to solve concrete problems, the process of reconciliation was begun. On the other hand, donors need to support the emergence of local governance in accordance with some overall strategy for dealing with the issue of central versus regional power in societies in which these issues are in dispute.

The intervening authorities and the host government can foster the role of local authorities by providing direct budgetary support and the authority at the local level to select and contract out small-scale reconstruction projects, including road improvements and schools. International donors and the host government need to provide proper financial and project oversight, including performance and financial audits, and insist on competitive bids. Because the intervening authorities will lack the staff to provide hands-on guidance and oversight, in many cases, activities designed to foster the development of local government should be subcontracted to NGOs. In mixed communities, local governments should be designed such that all groups have a voice. In these communities, the process of making local decisions about the provision of services can force antagonistic groups to work with each other and can hopefully lead to reconciliation.

Education and publicly provided health care are best funded at the national level so that regional differences in incomes and economic activity do not lead to dramatic differences in service quality. Authority over these institutions should, therefore, generally be split. The national government should set performance and budget guidelines and audit and monitor these institutions to see that these guidelines are respected. Because the principal of the local school and the director of the local clinic need to have budgetary and management authority and responsibility, local control should be confined to hiring, firing, and evaluating directors, not engagement by local government officials in the management of these operations. In many instances, it makes sense to contract out the provision of health services to nongovernmental providers. Bids need to be evaluated locally to ensure that the local authorities have confidence in the provider, and centrally to ensure that the government receives value for the money.

In several instances, international and host-country civil servants have created innovative programs to stand up local governments. They have focused on capacity-building and local government–level provision of services, in contrast to past practices, when development agencies had planned and administered local reconstruction projects. Several international actors are often involved in establishing local governments and encouraging local participation. In some cases, international military forces are the only international personnel in rural areas, and they work with locals to restore basic services. Some best practices have come from the creative instincts of these military officers. Others have been developed by specialized agencies that deploy as soon as security allows and adapt models from previous operations to local conditions. The UNDP, the World Bank, government agencies such as USAID and the UK Department for International Development (DFID), contractors, and NGOs focus on the development of local governance.

In Afghanistan, the United Nations has created a standardized package for local government that includes materials needed to establish a post office, police station, mayor's and governor's offices, and bank, as well as communication equipment. This package was complemented by a civil service package that included materials on literacy training, databases and computers, and a startup package of basic office supplies. The Office of Transition Initiatives in USAID provided substantial reconstruction money for the restoration of ministries, including materials such as paint, chairs, desks, office supplies, and books.

Key Actors

Several actors are involved in building governance capacity. In most nation-building missions, the UN or a lead nation governs directly or helps local leaders establish a government. Rarely do these leadership responsibilities fall to others. One exception is Bosnia, where the international community created an ad hoc international entity, the High Representative, following the signing of the Dayton Peace Accords.

Beneath the lead entity, a variety of international organizations are involved in governance: UN agencies such as UNDP; regional organizations such as the Asian Development Bank, the European Union, and OSCE; and other major international organizations such as the World Bank. Individual donor states usually become involved in governance through their international development agencies. NGOs and private contractors, which routinely work for the United Nations and donor states, assist in various governance activities. NGOs and contractors usually specialize in specific areas of governance, such as building civil services.

Because of its financial resources and expertise, the World Bank should take the lead in restoring utilities. The bank should provide utility experts to be included in the first contingent to enter the country. These individuals can be recruited and paid through donor-country assistance programs. On the advice of the World Bank, the head of the intervening authorities should appoint a high-level deputy to coordinate and manage this part of the assistance program.

Sizing and Costs

International Presence. Unlike the police and military components, there are no comparable benchmarks for numbers of international civil servants needed to help resuscitate the governments of postconflict societies. There is also little information on costs. This is due to the number of actors involved in governance, and partly due to variations in support by donor states. For example, Liberia, which drew broad support from the international community, received $253 per capita in assistance in 2005 and 2006 to help run the government. It has one civilian UN staff member for every 2,000 Liberians. In contrast, in the Democratic Republic of the Congo, the United Nations devoted $18 per capita in 2005 and 2006 and had one UN civilian staff person for every 20,000 people. From these examples, it is clear that the budget and staff allocated to these missions are based more on donor interest, available resources, and competing priorities elsewhere in the world than on any uniform needs assessment.

Resurrecting Government Services. To estimate the potential costs of providing education, health care, and government operations for one year, we analyzed existing spending patterns on the part of developing countries using data from the UN Development Programme's *Human Development Report 2004* on shares of GDP spent on education and public health; detailed budget information on expenditures on education, health, and government operations were taken from IMF Country Reports for 27 developing countries; information on per capita GDP at market exchange rates was calculated or extracted from data in the IMF's International Financial Statistics Browser and from the World Bank Country Statistical Information Database.[4] We found that, on average, developing countries spend 4.2 percent of GDP on education, 2.6 percent on public health, and 3.6 percent on general administration.[5]

These averages were used to generate best-practice estimates of donor spending needed to restart government operations in postconflict societies under the assumption that donors would have to pay for all government operations in the first year following a conflict. Because GDP is depressed in postconflict situations, the lower level of per capita incomes in the first year following a conflict may underestimate the level of support needed. We argue that due to difficulties in disbursing money quickly and effectively, this percentage is the level of aid likely to be effectively absorbed by the host country.

Table 6.1 applies this methodology to estimate what should have been provided for government services in two societies following conflicts: Namibia in 1990, a middle-income developing country; and

---

[4]   United Nations Development Programme, *Human Development Report 2004*, New York, 2004; International Monetary Fund, reports by country, information current in mid-2006; International Monetary Fund, International Financial Statistics Browser, available by subscription through the International Monetary Fund; International Monetary Fund, Country Statistical Information Database, information current in mid-2006. Data collected on the following: Argentina, Cambodia, Colombia, Costa Rica, El Salvador, Georgia, Ghana, India, Iran, Jordan, Kazakhstan, Kuwait, Kyrgyzstan, Namibia, Nepal, Nigeria, Philippines, Saudi Arabia, South Africa, Sri Lanka, Swaziland, Tajikistan, Thailand, Turkey, Uganda, Ukraine, and Zimbabwe.

[5]   We averaged data from 99 countries to calculate the share of GDP on education, 117 for share of GDP spent on public health, and 17 countries for share of GDP spent on public administration. Standard deviations were 2.06, 1.52, and 2.38, respectively. Sources for these data were United Nations Development Programme (2004); national budgets available from International Monetary Fund, reports by country, information current in mid-2006.

Table 6.1
**Estimated Costs of Restoring Government Services in
Two Postconflict Situations**

Country and Activity	Share of GDP (%)	Optimal Expenditure ($ millions)	Actual Total Assistance ($ millions)
Namibia, 1990			
Education	4.2	130.9	
Public health	2.6	80.7	
General administration	3.6	111.3	
Total	10.4	322.9	154.6
Sierra Leone, 2000			
Education	4.2	27.8	
Public health	2.6	17.1	
General administration	3.6	23.6	
Total	10.4	68.6	189.9

NOTE: All dollar amounts are in 2002 U.S. dollars. Amounts may not sum due to
rounding.

Sierra Leone in 2000, a poor developing country. If donors had covered
all the costs of providing education, public health, and general administration for one year after conflict ended in these two countries, they
would have needed to budget $323 million in the case of Namibia and
$69 million in the case of Sierra Leone in 2002 dollars. The differences
in expenditures are due primarily to differences in per capita incomes
and therefore labor costs in the two countries. The table also shows
how much assistance was actually provided to these two countries for
all purposes in the first year after the conflict ended.

How accurate and useful are these estimates? The figures for the
costs of education are probably the most precise. Percentages of GDP
devoted to education are fairly uniform across low- and medium-income
developing countries, averaging 3.98 and 4.28 percent, respectively.
Because education is so labor-intensive, using 4.2 percent of GDP yields
a fairly robust estimate of potential costs in this area, though it would

not cover the costs of a large program to repair or build new schools. The figures on public health expenditures are also useful, although this methodology underestimates the cost of importing pharmaceuticals and other medical supplies. In poor countries, citizens frequently cannot afford these items and therefore do without. In a postconflict environment, the international donor community would likely provide supplies, increasing donor costs. The figures for general administration are high. Many developing countries spend relatively large amounts on government administration; their government bureaucracies are often overstaffed. Estimates of the expenditures needed to run the government based on current expenditure patterns include these excess costs. The data collected for these estimates are derived from the budgetary categories of general public services, general administration, or civil administration These are catchall categories that are often ill defined and may contain expenditures on security or the armed forces that are estimated elsewhere in this volume. Finally, the sample size, 17, from which these expenditures were calculated is much smaller than the samples used to calculate the estimates for expenditures on education and health care with a corresponding reduction in reliability.

Despite these failings, this methodology provides a useful first estimate of the potential costs of funding education, health care, and government operations for one year postconflict. The methodology also should help control future spending in these areas. Postconflict societies are almost invariably poor. When the operation ends, the governments of these societies will have to fund these services. By sizing expenditures in accordance with per capita GDP, donors should help prevent inflation of wages and salaries of civil servants to levels that the country will not be able to support.

CHAPTER SEVEN

Economic Stabilization

To stabilize the economy after conflict and create conditions for economic growth, the intervening authorities need to create an environment in which individuals can safely and profitably engage in economic activity. In most instances, normal commerce will have broken down as the risk of assault, hijacking, kidnapping, or robbery makes daily life, especially travel, dangerous. Labor markets will have been disrupted as people leave some regions and overwhelm others, seeking secure places to live. Property will have been stolen or destroyed. Farms will have been abandoned. Utilities will have ceased to function as providers go unpaid and equipment is broken. The national currency will have been debased, and, because it is unable to collect sufficient taxes, the government may have resorted to printing money to finance its operations.

Key Challenges

Stabilizing the Currency. Sustained growth is virtually impossible in periods of very high inflation. During such periods, businesses and consumers spend much of their time attempting to preserve the value of their assets either by converting domestic currency into more stable foreign currencies, or by using it to purchase goods, services, or physical assets as quickly as possible. Because inflation makes possible large losses or windfall gains due to lags between sale and payments, financial success is often dictated more by the timing of payments than by improvements in products and services. Because of uncertainties concerning prices, businesses continually grapple with decisions about what is or is not profitable to produce. The increased uncertainty curtails investment and output. Curbing inflation is therefore an essential precondition for renewed economic growth.

Paying for It All. In the initial postconflict period, the local economy will be unable to generate sufficient tax revenues to pay for a level of government services that should be feasible once the economy has recovered. Attempting to raise tax revenues to a level sufficient to provide anticipated levels of government services is generally self-defeating: Increasing taxes may end up reducing revenues as economic activity is curtailed or gravitates to the untaxed, informal economy. As noted in Chapter Six, during this initial period, donors are often called upon to cover the gap between realistically attainable levels of tax revenues and the much higher costs of government operations. Establishing requisite levels of funding, identifying sources of these funds from donors, getting donors to honor their commitments, and monitoring and ensuring that donated funds are spent properly are necessary steps to ensure that government operations resume.

Building Capacity, Establishing Accountability, and Combating Corruption. Postconflict societies are mostly poor and undeveloped. Even among those government employees available to work, levels of competence will be low, and corruption high. Former employees have to be retrained and new ones hired. Revenue is the foundation of political authority. Audits of financial flows inside and outside the state help those who govern understand from where revenues are derived and where expenditures have gone. They help illuminate the nature of the resistance to political authority and how it is financed. An effective strategy to prevent or halt illicit economic activity and generate legal sources of revenue can be designed and implemented only if government officials can track financial flows.

Corruption is a particularly serious challenge. It has a supply side (those who give bribes) and a demand side (public officials who take them). Grand corruption involves high-level officials with discretionary authority over government policy, procurement decisions concerning large government contracts, or the sale of government assets. Petty corruption involves lower-level officials who make decisions about enforcing (or not enforcing) regulations. Corruption hampers economic growth, disproportionately burdens the poor, undermines the rule of law, and reduces respect for and the credibility of the government. It needs to be minimized if the economy is to recover rapidly.

Best Practices

Stabilizing the Currency

To curb inflation, the central bank must slow or temporarily stop printing money so as to reduce monetary emissions. Exchange rate policies can play a crucial role in the process of reducing inflation by restoring faith in the national currency and thereby changing inflationary expectations. In all postconflict societies, residents substitute foreign currencies, usually dollars or euros, for domestic currency for savings and larger transactions. When sufficient foreign currency reserves are available, the central bank can restore faith in the national currency by pegging it against a widely used, stable foreign currency, thereby bringing down the rate of inflation more quickly. Bosnia, for example, effectively reduced inflation by pegging its new currency, the K-mark, to the deutsche mark, and later the euro, through a currency board.

If sufficient reserves are not available from the IMF or from foreign currency loans or grants from foreign donors or other international financial institutions, the central bank must float the currency, curbing inflation through monetary policy alone. Among postconflict societies, Afghanistan, Haiti, and Mozambique floated their currencies. As the central bank gains reserves, it may manage the float so as to prevent large fluctuations in value. Mozambique's central bank has tempered exchange rate fluctuations by intervening in the foreign exchange market. Initially, Iraq had a floating rate, but as reserves have risen, the Central Bank of Iraq now operates an implicit peg.

Where a well-accepted foreign currency has replaced the local currency for daily transactions, citizens may favor its wholesale adoption. In Kosovo, the new monetary authorities, under the guidance of the IMF, replaced the Yugoslav dinar with the deutsche mark and then the euro, the foreign currency in widest use. El Salvador has replaced its former national currency with the U.S. dollar. However, in most cases, the monetary and fiscal authorities prefer to keep a national currency so as to preserve the option of adjusting the exchange rate to manage economic activity. There is also the practical matter of distributing and keeping an adequate supply of smaller bills and coins in circulation, if the issuing country is far away. In Kosovo, large quantities of small-denomination deutsche mark bills and even coins were imported into the country to provide sufficient currency for smaller transactions.

In some instances, the currency may have been so greatly debased that it is abandoned and replaced by a new domestic currency. Among postconflict societies, Congo and Sierra Leone have had several currencies. The Coalition Provisional Authority in Iraq replaced the national currency with a new one.

Whatever the choice of currency or exchange rate standard, a central bank or monetary authority must be created, reopened, or, if still operating, restructured. Where no monetary authority existed prior to the conflict, as in Kosovo and East Timor, one has to be set up from scratch. Central banks may have served as "piggy banks" for the previous regime or may have been looted during the conflict. These banks have to be reconstituted. New or restructured central banks have to issue currency, operate the foreign exchange regime, and oversee the financial system. To accomplish these tasks, bank managers need to be selected, offices found, the mint brought under central bank control, foreign currency reserves replenished, foreign exchange operations restarted, accounting systems set up and tested, and statistical collection systems reinstated and improved.

Training central bank staff and the provision of advice on the operations of central banks are core IMF functions. The spate of nation-building operations that followed the end of the Cold War has pulled in the IMF to assist with setting up or restructuring central banks in postconflict situations. Because of these experiences, the IMF is acknowledged as far and away the best lead agency for stabilizing the currencies and quelling inflation in postconflict situations.

In addition to providing technical assistance, the IMF frequently provides some funding under its emergency postconflict assistance programs. Although these funds tend to be dwarfed by bilateral assistance from donors, they are key to replenishing the reserves of the central bank and providing the resources needed to restart foreign exchange sales and trading by providing backing for the domestic currency. The IMF is the primary funder of the central bank; other donors tend to provide the central bank with funds for technical assistance, but only rarely for balance-of-payment support.

The IMF does not always have sufficient staff to help reconstitute central banks in postconflict situations. In most cases, the intervening authorities draw on staff from donor-country central banks, finance ministries, or treasuries, or they employ independent technical experts and consultants to assist in training, mentoring, and, in some cases, operating the new financial institutions.

Although the IMF often is and should be the lead agency for macroeconomic stabilization, it will need to coordinate with the intervening authorities, ensuring that its recommendations are consistent with other policies being pursued. For example, if smuggling operations finance the activities of local thugs, as they have in Bosnia and Kosovo, it does not make sense for the IMF to encourage the government to levy substantial import tariffs to raise revenues: Higher tariffs merely make the activities of local gangs that much more lucrative. As in most policy areas, coordination is needed not only in country but also with capitals and headquarters. In UN-led operations, the IMF should participate in coordination meetings at UN headquarters.

As the central bank is being reconstituted, the intervening authorities need to assist it in organizing and, in some instances, managing its operations. The primary tasks facing the central bank or monetary authorities in postconflict situations are

- controlling the emission of domestic currency
- ensuring that the domestic currency is not being counterfeited
- restoring the payment system
- facilitating or serving as a market for foreign exchange
- ensuring that the commercial banks become and remain solvent
- negotiating rescheduling or forgiveness of foreign debts.

Of these tasks, restoring the payment system and issuing a new currency to forestall counterfeiting are difficult and expensive. Standing up proper payment systems entails the creation of nationwide electronic networks (the most cost-effective, secure payment system). Currency conversion involves large, complicated nationwide operations. Donors can assist both in financing the capital and operating costs of the systems and in providing technical expertise in organizing and setting up operations. The IMF has the expertise to help set up foreign exchange markets. Because informal foreign exchange markets already exist, setting up an interbank market or auction run by the central bank is less challenging than some other tasks. The IMF also assists the central bank in tracking and controlling monetary emissions.

One of the most difficult tasks facing the central bank is to ensure that the commercial banks become and remain solvent. Ensuring that banks are run properly is difficult in any economy, but even more so in the immediate aftermath of a conflict. In many postconflict situations, one or more large banks, usually state-owned, have been bankrupted by the conflict. Resurrecting or closing down these banks is not an immediate priority, but the financial system will not function well until they are either liquidated or recapitalized. As bankrupt banks tend to be its responsibility, foreign advisors to the central bank are usually called upon to assist.

The central bank also has to begin guarding against future commercial banking problems. In transitional economies, banking problems ignored early on have led to banking crises and economic recessions four or five years after the initial recovery. Banking assets tend to be small in the immediate aftermath of the conflict, but setting up and employing an effective monitoring system at this juncture is important, as it will forestall crises further down the road.

In many postconflict situations, the central bank, in conjunction with the finance ministry, is called upon to begin negotiations on the repayment of sovereign debt. Even interim agreements, such as a moratorium on payments of principal and interest until such time as the country's economy is better able to service the debt, are useful at this stage. Such agreements eliminate the threat of seizure of government assets abroad because of nonpayment. The central bank also begins the process of reopening access to international capital markets. Despite these benefits, renegotiating foreign debt agreements should be given a lower priority than other tasks. Typically, the country has not been servicing its debt for some time. Continued nonpayment poses little additional cost to the country. Debt negotiations entail substantial amounts of time on the part of economic policymakers, time that could be better spent on improving central bank operations or overseeing the implementation of the budget.

Paying for It All

Local Revenues. Usually, the government in a postconflict situation is bankrupt. Government funds have been looted or stolen, tax collection has collapsed, and systems for dispensing funds no longer work. Raising funds, transferring funds, and ensuring proper payment of salaries and invoices are necessary for ensuring the provision of government services. In this environment, the intervening authorities and other donors often need to provide stopgap funding and resuscitate payment systems so as to make government operations possible.

Raising revenues is an ongoing challenge. Where tax systems already exist, they should be preserved so as to avoid having to rebuild them at a later date. However, where current taxes are expensive to collect or difficult to enforce, they should be abolished; new tax systems may need to be developed in their place. Care must be taken at this stage not to create or keep tax systems that are ineffective or have deleterious economic results. For example, business registration taxes are often designed to force business owners to pay bribes. The amount of tax collected is often negligible. High customs duties encourage smuggling and the growth of organized crime.

Natural resources often provide an easily tapped source of tax revenues. They have also been a source of conflict. The intervening authorities need to make securing natural resource deposits and the transportation links needed to export these commodities a high priority. Once secured, donors should work with host governments to set up financial controls to ensure that proceeds go to the government, not private pockets, and that they are spent appropriately. Donors have had some success in setting up national funds into which natural resource revenues are deposited. Chad and Sudan have set up oil revenue–sharing agreements with various communities as part of their efforts to resolve domestic conflicts. The international community has also set up certification schemes for commodities such as diamonds (in Sierra Leone and Liberia) and timber to reduce smuggling. Working with buyers to post contracts and contracted prices helps to reduce graft. These systems are often easier to set up immediately following a conflict when donors have more leverage and host-country leaders have not yet had time to firmly entrench themselves in these activities.

Sometimes the international community has pushed countries in postconflict situations to rapidly increase budget revenues so as to narrow budget deficits. Although it is important that government services be paid for with local tax revenues at some point, focusing on revenue generation in the immediate aftermath of a conflict should not be a priority. IMF pressure to increase budget revenues in Kosovo, Bosnia, and Macedonia following their conflicts may have been counterproductive. In most cases, economic activity is so depressed and the new government so weak that attempting to generate substantial sums from the local economy is a fool's game. The focus needs to be on restarting economic activity. Reducing rather than increasing barriers to setting up new firms or expanding existing operations should be the primary economic policy goal. Only after the economy begins to grow will the government have a clear picture of how and from which sectors to raise tax revenues.

Donor Support. Government expenditures do have to be financed. At this juncture, donors should play a key role in providing budgetary support. In many instances, only donors have the resources needed to pay the wages of government employees and to pay for government services.

The intervening authorities need to assess currently available government funds, abroad or in the treasury, and evaluate likely revenues that will be generated by the existing tax code under current economic circumstances to estimate the gap between local resources and the cost of providing anticipated levels of services. Donors then need to arrange for the immediate financing of this gap to ensure that the government is able to operate. Direct grants to the ministry of finance are among the best ways of achieving this goal.

These grants and other donated funds need to be tracked and audited. Donors should adopt common, simple tracking and reporting procedures and should request the same types of information. Demanding that host countries adhere to different, detailed reporting requirements for each donor defeats the purpose of the grants. Finance ministers from Albania, Bosnia, Cambodia, and Kosovo have complained about the time wasted in filling out the many different forms that donors demand.

Subsequently, the intervening authorities need to arrange for an initial needs assessment. The UNDP and the World Bank have developed an established approach. Useful, accurate, and consistent assessments require the cooperation of local authorities and may enlist the help of NGOs.

Donor conferences have become useful vehicles for mobilizing funding. Large sums were pledged to Afghanistan, Cambodia, and East Timor following donor conferences. The conferences identify those countries that are interested in assisting a particular effort; they elicit promises of levels of assistance, and they may delegate responsibilities for particular sectors and projects. It is usually best to have more than one conference. At the first conference organized for a particular effort, attendees should focus on generating sufficient funds for immediate assistance. Follow-on conferences help raise additional funds and channel assistance to areas of greatest need. The first conference should establish coordinating and monitoring committees. Donor coordinating committees reduce duplication of effort and funds and identify areas that are being neglected. They can also be used to pressure donors to fulfill their pledges; failure to follow through on pledges is a frequent problem. Committees should be chaired by the individual in charge of the intervening authorities or by a designated alternate. Representatives of the host government should also sit on the committees. To the extent possible, representatives from all major factions engaged in the conflict should be invited to participate.

The initial conference should not attempt to arrange for multiyear future assistance levels for economic reconstruction and development.

The economic and political environment is too fluid at this time to map out the levels and types of assistance that are likely to be needed three or more years out. The conference should set a future date for a follow-on conference, at which time additional assistance will be discussed and requested after a more detailed, better informed needs assessment is available. The participants should also assign an institution to conduct the future needs assessment and set deadlines for initiation and completion of that report.

The international community has often found it useful to pool donor assistance into trust funds, usually run by the World Bank or the UNDP. In the case of Iraq, two trust funds have been set up, one run by each institution. The two funds focus on sectors in which the lead institution has a comparative advantage: the UNDP on social welfare and the World Bank on economic development. Trust funds are potentially a more efficient funding source than a plethora of programs from individual donors. A single incorporated entity might be able to borrow against future donations to ease cash-flow problems. A fund should ease the audit and monitoring costs for the host government, as ministers would (hopefully) be badgered for information by only one entity. If host-country ministries need to respond to only one entity, it should be possible to set up regular reporting procedures more quickly and effectively. As audits of expenditures in postconflict countries have repeatedly exposed malfeasance, the more quickly such simple, transparent reporting procedures can be set up, the less likely it is that future scandals will occur. A representative appointed by the head of the intervening authorities should sit on the board of the trust fund so as to better coordinate decisions.

Donors and the emerging government need to be conscious of affordability issues from the moment the international community decides to intervene. When ministries have not yet been established, the intervening authorities should provide estimates of the number of local ministry staff that will be needed based on best practices in countries at similar levels of development. This approach was used in East Timor to good effect. Donors and the host government need to work out a government salary schedule that is sufficiently competitive to attract high-quality staff, but simultaneously will not break the budget.

Once staffing and a salary schedule have been decided, the intervening authorities and the host-country government will need to put together ministry budgets. If projected expenditures based on the initial staffing and salary proposals exceed likely future revenues, staffing or wage cuts will need to be made at this stage or long-term commitments will need to be sought from donors to cover the gap. It is much easier to restrain the size and salaries of the ministries at the start of an operation than to cut staff and expenditures at a later date.

The intervening authorities and the donor community affect the cost of local government operations through their own hires from the local labor market. In most postconflict situations, well-educated individuals who are fluent in languages spoken by the international bureaucracy (usually English) are in high demand. Competition between the host government and the intervening authorities for these individuals frequently either elevates host-government wages to unsustainable levels or results in well-qualified individuals working for international assistance organizations at relatively high salaries but in positions such as translation or driving, which fail to fully utilize their skills. This has been the case in Afghanistan, Bosnia, and East Timor.

The intervening authorities, donors, embassies, and NGOs should come to an agreement concerning appropriate wage rates for local staff that will not distort local labor markets. Together, they should set wage bands for occupations from which they commonly hire, taking into account competing local government pay scales. Another effective means of reducing disparities in wages between individuals working for the international community and those working for the local government are progressive income taxes. Although rates should not be punitive, instituting a two-tier income tax schedule with a fairly large initial exemption would reduce the relative attractiveness of working for the international community. Under no circumstances should either government employees or local staff who work for international organizations be exempt from local taxes, especially payroll taxes. Some analysts argue that international staff should also be liable for host-country taxes, but the complexities of making mobile international staff pay host-country taxes and the attraction to host-country governments of imposing high tax rates on this potential source of income make such a measure unworkable.

Building Capacity, Establishing Accountability, and Combating Corruption

Building an Effective Civil Service. Creating incentives and systems that induce government employees to provide quality services is difficult in any country; in postconflict societies, this task is daunting. Parties to the conflict see government jobs as spoils to be divided as part of the peace agreement, not as positions carrying responsibilities. Government employees perceive their jobs as sinecures that permit them to demand and receive bribes. Decisionmaking is highly centralized; routine decisions are made at the ministerial level. But communications, especially outside major cities, are poor, making implementation difficult. Where authority has been delegated, civil servants are reluctant to make decisions for fear of antagonizing those in power.

In light of these problems, personnel policies to make the civil service effective and independent need to be adopted early on. Policies need to be designed to assign responsibility, enforce accountability, and control financial flows.

One key measure is to devolve decisionmaking authority. Ministries should treat the service provider (school, clinic, precinct police station) as the operating unit. Principals, clinic directors, and police captains should be made responsible for all the operations at their facilities, from maintenance to staffing to operations. They should have the authority to hire, fire, and make decisions about expenditures. Simultaneously, the host government should be encouraged to make ministries as lean and flat as possible. If decisions have been devolved to the operating unit, there is little call for large ministerial staffs. The donor community's most effective mechanism in this regard is to limit funds and prioritize expenditures for the salaries of the frontline providers. There should be clear chains of command, with principals, clinic directors, and police captains reporting only to district or regional superintendents; other ministerial employees should provide support, not manage.

Responsibility entails accountability. Although managers should choose their own staffs, there is always a danger that some managers will choose applicants on the basis of family ties or the willingness of an employee to part with a share of his or her salary in exchange for a job, although the same holds true when higher-level officials make these decisions. These practices can be curtailed by insisting that hiring decisions be made by committees that include the manager's superior, other senior staff members, and members of the local government or community. When hiring, managers should have to choose among applicants who have met stipulated criteria for the job. This may involve passing a competency test or completing a training course with a passing grade. If parties to the conflict have been severely underrepresented in the civil service, affirmative action programs based on ethnicity or language may be used in hiring decisions. These need to be employed with care: They may reduce the sense of grievance in one community at the expense of exacerbating it in another.

Establishing workable financial controls without a banking system and in the absence of communications is a tall order. However, simple but robust financial controls can limit corruption. First, every school, clinic, police station, or other operating unit needs a budget. Initially, these can be drawn up crudely but effectively by creating personnel budgets and nonpersonnel operating budgets. Personnel budgets should be drawn up by setting head counts on the basis of estimates of the number of people to be served or protected. Uniform salaries for specific jobs should be set by the national government. This approach may have beneficial consequences for the more equitable provision of government services. If teacher salaries are set nationally, the lower cost of living in outlying regions make these areas more financially attractive, encouraging teachers to consider jobs outside major cities. Nonpersonnel operating budgets can be based on numbers of staff or people served.

To limit fraud, salary and other payments should be made by employees of the finance ministry rather than by the line ministry, and payroll and accounting clerks, employed by the finance ministry, should make all payments, not the director of the operating unit. If at all possible, electronic deposit systems should be used for payroll. These arrangements are remarkably versatile and can be used in very primitive financial systems. Simple but strict contracting procedures coupled with the dual authorization of expenditures, one from the manager and the second from the accounting clerk, followed by periodic audits, help control graft.

Early on, the intervening authorities should assist the government in establishing a civil service commission. The civil service commission should write or provide amendments to civil service laws, determine competencies for civil service positions, assess the competency levels of personnel, determine or revise the grading system for personnel, develop training and leadership programs, and create performance-review procedures.

The challenge for those who create or restore the civil service administration is to ensure that standards of professionalism, transparency, political independence, and public service are enshrined in law and practice. These goals have to be balanced against the need to rapidly recruit civil servants to operate the government. Pressure also comes from donors and political forces to bring ex-combatants into the government workforce. As opposed to programs specifically designed to disarm, demobilize, and reintegrate ex-combatants into society, programs that are often key to preventing a resumption of violence, creating permanent "jobs for the boys" triggers a host of problems for the future. By definition, DDR programs are short term: They are focused on drawing combatants away from their former units and reintegrating them into society. In contrast, creating permanent jobs for political supporters rots the integrity of the civil service. Resisting this pressure is often difficult, as these individuals may create more difficulties outside the tent than in. But a small, efficient civil service that will be affordable is preferable to creating a bloated bureaucracy.

In addition to ensuring that payroll obligations are met, the government, or, in the absence of a government, the intervening authorities need to establish a means of ensuring that civil servants perform their jobs. This step can be achieved by stipulating that wages will be paid only to people on the payroll who show up for work. Simple systems can be set up for monitoring who is coming to work. Dismissing incompetent or absent employees is more difficult but can be encouraged by giving parents of schoolchildren, medical patients, and crime victims venues in which to complain and to demand that service providers account for their actions by dismissing such staff. Spot-checks and performance audits conducted by nascent inspector general's offices can be used to verify that people are on the job. This system can be used simultaneously to ascertain whether clinics, police stations, or schools are open for business and to conduct a needs assessment of what supplies and improvements in physical infrastructure are lacking. This process serves as a means of holding individuals responsible for fixing problems once identified.

"Ghost" or absentee government employees, a problem in most developing countries, are even more prevalent in postconflict countries, where records have disappeared and audits are weak. Liberia and Sierra Leone have struggled to purge names from government payrolls following their conflicts. Employee censuses are a crucial first step in creating a more accurate payroll. Resuscitating accounting and payroll systems used in the past or, if unavailable, creating new ones is a crucial step. Establishing governmentwide pay scales and fixed numbers of positions so that salaries are controlled and employee costs can be budgeted are the next steps in this process.

The early introduction of simple financial management information systems, often operated by expatriates on laptop computers, is another early step toward establishing budgetary controls. These systems need to be kept simple but should be flexible enough for budgeting and accounting. It is better to have a set of robust, easily understood accounting and payment systems than a more sophisticated, single, integrated system that demands higher levels of technical expertise and more complex computer systems than are likely to be available. Civil servants need to be trained on these systems as soon as possible.

Contracting and Procurement. Governments not only generate services, they also purchase goods and services from outside vendors. Contracting and procurement of these services account for an appreciable amount of government spending. Best-practice policies for procurement contracts provide the host country with value for money; result in swift, simple, practical procedures; yield impartial, consistent decisions; provide accessible, unambiguous rules and procedures; and hold both the contracting agency and contractors accountable for their actions.

These practices not only yield best value, but they are among the best means of curbing corruption. Contracting and procurement decisions are easily influenced by bribes. Along with kickbacks related to nepotistic practices in government employment and bribery associated with obtaining government approvals, contracting and procurement are the largest sources of corruption in most societies. The World Bank has developed detailed policy guidelines and procurement manuals designed to elicit lowest-cost bids, ensure that the products and services delivered are of requisite quality, and avoid corrupt practices. Key lessons, applicable to postconflict situations, include the following:

1. The government must establish clear contracting procedures that apply to all government contracts. Contracts should be open for competitive bidding but should be differentiated by value. Smaller contracts should be handled in an expedited manner, though with proper financial controls.

2. The government should assign responsibility for planning large projects to cross-ministerial committees so that the most important stakeholders have a voice in the planning process: consumers and end users, suppliers, the finance ministry, and the line ministry. Plans need to be integrated carefully into current and long-term budget planning.

3. Prospective procurement of goods and services needs to be included in the annual budget. Once budgeted, the procurement authority should devolve to the operating ministry. The ministry of finance should not have leeway to arbitrarily sequester or retake appropriated funds.

4. Requests for proposals need to be publicly announced and posted so that all potential bidders have access to the same information. Evaluation criteria should be clearly posted.

5. Decisions should be made by committees of publicly designated individuals who do not have conflicts of interest with bidders. Once opened, the bids and the committee's evaluation of the bids should be publicly posted. The intervening authorities

can play a key role by appointing representatives to sit on these committees.

6. Responsible committees or individuals need to be designated to work with and monitor the contractor. Regular progress reports should be presented to the appropriate authority. The intervening authorities should integrate their reporting and audit requirements and those of other donors into this process. Governments in postconflict states complain bitterly of duplicative reporting requirements from donors, much of which involve requests for the same information but in differing formats.

7. Outside performance audits should be conducted before the project is accepted. Outside financial audits need to be conducted regularly, covering all expenditures. The intervening authorities can help cement these procedures into practice by assisting in enforcement and by insisting that the host-country government adopt and adhere to them.

Not only the host government has to adopt efficient contracting procedures: Virtually every intervention has suffered from contracting and accounting irregularities on the part of donors and the intervening authorities. Most of these occur after the immediate stabilization phase and do not involve the provision of humanitarian assistance. Despite complaints about the delays and red tape involved in following standardized procedures, there is no substitute for establishing transparent, open, competitive contracting procedures for the intervening authorities from day one. The savings in terms of investigative time, squandered resources, poor project delivery, and the financial credibility of the operation far exceed any supposed savings in time. Attempts to circumvent established contracting procedures frequently result in longer delivery times and more failures to deliver than if standard procedures had been used in the first place. (Witness the contracting problems in Iraq.) The World Bank can provide the intervening authorities, as well as the host government, with guidelines and procedures, draft contracts, and, potentially, links to the World Bank's own Web site for postings.

Combating Corruption. Corruption is the misuse of entrusted power for private gain. It can involve high-level officials with discretionary authority over government policies or lower-level officials who make decisions about enforcing (or not enforcing) regulations. Corruption impedes the development of democracy and the rule of law. In a democratic system, offices and institutions lose their legitimacy when they are misused for private advantage. While this is harmful in established democracies, it is even more so in postconflict situations. Accountable political leadership cannot develop in a corrupt climate. Corruption slows economic growth. It is often responsible for funneling scarce public resources to costly, high-profile projects at the expense of less spectacular but more necessary projects. It hinders the development of markets and distorts competition, thereby deterring investment. The effect of corruption on the fabric of society is the most damaging of all. It undermines the population's trust in the political system, political institutions, and political leadership.

The intervening authorities need to help curb corruption at all levels. They may provide legal advisors and consultants to help develop anticorruption legislation, design anticorruption public education campaigns, and empower domestic watchdog mechanisms and groups to monitor the government. In some cases, the intervening authorities may bring in international auditors to conduct audits and corporate management teams to run ministries and public enterprises. The intervening authorities should address and overcome the impunity enjoyed by criminalized political elites. International personnel may have to play a direct role in the criminal justice system for this purpose. Mission staff must be held accountable as well.

Outcomes

Data are both scarce and suspect during and following a conflict. Measuring improvements and connecting improvements to policies can be fraught with even more problems than usual in poor developing countries. For these reasons, our recommendations for best-practice policies in stabilizing the economy after a conflict are based as much on practitioner assessments as on analysis of economic and other data.

This said, some metrics reflect the effects of appropriate policies for stabilizing the economy. Stabilizing the national currency and reducing or halting emissions of the national currency in the aftermath of conflict have contributed to reducing and controlling inflation in a large number of postconflict situations, including Cambodia, East Timor, Haiti, Kosovo, and Sierra Leone (see Figure 7.1). The performance of these countries' governments is even more impressive considering that, during their respective conflicts, inflation had been very high and their central banks had ceased to function effectively.

Figure 7.2 indicates how important creating a secure environment and some macroeconomic stability is to economic growth. The average rate of growth in the first or second year after the end of a conflict runs 18.3 percent in our sample, which includes most interventions since World War II.[1] Even in Iraq, where security has been poor, growth was rapid in 2004, reaching 46.5 percent as better economic policies and an influx of foreign assistance and increased government expenditures resulted in a surge in consumption.

The extent of the initial rebound is dictated in part by the depth of the decline in output during the conflict. Regressing the depth of the cumulative decline in output on the rebound in the first year of recovery, we found that the decline accounted for roughly half (53 percent) of the rebound.[2] However, the importance of providing security and macroeconomic stability to restart growth cannot be overemphasized: Many of these countries experienced long periods of economic decline before the intervention, among them Bosnia, Cambodia, El Salvador, and Sierra Leone. Only after a modicum of security and

---

[1]   Previous RAND work, Dobbins, McGinn, et al. (2003), and Dobbins, Jones, et al. (2005) evaluated interventions in 15 countries. The average rate of growth cited above uses data from each of these case studies, with the exception of Eastern Slavonia and Somalia, for which no statistical data were available.

[2]   The estimated equation was Rebound in Year One = −0.53 × Cumulative Decline. The intercept was constrained to equal zero. The parameter estimate had a p-value of 0.00025 and the p-value for the equation using an F-test was 0.028. However, only 10 observations were available.

Figure 7.1
Inflation Following Conflict

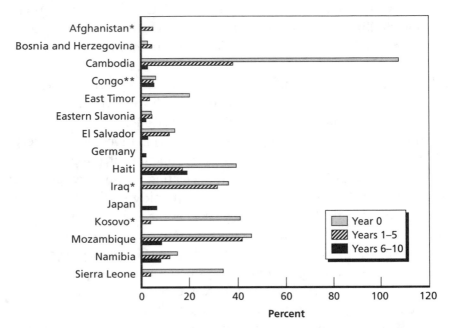

SOURCE: Data compiled from International Monetary Fund, International Financial Statistics Browser; International Monetary Fund, "Democratic Republic of Timor-Leste: 2005 Article IV Consultation—Staff Report; Public Information Notice on the Executive Board Discussion; and Statement by the Executive Director for the Democratic Republic of Timor-Leste," IMF Country Report No. 05/245, Washington, D.C., July 2005b, p. 31; Rakia Moalla-Fetini, Heikki Hatanpää, Shehadah Hussein, and Natalia Koliadina, *Kosovo: Gearing Policies Toward Growth and Development*, Washington, D.C.: International Monetary Fund, 2005, p. 81; International Monetary Fund, "Bosnia and Herzegovina: Statistical Appendix," IMF Country Report No. 02/60, Washington, D.C., March 2002, p. 13; International Monetary Fund, "Bosnia and Herzegovina: 2005 Article IV Consultation—Staff Report; Staff Supplement; Public Information Notice on the Executive Board Discussion; and Statement by the Executive Director for Bosnia and Herzegovina," IMF Country Report No. 05/199, Washington, D.C., June 2005a, p. 34.
NOTE: An asterisk (*) denotes that only data for year 1 following the conflict have been employed in the year 1–5 statistics because data for these subsequent years were not yet available; two asterisks (**) denote that the data from year 1 following the conflict have been employed in the year 0 statistics because year 0 data were unavailable.

RAND *MG557-7.1*

Figure 7.2
Prior Declines in Economic Output and Economic Growth in the First Year
Following an Intervention

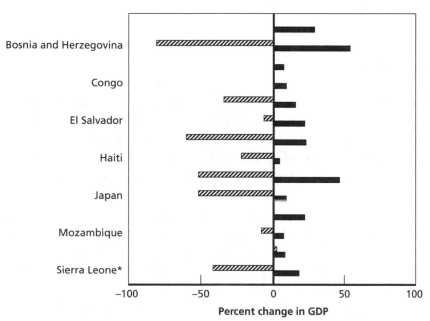

SOURCE: International Monetary Fund, International Financial Statistics; B. R. Mitchell,
International Historical Statistics: Europe 1750–1988, 3rd ed., New York: Stockton
Press, 1992; B. R. Mitchell, *International Historical Statistics: Africa, Asia, and Oceania*
1750–1993, 3rd ed., New York: Stockton Press, 1998; International Monetary Fund
(2005b, p. 31); Dimitri G. Demekas, Johannes Herderschee, and Davina F. Jacobs,
Kosovo: Institutions and Policies for Reconstruction and Growth, Washington, D.C.:
International Monetary Fund, 2002, p. 6; International Monetary Fund, "Bosnia and
Herzegovina: Selected Issues and Statistical Appendix," IMF Staff Country Report No.
00/77, Washington, D.C., June 2000, p. 118; International Monetary Fund, "Islamic
Republic of Afghanistan: Fifth Review Under the Staff-Monitored Program and
Request for an Extension," IMF Country Report No. 05/371, Washington, D.C., October
2005d, p. 19; International Monetary Fund, "Iraq: Statistical Appendix," IMF Country
Report 05/295, Washington, D.C., August 2005c, p. 3.
NOTE: An asterisk (*) denotes that data are for the second year after the intervention
(Germany, 1947; Kosovo, 2001; and Sierra Leone, 2001) because of lack of data or
because the immediate aftereffects of the conflict resulted in continued declines in
output during the first year.
RAND *MG557-7.2*

macroeconomic stability were restored did growth resume. Since the end of their respective conflicts, these countries have enjoyed a period of strong, sustained growth despite the many other problems with which they are plagued.

Key Actors

The IMF is far and away the best institution to help the host country stabilize its currency and control inflation. Donor-country finance ministries and central banks can assist by providing technical assistance, especially staff, to mentor and train host-country civil servants. Technical assistance is also needed to set up payment, statistical, and other systems.

The intervening authorities need to take the lead in restarting government operations. Although donors provide staff, funds, and programs, the intervening authorities need to provide direction as well as coordination. Restarting government operations requires the largest numbers of international staff. Key staffing needs include budgetary, accounting, and tax experts for the finance ministry, and public health and education experts for those two ministries. These can be recruited from the large pool of international consultants engaged in development work.

Donor conferences are usually organized by the country or countries that have taken a lead role in the intervention. The World Bank and the UNDP are best suited to provide a needs assessment in preparation for such a conference. The lead nation usually takes responsibility for pushing donors to honor their commitments as well. Trust funds have been useful in Cambodia, East Timor, and elsewhere to coordinate assistance. The World Bank has the most experience in running these funds and, in our view, is the most appropriate body to organize and staff them.

Costs

Resuscitating the Central Bank. Since 1962, the IMF has provided emergency assistance to help member countries with urgent balance-of-payments financing needs in the wake of natural disasters.[3] In 1995, this program was extended to states emerging from conflict. Countries are eligible to receive such funds if institutional and administrative capacity has been severely disrupted and they have an urgent need for funds because of balance-of-payments pressures. However, the country must still have sufficient capacity for planning and policy implementation. It must also agree to follow up with a more detailed policy program under one of the IMF's regular lending facilities.

These programs help finance government budget deficits and provide foreign exchange for importers to purchase goods and services from abroad. Recipients also receive technical assistance from the IMF to rebuild the capacity to implement macroeconomic policies, including statistical capacity, establishing and reorganizing fiscal, monetary, and exchange institutions to help restore the ability of the government to tax and make expenditures, and for payment, credit, and foreign exchange operations. The program not only provides funds directly, but the imprimatur of the IMF often opens up credits from other sources that can be used to reinvigorate foreign exchange markets and thereby stabilize the currency. Assistance has been typically limited to 25 percent of the member's quota in the IMF, although amounts up to 50 percent of quota can be and have been provided in certain circumstances.

The program has become a key source of funds for immediately stabilizing economies in postconflict situations. Table 7.1 shows the amounts of all the programs to date in terms of total dollars, as a share of GDP, and per capita value. As shown in the table, the loan amounts tend to be relatively small, primarily because the economies and the

---

[3] International Monetary Fund, "IMF Emergency Assistance: Supporting Recovery from Natural Disasters and Armed Conflicts," fact sheet, Washington, D.C., December 2005e.

Table 7.1
IMF Loans for Postconflict Emergency Assistance

Country	Year	Amount (millions of US$)	GDP (millions of US$)	Loan as Share of GDP (%)	Population (thousands)	Per Capita Value of Loan (US$)
Bosnia and Herzegovina	1995	45.0	2,785.8	1.62	3,420.1	13.16
Rwanda	1997	12.2	1,868.5	0.65	6,180.0	1.97
Albania	1997	12.0	2,294.5	0.52	3,082.7	3.89
Rwanda	1997	8.1	1,868.5	0.43	6,844.7	1.18
Tajikistan	1997	10.1	1,123.9	0.90	5,931.7	1.70
Tajikistan	1998	10.0	1,320.1	0.76	6,010.7	1.66
Republic of Congo	1998	9.6	1,949.5	0.49	3,221.9	2.98
Sierra Leone	1998	16.0	672.4	2.38	4,278.6	3.74
Guinea-Bissau	1999	2.9	224.5	1.29	1,327.7	2.18
Sierra Leone	1999	21.4	669.4	3.20	4,376.2	4.89
Guinea-Bissau	2000	1.9	215.5	0.88	1,365.7	1.39
Sierra Leone	2000	13.3	635.9	2.09	4,509.0	2.95
Republic of Congo	2000	13.6	3,219.9	0.42	3,437.8	3.96
Fr. Republic of Yugoslavia	2000	151.0	8603.0	1.76	10,646.1	14.18
Burundi	2002	12.7	628.1	2.02	6,818.1	1.86
Burundi	2003	13.4	595.5	2.25	7,036.7	1.90
Central African Republic	2004	8.2	1,288.5	0.64	3,986.0	2.06
Iraq	2004	435.1	25,539.0	1.70	27,139.6	16.03
Haiti	2005	15.5	3,650.2	0.42	8,326.3	1.86
Average		42.74		1.29		4.40

SOURCE: International Monetary Fund (2005e).
NOTE: Amounts may not sum due to rounding.

members' quotas in the IMF are small. On a per capita basis, they have averaged $4.40 per person in the recipient countries.

IMF loans for postconflict emergency assistance provide a useful measure of how much is needed for monetary stabilization efforts. Although in granting these loans, the IMF has restricted them to 25 to 50 percent of a country's IMF quota, quotas are determined by the size of a country's GDP, international trade and investment flows, and a country's foreign currency reserves. Thus, loans granted under the postconflict emergency assistance program are sized roughly in accordance with the country's economy and ability to absorb the assistance. Loans have run from 3.2 percent of GDP for the small economy of Sierra Leone in 1999 to 0.42 percent of GDP for the larger economy of the Republic of Congo in 2000. Loans have averaged 1.29 percent of GDP.

We have used this average of 1.29 percent as a guide to the level of assistance needed to initially stabilize the currency and resuscitate the central bank following a conflict. Although the IMF will need to tailor the size of each loan to the specifics of the country involved, we believe 1.29 percent of GDP provides a good rule to gauge the level of assistance needed.

Shifting from Donations to Taxation. As the host-country government develops its own capacity to levy and collect taxes, the donor community should shift from being the primary source of funding for the government's operating budget to plugging funding gaps that the host government is still unable to fill. Transferring financing from donor contributions to host-country tax revenues is no easy task. The donor community needs to work with the host government to ensure that government expenditures, especially the government payroll, can eventually be covered through a reasonable level of taxation. If the government is unlikely to be able to generate sufficient revenues to provide adequate levels of public service for the foreseeable future, the host government and the donor community should carefully assess current and projected expenditures. If expenditures seem to be in line with the need for teachers, health care workers, police officers, and other government employees, the donor community should commit itself to making up the shortfall between likely revenues and projected spending for an extended period of time, giving the finance ministry and the economy the breathing room needed for the country to become self-sufficient. If expenditures appear to be inflated, the donor community should work with the host government to trim staff or wage scales.

Grant aid to support the operating budget is the best means of bridging funding gaps at this time. It keeps the donor community engaged in monitoring the provision of public services and controlling expenditures, especially expenditures on government employment. It also serves to prevent the creation of punitive tax regimes, which encourage bribery and smuggling while retarding economic growth.

Bosnia, despite its many problems, provides a guide to the speed with which expenditures can be shifted from donations to taxation. In many countries, lack of donor interest has been a binding constraint on assistance: The level of assistance is determined by willingness to contribute rather than by assessment of need. Because of the importance of Bosnia to the wealthiest donors (the United States and the European Union), the country was singularly well funded. Figure 7.3 plots two estimates of foreign assistance to Bosnia as a share of government expenditures. As detailed in the figure, foreign assistance accounted for a very large share of government expenditures early on, then trailed off fairly quickly as the economy recovered. By 2005, it covered just 6.4 percent of total expenditures.

Using the expenditure path illustrated in Figure 7.3 as a guide, assistance would initially account for most government expenditures in a postconflict situation, falling to about a quarter of the total in the fourth year, and tapering off thereafter. However, in many postconflict countries, Afghanistan, Liberia, and Sierra Leone, to mention three, the recovery in tax revenue has been far slower than in Bosnia. Consequently, the international donor community should be willing to cover a greater share of government operating costs for a longer period of time than in countries in which the government has more resources to finance these expenditures itself.

Figure 7.3
Foreign Assistance as a Share of Government Expenditures in Bosnia

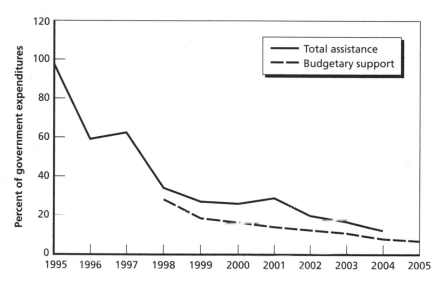

SOURCE: International Monetary Fund (2005a, pp. 29, 34).
RAND *MG557-7.3*

In Table 7.2, we project hypothetical appropriate levels of assistance for Namibia and Sierra Leone. Using the same factors as in Chapter Six, we project the cost of fully funding health, education, and public administration at reasonable levels for these two countries during the first five years following the end of their conflicts, 1989 and 1999, respectively. We then calculate what would have been reasonable levels of foreign assistance to cover these expenditures, employing the higher spending patterns exhibited in Bosnia.

Table 7.2
Estimated Costs of Supporting Government Services in Namibia and Sierra Leone

Country	Year 1	Year 2	Year 3	Year 4	Year 5
Namibia					
GDP ($ millions)	3,117.1	3,177.6	3,530.8	3,215.1	3,434.9
Appropriate expenditures on education, health, and administration ($ millions)	322.9	329.2	365.8	333.1	355.9
Share of international community (%)	97.2	61.8	61.8	33.7	26.2
International community contribution ($ millions)	313.8	203.3	225.9	112.2	93.2
Sierra Leone					
GDP ($ millions)	661.9	819.0	936.0	971.9	1,030.8
Appropriate expenditures on education, health, and administration ($ millions)	68.6	84.8	97.0	100.7	106.8
Share of international community (%)	97.2	61.8	61.8	47.7	33.7
International community contribution ($ millions)	66.6	52.4	59.9	48.0	36.0

SOURCE: RAND calculations.

NOTE: All dollar amounts are in constant 2002 U.S. dollars. Amounts may not sum due to rounding.

CHAPTER EIGHT

Democratization

The prime objective of most nation-building missions is to make violent societies peaceful, not to make poor societies prosperous or authoritarian societies democratic. Nevertheless, the three are interconnected, and most successful missions accomplish all three, albeit to different degrees. Successful transformations of violent societies into peaceful ones are thus almost always accompanied by some degree of economic development and political reform. These missions invariably begin in circumstances in which existing systems of governance have largely or totally collapsed. In some cases, this is the result of civil war. In others, it is the result of the intervention itself. Whatever the cause of collapse, a new or renewed system has to be constructed. In rare cases, traditional nondemocratic institutions may retain enough local and international legitimacy to provide a viable basis for renewed governance, the 1991 restoration of Kuwait's monarchy being the prime example. In most instances, however, traditional alternatives to representative democracy will have disintegrated or been discredited beyond redemption. Thus in most cases, the creation or re-creation of institutions deriving their authority from popular suffrage offer the intervening authorities the only practical means of transferring power back to an indigenous government and leaving behind a peaceful society.

Liberal democracies are arguably more pacific than are other types of political systems. At least they seldom go to war with each other. Liberal democracies are also less likely to become embroiled in civil war or perpetuate genocide.[1] Newly emerging democracies, on the other hand, are often prone to external aggression and internal conflict.[2] The quality and duration of the transition is thus quite important. So is the character of the newly introduced institutions. In societies sharply divided along ethnic, religious, or even economic lines, majority rule is likely to be hotly contested. Thus the design of any new institutional structure needs to be adapted to the unique characteristics of the society in question. Safeguards for minorities and checks on majorities need to be designed to ameliorate rather than exacerbate existing fissures.

Key Challenges

Understanding the Obstacles and Opportunities. Failed states would appear to be poor candidates for democratization, possessing few of the factors tending to favor the growth of representative government. They are likely to be poor, ethnically divided, socially stratified, and surrounded by other states in a similar condition. Nevertheless, unpromising candidates have made the transition, perhaps not all the way to liberal democracy, but to representative systems that hold reasonably fair elections on a regular basis and that alternate power among contesting parties. An understanding of the difficulties and a realistic assessment of the possibilities serve as the proper starting point for any effort to promote such a process.

Structuring Representative Institutions. In countries where democratic institutions are weak and few, building a representative system of government is a long, difficult process. In most postconflict societ-

---

[1]   See, for example, Michael W. Doyle, *Ways of War and Peace: Realism, Liberalism, and Socialism*, New York: W. W. Norton, 1997; Bruce Russett, *Grasping the Democratic Peace: Principles for a Post–Cold War World*, Princeton, N.J.: Princeton University Press, 1993; and Spencer R. Weart, *Never at War: Why Democracies Will Not Fight One Another*, New Haven, Conn.: Yale University Press, 1998.

[2]   Edward D. Mansfield and Jack Snyder, *Electing to Fight: Why Emerging Democracies Go to War*, Cambridge, Mass.: MIT Press, 2005; Jack Snyder, *From Voting to Violence: Democratization and Nationalist Conflict*, New York: W. W. Norton, 2000.

ies, years of repression and violence have fostered a culture of "guns and greed," which must be supplanted by a political culture that fosters public discourse rather than violence as the channel of competition for wealth and power. Political institutions and legal codes often need to be created from scratch. The flow of public information has often been usurped by warring factions and used to enforce divisions and strengthen political power. The maturation of political processes, civil society, and a media that ensures transparency and accountability is a prerequisite for durable political institutions and a viable peace.

Constitutional Design. Writing or revising a constitution is a significant challenge in postconflict countries. Since postconflict countries are in serious disarray not just physically but socially and ideologically, getting all factions to agree on the text of a new constitution often requires heavy external engagement. The process is marked not only by the debate and grave consideration inherent in such a solemn task, but also, and less inspiringly, by arm-twisting, threats, and behind-the-scenes horse-trading.

Developing Civil Society. Postconflict countries usually lack strong civil societies that can promote government accountability. During periods of conflict, civil society groups, to the extent that there are any, often go underground or into exile or they become targets of violence. Resuscitating, fostering, and protecting these groups while dampening ethnic or religious tensions is one of the most difficult tasks facing the intervening authorities.

Creating a Free Press. Free, independent, and professionally competent media are usually in short supply following a conflict. When Cambodian factions agreed to a peace settlement in 1991, for example, all journalists had been employed by the communist government, which imposed strict controls. Other journalists, part of the opposition press, worked out of refugee camps along the Thai-Cambodian border or from locations abroad. The press has to become emboldened to cover sensitive political issues while learning the importance of objectivity and accuracy.

Organizing Elections. Nothing short of elections is likely to provide a government with the broadly based support and generally accepted legitimacy needed to rule once the intervening authorities have departed. On the other hand, premature elections can often reinforce ethnic and sectarian cleavages, promote divisive political positions, and even spur a return to violence. Elections do not necessarily produce governments committed to resolving disputes through negotiation and compromise—or, for that matter, governments committed to preserving democracy. If the parties that win these elections remain dedicated to the destruction of their rivals or if they seek to undermine the democratic institutions that brought them to power, elections may work against the goal of establishing a stable and peaceful society. If the parties that contest elections attempt to build popular support by appealing to intercommunal fears and hatreds, the election campaign can rekindle the very conflict that the intervening authorities sought to mitigate.

Best Practices

Understanding Obstacles and Opportunities

There are a number of general factors that tend to make democratization more or less difficult. The first is the *regime type* in surrounding countries. Authoritarian regimes surrounded by democracies are more likely to democratize than are authoritarian regimes surrounded by other authoritarian regimes.[3] The causal mechanisms underlying this tendency remain unclear. It may be caused by peer pressure or peer envy. Or it may be caused by democratic norms, which can take hold more rapidly if a culturally similar neighbor sets an example. The point, however, is that nation-building in countries surrounded by authoritarian regimes is likely to be more challenging than it would if neighboring countries were functioning democracies.

International pressure can play a significant role in creating a successful move to democracy.[4] Pressure has been most effective when it

---

[3]   Kristian Skrede Gleditsch, *All International Politics Is Local: The Diffusion of Conflict, Integration, and Democratization*, Ann Arbor, Mich.: University of Michigan Press, 2002.

[4]   Robert A. Dahl, *Polyarchy: Participation and Opposition*, New Haven, Conn.: Yale University Press, 1971, p. 197; Samuel P. Huntington, *The Third Wave: Democratization in the*

has come from more powerful countries and international organizations such as the United Nations. Some authoritarian regimes have been supported by external assistance, especially from larger countries and through diaspora communities. Geopolitical shifts may alter these relationships by drying up sources of revenue or fostering new pressures toward political liberalization, leading to democracy.[5] At the end of the Cold War, several states experienced pressures to democratize because of cuts in military aid from the United States or the former Soviet Union, accompanied by bilateral and multilateral pressures toward liberalization. The salience of this factor is likely to vary according to the degree of dependence on foreign support and the availability of compensatory sources of government revenues, such as those from natural resources or from other alternatives.

Democratization tends to occur in *waves*, with a series of clustered openings followed by a period of retrenchment.[6] The causal mechanisms driving democratization waves are somewhat unclear. However, contagion effects may endow waves with a force of their own—opposition movements often draw inspiration or adopt strategies from recent international developments. The intervening authorities can sometimes ride the wave, propagating techniques and political measures that facilitated successful democratization in a different postconflict setting. The intervening authorities may also wish to bring officials and individuals who participated in a successful democratization effort in a neighboring state into the host country as advisors to institutions and politicians. In these ways, the presence of a broader democratic wave can increase the likelihood of democratization.

Theories of modernization posit that *economic development* promotes democracy by facilitating the emergence of a middle class with sufficient time and resources to push for more representative institutions. This suggests that intervening authorities involved in nation-building should view economic development as an opportunity for

---

Late Twentieth Century, Norman, Okla.: University of Oklahoma Press, 1991, pp. 85–100.

[5] Laurence Whitehead, ed., *The International Dimensions of Democratization: Europe and the Americas*, New York: Oxford University Press, 1996.

[6] Huntington (1991, pp. 3–30).

strengthening the democratization process. Seymour Lipset first noted in 1959 that, in both Europe and Latin America, democratic states tended to be more economically developed across a range of indicators, including per capita GDP, literacy, penetration of modern goods, and urbanization.[7] Subsequent studies have indicated that this trend holds more globally and that economic growth tends to contribute to the creation of democracy, not vice versa.[8] Other factors that have been cited as contributors to democratization include the strength of civil society, egalitarian income distribution, and a market-oriented economy.[9]

The perceived *legitimacy* of the regime is an important determinant of whether democratization will be successful. The imposition of a government by an intervening authority may result in its eventual overthrow if it is not viewed as legitimate over the long run. A government viewed as illegitimate by the population is a major obstacle to democratization no matter how fairly elected. While legitimacy itself is difficult to measure, the symptoms of failed legitimacy are well known: sagging support in public opinion surveys, rampant corruption, economic stagnation, unsuccessful foreign policy initiatives, and loss of support from domestic constituencies such as religious authorities.

A country cannot remain democratic without a *credible opposition movement*. The movement should have at least some semblance of organization and cohesion. The bargaining process that usually ensues between the government and a strong opposition movement is an important pathway to democratization.[10]

---

[7]   Seymour Martin Lipset, "Some Social Requisites of Democracy: Economic Development and Political Legitimacy," *American Political Science Review*, Vol. 53, No. 1, March 1959, pp. 69–105.

[8]   See, for example, Robert J. Barro, "Democracy and Growth," *Journal of Economic Growth*, Vol. 1, No. 1, March 1996, pp. 1–27; Ross E. Burkhart and Michael Lewis-Beck, "Comparative Democracy: The Economic Development Thesis," *American Political Science Review*, Vol. 88, No. 4, December 1994, pp. 903–910.

[9]   Adam Przeworski and Fernando Limongi, "Modernization: Theories and Facts," *World Politics*, Vol. 49, No. 2, January 1997, pp. 155–183 [pp. 159–160]; see also, among others, Huntington (1991).

[10] Adam Przeworski, *Democracy and the Market: Political and Economic Reforms in Eastern Europe and Latin America*, New York: Cambridge University Press, 1991.

The effectiveness and role of the *security apparatus* affects the probability that a postconflict society will become a successful democracy. Low morale, high desertion rates, a history of military takeovers of government, or legal provisions providing the military with high levels of political autonomy are danger signs. An incompetent or excessively politicized security apparatus can be a major obstacle to democratization.

The intervening authorities can affect only some of these conditions. The authorities can bring international pressure to bear—and indeed this is often the manifestation of that pressure. They can provide security, thereby allowing goods, services, people, and ideas to circulate freely. They can provide assistance that can further accelerate economic growth. They can facilitate the emergence of an organized political opposition. They can reform the state's security apparatus. But they may not be able to transform the nature of neighboring regimes. They will not have the time or money needed to significantly enlarge the middle class. Nor, in a period of a few years, is the overall level of social development likely to be lifted very much. Aspirations for the society's political transformation need to be guided accordingly, recognizing the conditions of poverty, corruption, ignorance, and sectarian discord from which the new institutions will need to emerge and which they cannot entirely transcend.

Structuring Representative Institutions

In some cases, the intervening authorities will begin with sovereign powers, as was the case in Kosovo, East Timor, and Iraq. Alternatively, the intervening authorities may share oversight duties with an existent indigenous regime, one that will have agreed, perhaps as a condition for the intervention, to give way in due course to a more permanent government. Sometimes that transition can take place via elections held under existing constitutional arrangements. Frequently, however, that legal framework will have broken down or been discredited, necessitating the fashioning of new institutions.

In considering constitutional revision, the first step is to analyze the sources of violent competition in the society. Who is competing, and for what? How can that competition be diverted from violent into peaceful channels? How can the contenders be brought into the new system? What institutional arrangements are most likely to enjoy broad public support while adequately accommodating the needs of the various power centers in the society, thereby reducing the prospect of violent resistance?

By its very presence, an intervening force will shift power relationships within the host society, strengthening some claimants and weakening others. If heavily committed and generously resourced, intervening authorities may occasionally be able to entirely dispossess one ruling elite and empower another in an enduring fashion. After World War II, the Nazi party was banned in Germany and thousands of its members were barred from political participation. An attempt to replicate this experience in postinvasion Iraq, where the U.S. troop presence was more than 20 times smaller in proportion to the population than it had been in Germany, proved less successful. Even after World War II in Japan, which was occupied much more lightly than Germany, the U.S.-led purge of officials associated with the wartime regime was much more modest and almost entirely reversed by the Japanese authorities as soon as the occupation ended.

In most circumstances, the intervening authorities will be better advised to try to bring all the claimants to power in the society into the political process. The threat of coercion may be employed for leverage, but the main objective in most cases should be to allow the main contenders to continue their competition under new rules that favor peaceful over violent means, giving all a chance for and, indeed, a share of, power.

There are many options for doing this. Democracy comes in a variety of shapes. There are federal and unitary states, parliamentary and presidential systems. Given free rein, intervening authorities will be tempted to replicate their own system of government rather than search for one most suitable to the recipient society. By the same token, local populations will often be inclined to opt for the system with which they are familiar, even if it has served them poorly in the past. In most cases, it will be better to adapt the familiar to new circumstances than to attempt to impose a wholly new construct. The Afghan constitutional process set out in the December 2001 Bonn Agreement, for example, drew heavily on traditional Afghan modalities for national decisionmaking. This clearly enhanced the legitimacy of the process in the eyes of the population as it went forward. By contrast, the roadmap set out in 2004 for Iraq's transition to democracy new and unfamiliar concepts, most notably federalism. While a decentralized authority of that sort undoubtedly had a logic, and it was strongly demanded by the Kurdish minority, it has been violently resisted by the Sunnis and regarded with some suspicion by the Shiite majority.

In ideal circumstances, the march toward renewed sovereignty occurs in graduated stages. First, the contending forces are disarmed, demobilized, and reintegrated. Then civil society and independent media are given resources and time to grow. Political parties are organized under new rules. Ministries are organized and staffed with professionals. Security forces are reorganized and trained. Local elections are held, and grassroots democracy takes hold. And then, as the capstone, national elections are held, and full sovereignty is returned to a freely elected government.

This ideal sequence is likely to be fully realizable only in circumstances in which the population is acquiescent and the intervening authorities are well resourced. More often, the intervening authorities will not be equipped to provide the full panoply of interim governance, while the interim indigenous regime, if there is one, will be weak, inept, and corrupt, else the intervention would not have been necessary in the first place. In some cases, the contending parties will not be ready to disarm and cannot be forced to do so. In such circumstances, elections may, in fact, be a requirement for forming a new government with adequate coherence and authority to deal with the society's most urgent problems.

Most postconflict societies benefit from the development of new political leaders. Former leaders may have often based their power on armed gangs or may have come to power by manipulating ethnic or religious tensions. To create a durable political system under the new regime, new actors are needed. The intervening authorities can encourage the development of new local leaders by devolving responsibility for the provision of government services to local authorities and by encouraging local input into decisions. The intervening authorities must also ensure that leadership develops among all factions. NGOs can be especially useful in developing leadership in local communities and among women and minority groups. Members of the diaspora can also be useful in developing or supplementing local talent.

Constitutional Design

It is important for long-term stability and societal reconciliation to have broad popular participation in—and legitimation of—the constitutional process. International intervention cannot succeed and the institutions it establishes cannot be viable unless there is participation and ownership on the part of the people. This is why the process of constitution-making should be democratic and broadly participatory. It should include not just the election of a constituent assembly or the penning of a constitutional referendum, but also the involvement of the widest possible range of stakeholders in the relevant discussions and in procedural planning. It should also include the organization of an extensive national dialogue on constitutional issues and principles.[11] As Jamal Benomar observes, "Constitutions produced without transparency and adequate public participation will lack legitimacy."[12] And illegitimate constitutions bode poorly for future stability.

While there should be as much continuity as possible with preexisting constitutional traditions, many conflicts are partly caused by the weakness or failure of the preceding institutional arrangements. Sometimes, significant innovation in institutional design is needed. In some cases, this means the devolution of power, if not federalism, to assure each group a stake in the system. It might also mean a new type of electoral system to ensure fair and balanced representation without too much fragmentation. The choice of executive structure (e.g., parliamentary or presidential), electoral system (e.g., proportional repre-

---

[11] Larry Diamond, "Promoting Democracy in Post-Conflict and Failed States: Lessons and Challenges," paper presented at the National Policy Forum on Terrorism, Security, and America's Purpose, Washington, D.C., September 6–7, 2005.

[12] Jamal Benomar, "Constitution-Making After Conflict: Lessons for Iraq," *Journal of Democracy*, Vol. 15, No. 2, April 2004, pp. 81–95 [p. 89]. An interesting exception to this rule is the Japanese constitution, which was written entirely by Americans and remains unamended to this day.

sentation, majoritarian, or a combination of both), and the degree of devolution of power have significant implications for future stability. Also important is the degree to which the constitution effectively constrains abuse of power and empowers an independent judiciary and other countervailing institutions.

There are at least two broad options for power-sharing that intervening authorities should consider during the constitutional process. One is the *consociational* approach.[13] This has been employed by states that have internal divisions along ethnic, religious, linguistic, or other lines, yet nonetheless manage to remain stable due to consultation among the elites of each of its major social groups. Thus, consociational democracies are characterized by grand coalitions and proportionality in the electoral system, as well as in the distribution of public offices and scarce resources. Examples include Switzerland, India, the Netherlands, Lebanon, and Malaysia. The consociational approach assumes that, since ethnic, religious, linguistic, or other social divisions can be destabilizing, cooperation across these divisions can bring about long-term political stability. The other approach is to design a political system in which a majority of the population can be assured a certain degree of primacy in society, but to build in crosscutting limitations and incentives to ensure moderation.[14] Both approaches have some merit. Intervening authorities in postconflict situations should push for political institutions that give each major contending group a stake in the future system (through some mechanism of sharing or devolving power) and that diminish the potential for one group (majority or plurality) to dominate the system indefinitely and abuse and aggrandize power.

---

[13] See, for example, Arend Lijphart, "Constitutional Democracy," *World Politics*, Vol. 21, No. 2, January 1969, pp. 207–225; and Arend Lijphart, *Patterns of Democracy: Government Forms and Performance in Thirty-Six Countries*, New Haven, Conn.: Yale University Press, 1999.

[14] See, for example, Donald L. Horowitz, *Ethnic Groups in Conflict*, Berkeley, Calif.: University of California Press, 1985; and Donald L. Horowitz, *A Democratic South Africa? Constitutional Engineering in a Divided Society*, Berkeley, Calif.: University of California Press, 1991.

Developing a Civil Society

Civil society occupies the political space between the individual and the government. It includes NGOs, associations, and social groups that contribute to a democratic society and nonviolent political transition from war to peace. These organizations have several functions:

- They enable citizens to have an impact on government decisions without necessarily competing for political power or resorting to violence.
- They give a voice to minority and other marginalized groups.
- They help increase government transparency, accountability, and responsiveness.

In light of the significant role that civil society plays in supporting and monitoring both local and national governance, international and local authorities should establish legal regulations to protect and develop such organizations. Civil society development should be supported with funding, training, and advocacy. Civic education organizations should be equipped and trained to carry out voter education and get-out-the-vote campaigns. A strong, diverse civil society can provide the foundation for a viable postwar democratic transition that is just and sustainable. Its absence can result in the resurgence of conflict and repressive governance. Nation-building operations create a window of opportunity for international and domestic civil society organizations. They provide an opportunity to firmly establish civil society. But they can also create false expectations and undermine long-term reconstruction if the international community and international civil society organizations quickly withdraw support following the end of the conflict. A legal framework and a civil society that can exist without external support over time are required. In many postconflict societies, civil society organizations are at work prior to the war. When present, the international community should utilize already existing capacity and build on that foundation.

Assistance to civil society often gains momentum late in the nation-building mission, since more immediate humanitarian needs may take precedence in the early stages. In Afghanistan, Counterpart

International conducted an assessment of civil society in 2005, four years into the mission, as part of the USAID-supported Initiative to Promote Afghan Civil Society. Key recommendations included the following:

> Efforts to support civil society must take into account the diverse nature of Afghan [civil society organizations] and their varied needs, resulting in a flexible offering of capacity-building approaches;

> Despite their limitations as non-representative, mostly male bodies, shuras and ulemas should be fostered because of their credibility with communities and the resulting potential for making important contributions to anchoring civil society as a force in Afghanistan.[15]

> The capacity-building strategy should introduce graduated grants—starting with small "learning grants" for new organizations and building up to larger grants.[16]

> Support for the adoption and implementation of an NGO Law should remain a high priority as it is a critical element of a functioning civil society in any country.[17]

These recommendations reflect familiar themes found in other nation-building operations. Legal foundations, capacity-building services, funding, and recognition of traditional structures are now key pillars of civil society development programs.

While law is important, civil society often functions well without regulation. In some cases, civil society may actually function in spite of regulations. In Cambodia, organizations mushroomed during the war

---

[15] Counterpart International, *Afghanistan Civil Society Assessment*, Washington, D.C., June 3, 2005, p. 8.

[16] Counterpart International (2005, p. 8).

[17] Counterpart International (2005, p. 8).

and the postconflict UN operation. Many had been established in the refugee camps lining the Thai border. But they were not recognized by the government or by political parties, and they had no basis in law.

Many international NGOs entering postwar countries fail to create strong local capacity because they largely employ foreign personnel. The goal should be to foster and leave behind strong local organizations once they depart. Local civil society organizations should be trained, equipped, and supported. The international community should help create capacity within civil society organizations that allows them to function according to the rules and procedures set by their boards. Only well-structured organizations can survive "abandonment" once international organizations leave. Many civil society organizations face financial difficulties as a result of the departure of international partners. A package of incentives and programs may be required to ensure the financial health of such organizations. Speed of funding in the initial postconflict period is important. In the rapidly changing environment of postwar societies—which may include riots, elections, and humanitarian disasters—international donors should develop the capability to deliver rapid support to local civil society organizations. International and local authorities should also encourage citizens and local businesses to contribute to worthy organizations in cash or in kind.

While civil society can make an important contribution to the emergence of effective representative government, it cannot offer an alternative. Donors should be wary of using NGOs to deliver services that should be provided by the state. Working through such organizations may improve both the quality of the services delivered and accountability for the use of donor funds, but it will do nothing to enhance the capacity of the local government.

Creating a Free Press

Independent media play a key role in providing information and analysis of elections, candidates, parties, and platforms, as well as reports on problems during elections, offering a forum for alternative views, interpreting political or technical information for public consumption, helping the public make informed choices, holding public officials accountable through responsible reporting, and serving as a forum for peaceful debate among those who might have resorted to violence. The intervening authorities may establish media outlets to meet the need to convey information to the public immediately, to dispel rumors, and to counteract the effects of hate speech and inflammatory propaganda. Outlets may take the form of radio stations, television stations, newspapers, or magazines. The establishment of an international media outlet does not replace the need to nurture indigenous media, but it acknowledges that the latter task may take a substantial amount of time.

The intervening authorities should gather information about the state of the media prior to and after the conflict, including media facilities. Television and radio studios, presses, and communication systems are often targeted and damaged during conflict. Donors require knowledge about who controls or supports the media, including outside countries, political parties or factions, warlords, and criminal organizations. These assessments need to take into consideration what is being broadcast from outside the state and from where. Examples include Iranian media campaigns in Iraq, Serbian and Croatian campaigns in Bosnia, and Albanian campaigns in Kosovo.

Once an adequate assessment has been made, international and local authorities can make decisions about how to develop the media, including whether to focus on private or public media outlets. A key issue is funding, as even private media outlets may not be able to support themselves. Key tasks include the creation of a legal framework for media operations, such as a licensing structure, professional standards, and associations for publishers, editors, and journalists; construction and rehabilitation of publishing houses, presses, transmitters, and other media equipment; and training and education programs for publishers, broadcasters, and journalists.

The intervening authorities may establish or fund media outlets to counter hate propaganda and inflammatory statements, and disseminate critical information about transitional activities that affect the population. These efforts are often designed to preempt or compete with media outlets controlled by warlords, ethnic factions, or other opponents of peace. The intervening authorities may need to fill the vacuum in the provision of critical information to the population about nation-building activities, especially when free and independent media are lacking. Examples include information on the movement of peace-keeping forces, land mine awareness, refugee returns, food and shelter programs, and voter registration and other election information. These media programs help counteract rumors that lead to violence and help expose the activities of those spoilers opposed to the peace process. They are now considered a permanent feature of the initial phase of nation-building operations. Additionally, the intervening authorities should strengthen local indigenous media outlets as part of a broader effort to build a vibrant civil society.

Media supported or controlled by the intervening authorities may be viewed as biased. In addition, media outlets run by the intervening authorities may attract local talent away from the local media, weakening these outlets and leaving a vacuum when the international intervention is over. At the same time, indigenous media outlets are likely to be associated with contending political factions. The challenge is to navigate between the short-term requirement for providing immediate, critical information to the public and the longer-term imperative of creating healthy, free, independent media.

The intervening authorities need to examine the current capacity of the media to print, distribute, and transmit news, as well as the capacity for media education and training. Before designing a media strategy, several questions must be answered. Who are the main actors in the crisis? Who are the opinion-makers? How does the population get information? Do the citizens have radios, televisions, and access to print media? What is the literacy rate among the population?

The control of transmitters after the conflict is a particularly sensitive issue. In Bosnia, Croatia and Serbia established separate units to help Bosnian Croats and Bosnian Serbs begin broadcasting radio and television programs. The decision to help each community separately served to fuel further fragmentation of society in Bosnia following the conflict. The parties continued to spread their doctrines of intolerance and hate. In countries that had strong public broadcasting systems prior to the conflict, the intervening authorities should analyze the past role of these systems and make decisions about the continuation of funding and support. In some areas of conflict, public broadcasting agencies were used as propaganda tools. In post-Taliban Afghanistan, parts of the population perceived the state media as biased in favor of the Northern Alliance. In postwar environments such as in Kosovo and Bosnia, the international community advocated the establishment of a public broadcasting corporation modeled after the BBC. A media strategy should address whether both private and public media are going to be promoted, developed, and funded. For the longer term, a media strategy must encompass how advertising and other revenue streams will create self-sustaining media. Revenues will reduce the dependence of the media on international donors or local political parties.

One of the main challenges in building free, independent media is establishing an impartial, transparent legal regime that upholds freedom of speech, establishes fair licensing practices, permits independent media to operate without harassment, and minimizes the advantages that public media may have over private providers. Laws and regulatory regimes often take longer to realize than other goals of donor activities affecting the media. In some cases, postwar governments fail to enact legal measures to support and guide media. In Bosnia, the OSCE was given responsibility for organizing the first postwar elections. Upon arrival, the OSCE discovered that the same leaders who had prosecuted the war remained in control of the media. To ensure fair elections, the OSCE established the Media Experts Commission as a subcommission to the Provisional Election Commission. It issued a set of rules and regulations that directed the media to publish accurate information and to refrain from broadcasting incendiary programming. The Media Experts Commission also ordered the three television systems, which were controlled by the ruling parties of Bosnia's three entities, to provide opposition political parties with the same amount of advertising time as they did the ruling parties and to run election notices and advertisements issued by the international community.

In many war-torn environments, journalists have worked only under authoritarian regimes and state-controlled media outlets. The business aspect of running sustainable media organizations may need to be taught through training courses. The establishment of a center that provides a variety of services and allows providers to coordinate their activities with the work of local journalists has been a successful model for media development in postwar societies. In Afghanistan, the United Nations Educational, Scientific and Cultural Organization (UNESCO) helped establish a single independent media training and resource facility, the AINA Media and Culture Centre in Kabul, which improved coordination among donors and NGOs. Several organizations, such as the Institute for War and Peace Reporting, opened offices in this facility, as did local newspapers, magazines, and NGOs. UNESCO later funded an Internet connection and supplied computers. The BBC conducted a training program through its media training facility at Radio-TV Afghanistan. In Bosnia, the Open Society Institute and the BBC established a broadcast training school, where young journalists came from all over Bosnia to receive training from BBC producers and journalists.

Intervening authorities can revive or create university programs that provide professional education for students in journalism and communications. In Cambodia, the Asia Foundation initiated a one-year certificate program in journalism at the University of Phnom Penh. Two of Cambodia's most respected journalists taught a new generation of aspiring journalists. The Institute for War and Peace assisted Kabul University in developing a journalism program. In Rwanda, the National University of Rwanda's School of Journalism contributed to the development of professional journalism following the conflict. In Kosovo, Press Now and Internews provided training on how to cover elections to local radio journalists. In East Timor, Internews conducted hands-on media training, mentoring, management programs, and technical assistance inside media outlets across the country.

Building and supporting associations for media professionals is another critical tool to encourage media development, promote professional standards, and encourage continuing education in a postconflict setting. In Cambodia, the Asia Foundation worked with the Khmer Journalists Association to promote professionalism and ethical standards. In Sierra Leone, the Sierra Leone Association of Journalists and the Guild of Newspaper Editors received training and help in building their associations.

Finally, intervening authorities may have to discourage or prevent indigenous media outlets from broadcasting propaganda that increases ethnic tensions and raises the likelihood of conflict. After early efforts failed to prevent ethnically slanted and inflammatory media broadcasts in Bosnia, NATO troops seized television broadcast towers in Serb-controlled areas of the country. In this case, the show of force succeeded in moderating the future behavior of Serb broadcasters.

Organizing Elections

One highly desirable prerequisite for elections is the completion of the DDR of former combatants, which is explored in more detail in Chapter Two. Whenever possible, design and implementation of a DDR program should be among the earliest priorities of any nation-building mission. Cases may arise, nevertheless, in which the intervening authorities lack the power and the contending parties the will to disarm, as was the case in Cambodia in 1991 and in Iraq beginning in 2003. In such circumstances, the only option may be to hold the elections and hope for the best.

Under ideal circumstances, it is preferable to postpone national elections until security has been established, the contending parties have been disarmed, political parties have been organized, civil society developed, and local elections held. By holding local elections first, national political parties and their leadership have time to mature. The population has time to develop trust in and experience with the political system. New leadership has an opportunity to emerge and gain experience. On the other hand, empowering local officials before doing the same at the national level can be problematic when the proper relationship between the central and local governments is in dispute or where strong sectarian differences have contributed to civil strife.

Several questions are worth asking in seeking to determine the ideal time for elections. First, can the society be governed adequately without early elections? In situations in which the indigenous elements pressing for early elections are strong and the intervening authorities' capacity to govern is weak, as was the case in Iraq in 2004, there may be little choice but to accede to those demands. Second, will the government likely to emerge from the elections be more or less effective than whatever government currently exists? Third, is the result of the election likely to be stabilizing or destabilizing? In societies badly divided along ethnic, religious, or class lines, elections are likely to increase polarization. In such cases, provisions for protection of minorities and limitations on the power of the majority may need to be put in place before the balloting commences.

Intervening authorities will need to provide a budget for elections and help raise the necessary funds. Both local and international observers should be recruited and trained to monitor elections to diminish the incidence of fraud and mismanagement. Information about the voting process and on the results of the election should be disseminated across the country in a fashion that is accessible to all people. Two goals drive this process: the encouragement of peaceful participation and the engagement of previously disenfranchised or marginalized sectors of society. By making the election process and results transparent and public, accusations and misconceptions of fraud or other problems can be minimized. The intervening authorities should also help establish electoral commissions to adjudicate disputes that may arise over elections.

Robust security is important to the successful conduct of elections. Elections provide targets of opportunity for opponents of the peace process. Voter and candidate intimidation, threats and violence against election workers, and other forms of violent protest routinely occur in postconflict states. International and local authorities should deploy enough military and police personnel to ensure a secure environment for elections and election campaigns.

Afghanistan's Electoral Work Plan, prepared by the United Nations Assistance Mission in Afghanistan, offers one template for setting conditions for what turned out to be rather successful elections. It linked the achievement of elections to the larger state-building mission in Afghanistan. The plan delineated a series of tasks that had to be undertaken and completed in advance of elections, such as

- ensuring a credible political environment, including legislation on elections, political parties, access to media, and monitoring and reporting on human rights

- establishing a reasonable degree of security, including the training of 30,000 Afghan police officers and coordination between national and international military forces
- specifying targets for the disarmament, demobilization, and reintegration of former combatants before the elections, including demobilization of at least 40 percent of the estimated 100,000 ex-combatants and cantonment of all heavy weapons
- completing key technical preparations for each phase of the electoral process.

Elections are commonly administered and overseen by election commissions. Transparent, impartial operation of these bodies is a critical factor in the success of elections, especially in states where there has been little experience with elections and where there is significant ethnic, religious, or tribal friction. The intervening authorities should strive to include representatives of disenfranchised groups on the electoral commission, including women. In some cases, the commission may also include international members in an effort to enhance its impartiality and expertise. The intervening authorities should act to protect the independence of the electoral committee from outside control or manipulation; take measures to facilitate voter and candidate registration, including among displaced persons; and provide information on voting procedures and other information about the election in all major languages and using radio broadcasts and placards where illiteracy rates are high. The intervening authorities should also help design rules regarding permissible sources of financing for elections.

Key Actors

The United Nations is the best source of expertise on the development of transitional and permanent political systems. The OSCE has developed considerable expertise in the promotion of civil society, the establishment of independent media, and the development of political parties, though its activities have so far been limited to Eurasia. Several nations, including the United States and Germany, maintain organizations affiliated with their own political parties that specialize in helping to set up political parties in emerging democracies. The IFES (formerly the International Federation for Election Systems) has organized elections in dozens of countries around the world under the most challenging of conditions.

Costs

Intervening powers are likely to be called on to fund some or most of the expenses for elections, including the costs of helping build political parties, providing voter information, and organizing caucuses or primaries for the first several years following an intervention. The indigenous government, if there is one, is likely to lack sufficient funds to cover the costs of designing, securing, and holding elections. Of these costs, providing protection for voters and candidates typically accounts for approximately half of the total. Raising the funds necessary to mount elections should begin well in advance of the date on which voters go to the polls. A United Nations trust fund has often been the most effective way to provide funding.

The cost of organizing elections has historically varied from a high of $20 per registered voter for the 2004 presidential elections in Afghanistan and the 2001 local municipal elections in Kosovo to a low of $2.20 per registered voter for the 2002 local commune elections in Cambodia. Figure 8.1 illustrates the costs of running elections in six postconflict societies: Afghanistan, Kosovo, Haiti, Cambodia, Mozambique, and Bosnia.[18] The average cost is $12 per registered voter.

For planning purposes, we recommend that the intervening authority plan to spend the average of these past costs: $12 per voter. Actual costs would be subject to several variables, such as the level of violence. To illustrate, we evaluated the hypothetical costs of holding an election in Macedonia following an intervention. In 2006,

---

[18] The elections were the 2004 presidential elections in Afghanistan, the 2001 local municipal elections in Kosovo, the 2005 local municipal elections in Haiti, the 2002 local "commune" elections in Cambodia, the 2004 presidential elections in Mozambique, and the 1996 national elections in Bosnia.

Figure 8.1
Cost of Organizing Elections

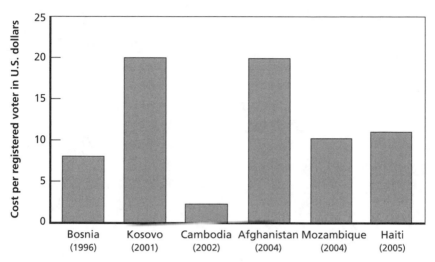

SOURCE: IFES and United Nations Development Programme, *Getting to the Core: A Global Survey on the Cost of Registration and Elections,* Madrid and Washington, D.C., 2006.
RAND *MG557-8.1*

Macedonia had a population of 2 million and approximately 1,741,449 registered voters.[19] Using an average of $12 per registered voter, we estimate that it would cost approximately $21 million to design, secure, and implement countrywide elections in Macedonia.

---

[19] IFES, Election Guide: Macedonia, guide for 2006 Macedonia parliamentary elections, Washington, D.C., 2006.

CHAPTER NINE

Development

In most postconflict economies, the first and second years after an intervention are ones in which the economy grows rapidly, a consequence of the end of conflict, improved economic policies, and inflows of aid. Following this initial spurt in economic activity, when refugees and displaced people return and rebuild their homes and businesses, more traditional problems of development arise. Host governments are confronted with the tasks of creating conditions conducive to business and economic growth; improving human capital; providing government services cost-effectively; and creating conditions for the efficient provision of electric power, telecommunications, water, and other utilities. These tasks have to be achieved in the context of a country in which the central bank and economic ministries have only just begun to function, individuals and businesses still fear renewed strife, regions of the country remain cut off because of the dilapidation of roads and the absence of telecommunications, and utility service levels are rudimentary and intermittent.

Key Challenges

Controlling Inflation and Establishing Budgetary Balance. Societies in conflict experience high rates of inflation. Inflation rates ran in the thousands of percent in Bosnia. In Sierra Leone and Cambodia, rates exceeded 100 percent. In countries with high rates of inflation, growth is more erratic and slower than in comparable countries with lower rates.[1] High rates of inflation introduce greater uncertainty, discouraging investment; they impede the functioning of long-term capital markets because of rapid declines in the real value of loan principal; and they increase the costs of doing business as leads and lags in payments result in substantial windfall gains or losses. In light of these costs, reducing inflation should be a priority following conflict, especially because reducing inflation is universally popular and a sign that times have changed for the better. But the root cause of inflation is usually imbalances in the budget. Faced with pressures to increase spending and a lack of revenues, governments of states in conflict force the central bank to cover their bills by printing money. Although money creation can be stopped, if deficits persist, they have to be financed. If unchecked, fiscal imbalances will eventually derail initial progress on reducing inflation. The creation of incentives and systems to prevent fiscal imbalances is a crucial component of policies to curb inflation.[2]

Creating an Environment Conducive to Economic Growth. During conflict, regulatory and tax systems frequently collapse. As the economy stabilizes and the government reconstitutes itself, the state resumes collecting taxes and attempts to enforce health, safety, environmental, and other regulations so as to improve public welfare. For political reasons, the state may also attempt to reimpose price, exchange rate, import and export controls, or resuscitate centralized marketing organizations for commodities such as cacao, coffee, or diamonds.

If rapid economic growth is to be sustained, the intervening authorities must assist postconflict governments in creating simple, transparent, easily enforceable tax and regulatory systems. Businesses in postconflict societies face a myriad of difficulties, ranging from lack of security to making payments on receipt and shipment of goods. When postconflict governments compound these difficulties by resuscitating pernicious tax and regulatory systems that are exploited to extort bribes, economic growth is retarded and distorted. The govern-

---

[1]   Stanley Fischer, Ratna Sahay, and Carlos Végh, "Modern Hyper- and High Inflations," IMF Working Paper 02/197, Washington, D.C.: International Monetary Fund, January 31, 2003, p. 41.

[2]   Fischer, Sahay, and Végh (2003, p. 31).

ment also needs to lay the groundwork for collecting adequate taxes to protect consumers while inhibiting the ability of civil servants to demand bribes.

Operating, Reconstructing, and Investing in Utilities, State-Owned Enterprises, and Infrastructure. Immediately following the conflict, the intervening authorities and host-country government often need to jump-start the provision of utilities such as electric power, water, garbage pickup, sewage, and telecommunications by supplying funds, fuels, and spare parts. State-owned enterprises, which may be major employers or produce key exports, also may need to be put back on their feet at this time. Once rudimentary operations resume, the intervening authorities need to turn their attention to working with the host government to create conditions for the efficient operation of utilities and state-owned enterprises. The solvency of these enterprises is a key problem in many developing countries—even more so in postconflict societies, where payment collection has often collapsed. If utilities and state-owned enterprises generate sufficient revenues to cover costs, ensuring their financial health, they become a source of economic growth as service is improved and expanded and investments are made in new capacity. If utilities and state-owned enterprises are operating inefficiently and unprofitably, they can easily retard growth as consumers and businesses are unable to access electric power, water, or sewage treatment services and the budget is burdened by losses. Poorly functioning utilities also contribute to the spread of disease and high infant-mortality rates.

Estimating and Phasing Donor Assistance. Following the initial postconflict period, the role of international donors shifts from humanitarian assistance and emergency stopgap funding of government operations to more traditional development assistance. Even in very poor countries, donors expect that funding needs will begin to decline at some point in time. Donors need to work with the host government to identify financial needs, encourage potential donors to commit to financing these needs, evaluate the efficacy of past expenditures, ensure that funds have been spent appropriately, and coordinate with the government to phase out assistance in areas where the local government has developed the capacity to fund and deliver services on its own.

Best Practices

Controlling Inflation and Establishing Budgetary Balance

Controlling Inflation. As discussed in Chapter Seven, host-country governments that have been successful in reducing inflation have followed a standard recipe. In conjunction with the intervening authorities, they have created independent, professional central banks or monetary authorities, which have constrained emissions of money.

Coupled with the creation of a solid institutional framework, countries have utilized various exchange rate regimes to control inflation. In some postconflict nations, inflationary expectations have been broken by targeting or pegging the exchange rate to a foreign reserve currency. Pegs tend to be popular, as they introduce some financial stability into what has been an unstable economy. Countries that adopt pegs tend to be small, their economies are closely tied to one of the major reserve currency areas, a major foreign currency tends to be used pervasively in day-to-day transactions, and the country has sufficient reserves available to support a pegged exchange rate regime (usually provided by the donor community or from remittances). In other postconflict societies, floating rates in conjunction with tight constraints on monetary emissions have been successful. These countries tend to be less integrated into the global economy, more reliant on exports of just a few commodities (sometimes only one), may have larger economies, or may lack the reserves to support a pegged system.

Despite their short-run utility, pegged exchange rates may outlive their usefulness after the immediate postconflict period. As the economy recovers, the supply and demand for foreign currency will likely undergo substantial changes because of resumption in exports, declines in donor assistance, or change in the demand for imports. These changes may make it difficult for the monetary authority to sustain a peg.

At this point, the central bank, in conjunction with the IMF, may well wish to move from a hard peg to a managed float. A managed float introduces elements of exchange rate risk into the calculus of lenders and borrowers, forcing them to better match assets and liabilities to reduce this risk. When banks and businesses believe that the exchange rate will not change, they tend to borrow in whichever currency offers the lowest interest rates, usually foreign currency, and lend in whichever offers the highest, usually the local currency. If the exchange rate depreciates, borrowers often go bankrupt, as they can no longer cover loan payments in foreign currencies from earnings in the depreciated domestic currency.

More flexible exchange rates also permit the economy to adjust more easily to changes in prices of imports and exports. As assistance tapers off, postconflict countries may choose to let their currencies depreciate so as to encourage exports and discourage imports. Mozambique, Namibia, and Sierra Leone have successfully used exchange rate flexibility to manage their external balances.

Successful means of shifting from a pegged to a floating system include the creation of an intrabank market, followed by the gradual withdrawal of the central bank from market-making activities. Initially, the central bank may limit exchange rate fluctuations to a range around a peg. It may then expand and eventually eliminate the range, letting the rate float. Alternatively, the central bank may set implicit or explicit bands within which the currency may fluctuate. Except for very small economies or economies closely integrated with the economies of one of the major reserve currencies, more flexible exchange rate systems provide more resilience for countries emerging from an extended conflict.

Establishing Budgetary Balance. Controlling the budget, although superficially straightforward, is one of the most difficult tasks for any government. Interest groups and ministries continually press for higher budgets while taxpayers lobby for lower taxes. Permitting the budget to operate in deficit is often the easiest course of action. But preserving fiscal balance is key to preventing a recurrence of inflation,[3] funding government services, and creating a business climate conducive to economic growth.

The challenge of preserving fiscal balance is much greater for nations in the aftermath of a conflict than it is during the normal course of events. Sources of revenue other than donor finance are extremely limited. Procedures for budgeting, procuring, and dispensing funds have fallen apart. Government employees and service providers have disappeared. Donor funding is often slow in coming and fluctuates frequently as assistance agencies add or subtract funds. Managing the budget is one of the most difficult tasks facing the host country and intervening authorities, but it is also among the most important.

Expenditures. As schools reopen, clinics expand their activities, and government offices again begin to function, the intervening authorities and host government must quickly turn to budgeting for these operations. This entails sizing government operations (and donor budget support) correctly. If salaries and payrolls are not constrained during the first years of recovery, the host government may find itself unable to pay government workers, forcing layoffs and cutbacks a few years further on when donor finance and presence tapers off. Some governments such as Congo's, reluctant to make these adjustments, become insolvent. Reductions in staffing have resulted in demonstrations or riots. The violence in East Timor in 2006 was triggered when the government laid off soldiers. By restraining salaries and payrolls when government services are restored, this problem can be avoided or at least made less likely.

The most effective means of controlling government expenditures on the civil service is to limit government to core activities. In the first years following a conflict, it may make sense to limit the number of ministries (and ministers) that provide services to education, public health, transportation, energy, and security (usually justice, interior, and defense). The government will also need to pay for the operations of the ministries of foreign affairs and finance, the cabinet office, and, in countries where the planning ministry is responsible for large infrastructure projects, the planning ministry. Households and businesses

---

[3]   Fischer, Sahay, and Végh (2003, p. 25).

then have to fend for themselves to obtain other services. Such an approach helps control ministerial bloat.

In the ministries responsible for these services, the host government needs to set head counts based on the level of services to be provided. The government should calculate administrative and support staff numbers needed per 100 first-line providers. Initially, this approach yielded success in East Timor, where a decision by the World Bank to set staffing levels commensurate with the level of work left the East Timorese with a lean, effective bureaucracy by developing-country standards. Each individual had a clearly defined position, tasks, and authority, making policy decisions easier to implement and monitor. Such an approach also helps curb charges of favoritism, as the formerly disenfranchised should receive the same levels of service, at least in terms of staffing, as should better-positioned groups.

Once head counts are established, wage scales need to be adopted and tied to positions within the civil service. Scales need to be set tightly to prevent bracket creep, but high enough to attract well-qualified staff. Once a head count and wage bill are set, the finance ministry should enforce budget constraints by limiting the size of the ministry payroll to that set in the budget. If the ministry succeeds in circumventing the head count or salary controls, the finance ministry provides a third line of defense by controlling the funds transferred. In the best systems, the finance ministry handles the payroll as well as overall funds, limiting the ability of the ministry to create "ghost" employees or to finance higher wages for individuals with government connections by not paying teachers, nurses, or fire personnel. The appointment of chief financial officers for each ministry who are personally responsible for ministry expenditures and conducting annual external audits also helps constrain expenditures. The use of inspectors general to evaluate operations and controls is also helpful.

Assigning international civil servants as mentors to senior and, in some cases, mid-level civil servants is the most effective way of ensuring that government services are delivered while local control is restored. Mentoring is difficult: Mentors and local civil servants have to learn how to work with each other. Providing well-defined guidelines concerning authority and decision approval procedures and for "graduation," the shift of authority from the international civil servant to local control, makes this relationship clearer and easier to manage. Although these relationships are replete with tensions, in countries where the government has ceased to exist, mentoring relationships provide an opportunity to train local civil servants, monitor performance, and preserve local input while jump-starting the operations of government. By establishing clear deadlines for the transfer of authority, the relationship also forces the international civil servant to focus on the transition and working with his or her local counterpart rather than on the execution of daily tasks.

Taxation. During the course of the conflict, tax collection has usually collapsed. Although providing government services and utilities is more important, as the economy recovers, the state must begin to generate tax revenue to augment and then replace donor funding. At this juncture, creating an equitable, efficient system for collecting taxes becomes a priority.

Donor financing should provide a cushion for the government, making it possible to impose taxes slowly and methodically. The first order of business is to evaluate the former tax system in terms of perceived equity, revenue collected, ease and cost of collection, propensity to encourage bribery, and distorting economic effects. In some instances, taxes have contributed to conflict. Taxes on crops, gems, minerals, or imported fuels or foodstuffs may have engendered support for insurgencies, especially if they are perceived as being directed at a specific ethnic or regional group or if the local community feels that it does not receive an equitable share of revenues.

Despite recent criticisms, resource taxes have been effective in terms of equity, value, and ease and cost of collection. Jump-starting these operations and the accompanying tax flows should be a major priority for the host country and intervening authorities. Where commodities are mined or pumped from large, single locations, collection can take place at the point of export. The producer, usually a large company, transfers royalties, export taxes, and other payments directly to the treasury. Graft can be controlled in part by independent external audits that compare anticipated tax revenues based on sales to actual revenues. These audits and calculations should be disseminated to the public. Responsible officials need to be held accountable for any discrepancies by inspectors general and the legislature. Agreements with key purchasers of these products, for example, international oil companies or diamond importers, to publicly report payments provide an additional check on revenues.

A more difficult task is to collect tax revenues from exports of goods produced by small operations. The developing world is rife with the failure of central purchasing organizations to procure, process, and export products grown, raised, or mined by individuals. The production of higher-value products such as coffee and cacao has been stunted by inefficiencies and high taxes, implicit or explicit, imposed by these organizations. These taxes encourage farmers to evade the system by selling to private traders who then smuggle the product out of the country. Smugglers can become the nucleus of armed opposition to the current regime. Even less successful has been the taxation of sales of alluvial diamonds. Because of their high value and small size, diamonds are easily smuggled. In Angola, Congo, Sierra Leone, and elsewhere, insurgents have financed their operations through control of the alluvial diamond trade.[4]

Taxes on commodity exports need to be levied in a manner that is simple and does not discourage production nor encourage smuggling. If imposed intelligently, these taxes can become important sources of revenue while depriving spoilers of income. First and foremost, the intervening authorities and the host government need to reassert control and establish security in producing regions. These are not one and the same. Reasserting control involves expelling rebel forces. Establishing security means ensuring that local growers and miners are protected from theft and assault. Establishing security for producers begins by setting up secure markets. By ensuring a safe place in which to sell, the government will attract sellers and buyers. The government also needs to ensure secure transport for wholesalers to major hubs from which the product can be exported. If roads are secure and port facilities fairly efficient, the government can win back business from smugglers. If

---

4   Louis Goreux, "Conflict Diamonds," Africa Regional Working Paper, No. 13, Washington, D.C.: World Bank, March 2001.

the government can provide wholesalers with secure, efficient transport links, it can levy taxes at the wholesale level, the most efficient place to collect revenue. Trying to collect taxes directly from small-scale producers entails great effort, usually antagonizes large numbers of miners and farmers (thereby increasing support for insurgents), and generates less revenue. Taxes based on weight or quantity of goods are simpler and less open to corruption by tax collectors than are those imposed on revenues.

The problem is trickier for higher-value items such as gems and precious metals. Here, the government would generally like to levy a tax on the value of the product. In this case, the government not only has to provide secure transport links, but it also has to work with purchasing nations to obtain data on actual sales revenues. If reputable purchasing agents from countries with stringent anticorruption standards can be induced to set up shop within the country, the government can levy taxes at the point of purchase, turning to the purchasers rather than miners for revenues. Governments, especially those in countries emerging from conflict, have yet to find effective means of taxing these items, though keeping export tariffs low is important for discouraging smuggling through other countries.

In nations where control of the borders has been reestablished after a conflict, a fixed, low import duty can be a useful means of collecting revenues. Revenues can be sizable, costs of collection moderate, and economic distortions limited if rates remain in single digits. Import tariffs do not work well if control over the country's borders has not been reestablished; tariffs rates vary considerably; exemptions, including on donations, are common; or the country sets up special free-trade zones. In these instances, customs agents often seek bribes to move goods from one category to another. When tariffs are relatively high or borders difficult to patrol, as in Bosnia, criminal gangs smuggle, creating security as well as revenue problems for the government.

Income taxes on the total compensation of individuals, in paid salaries or wages, are useful as a means of both collecting revenue and limiting the attractiveness of government jobs. Wage-bracket creep in government is difficult to combat. By levying a progressive income tax on an individual's entire compensation package, a host-country government can recapture some of the above-market wages that are sometimes earned in the public sector in these countries.

Excise taxes on tobacco, alcohol, automobiles, and gasoline and other fuels are useful means of raising revenue. These products are often consumed in greater quantities by upper-income individuals. Taxes have the added benefit of discouraging the consumption of substances detrimental to one's health.

Value-added tax (VAT) is not the tax of choice in the immediate aftermath of a conflict. It has become popular in developed countries because of its self-enforcing features: VAT paid on production inputs is refundable when the final product is sold. However, VAT is complicated, difficult to levy on small businesses, and refunds are open to abuse. Sales taxes are often easier to collect, especially if levied on permanent establishments only or at the wholesale level. Trying to collect sales taxes from street merchants is costly and ineffective in any society; collection efforts also antagonize an important political constituency. When street vendors are the major purveyors of retail trade, as is usual following a conflict, levying sales taxes at the retail level is a nonstarter.

Once a set of taxes has been selected, the tax collection system needs to be revived. The revenue collection agency should be housed in the ministry of finance and the minister should oversee the agency. Tax collectors should not have prosecutorial authority, but should refer cases of noncompliance to special prosecutors. Tax disputes should be tried as civil matters. The creation of tax courts is sometimes a useful means for expediting cases and limiting corruption, but, in most postconflict situations, this detracts from developing the court system, an area that generally does not get enough support from donors. To the extent possible, collection should take place at the point of payment and at wholesale rather than retail levels. For example, gasoline taxes should be levied at the port of entry, if imported, or at the refinery gate. Wage taxes should be deducted prior to payment of wages. The more automatic the payment and the fewer hands through which payments pass, the better.

Deficit Finance. One of any intervening authority's major responsibilities is to ensure a balance between tax revenue and donor budget support, on the one hand, and budget obligations on the other. In cases of anticipated imbalance, the intervening authorities need to intervene to provide more support or to limit government spending.

In the immediate aftermath of a conflict, taxes are unlikely to generate sufficient revenues to finance government services at a level commensurate with the size of the population and likely future levels of income. Pushing hard to increase tax revenues at this stage is counterproductive, as economic activity is too low to cover the costs of government operations. But after a few years of economic growth, the government should be able to generate enough tax revenues to cover the costs of providing basic services. Until that point, the donor community should cover the deficit.

Donor funding of government deficits through loans or grants can be beneficial for fiscal discipline. Through the power of the purse, the donor community, especially the international financial institutions, can play a key role in keeping expenditures under control. IMF programs contain mutually agreed-upon performance targets, which usually include budgetary expenditures and deficits. When host governments face a credible threat of losing funding because they have fallen out of compliance, unpalatable decisions are made. For example, the interim Liberian government finally agreed to the formation of a financial control board with foreign representation, the Governance and Economic Assistance Program, only after facing a credible threat of a cutoff in funding.

Developing the Financial Sector. By the end of a conflict, banking systems have generally ceased to function. In the cases of Cambodia, East Timor, Haiti, Liberia, Mozambique, and Sierra Leone, the financial systems had all but disappeared by the time the countries emerged from conflict. Payment systems had disintegrated and those banks that were not closed were usually insolvent. Their deposits had been looted by insurgents or by the government. Their assets had disappeared as borrowers had gone bankrupt and collateral for loans had been stolen or destroyed.

Once the economy stabilizes, financial activities resume. Initially, the most important activity of banks is to make payments and provide a safe haven for depositing cash. The intervening authorities often play a major role in spurring the development of these activities, as they need to be able to transfer funds from abroad and make payments and grants inside the country. Deposit-taking, payments, transfers, and foreign exchange conversion are the principle activities of banks at this time. Eventually, banks begin to lend again, primarily for inventory and trade finance. This lending tends to be collateralized. Subsequently, banks move into consumer lending, often for household durables and motor vehicles. Corporate lending follows. Because of difficulties in assessing creditworthiness, banks are careful about extending loans to small businesses, though donors often provide funds for special programs targeting smaller businesses or supporting microfinance programs. Once financial markets have stabilized and inflation is firmly under control, mortgage finance and uncollateralized lending may become possible.

The financial sector should *not* receive substantial funding from the donor community to support lending following a conflict. Much of the development of the financial sector in a postconflict society is driven by market forces. Although stages overlap, the progression outlined in the previous paragraph should not be circumvented. With the exception of microlending, which has had some successes, experiments in accelerating the expansion of credit through the provision of subsidized loans or by encouraging banks to lend to less-than-creditworthy borrowers tend to end badly. Because the economy is in such flux and credit histories are so short, lending is especially hazardous in the immediate aftermath of a conflict. Financial institutions lack the information and safeguards necessary to lend sensibly and safely. At this juncture, household savings and retained earnings suffice to fund the development of the small-scale activities that characterize the initial recovery. The early rapid rates of economic growth tend to generate sufficient profits for entrepreneurs to finance initial investments.

The international community does have a role to play in creating an environment in which a domestic financial sector can grow and thrive. As the financial sector develops and lending resumes, the monetary authorities need to ensure that lending decisions do not hold problems for the future. The bankruptcy of major banks, threatening a collapse of the financial system, is a major cause of recession throughout the world. In transitional economies, banking problems ignored early on have led to banking crises and economic recessions four or five years after the initial recovery. Fortunately, banking assets tend to be small in the immediate aftermath of a conflict; setting up and implementing an effective system for supervising all financial institutions early on will forestall crises further down the road.

If the government and monetary authorities are to create conditions for the development of an efficient financial sector while avoiding major banking insolvencies, they need to create a transparent, easily understood set of laws and regulations governing financial transactions. They also need to create conditions for the rapid, fair settlement of disputes concerning transactions. International assistance agencies and the IMF have created templates for laws and regulations needed for the financial sector. These are relatively easy to adapt and adopt in postconflict nations.

As the legal and regulatory framework is being created, the monetary authorities need to hire and train inspectors and develop a rigorous program of bank inspections. Care needs to be taken to make banking regulations easy to understand and enforce. Because the economy is in such flux and well-trained bank examiners are in short supply, the monetary authorities cannot rely on supervision alone to detect credit problems in banks. Setting relatively high capital requirements for existing and new banks provides insurance against a lapse in supervision. Because they also face the prospect of losing substantial amounts of their own money, owners of heavily capitalized banks tend to be less willing to take unwarranted risks with depositors' money than are more lightly capitalized banks. Care needs to be taken to ensure that committed capital is actually injected into the banks by insisting that capital be on deposit at the central bank or at trusted international banks.

Although these measures are useful, the most successful policy for preventing future banking crises is to give well-capitalized foreign banks the opportunity to compete for the domestic market on the same basis as domestic banks. Well-capitalized foreign banks bring great advantages to the host country: They have already developed the credit evaluation, accounting, settlement, and payment systems needed to operate a modern bank efficiently and securely. Several, like Standard Chartered Bank, have past experience in postconflict societies, which they can bring to bear in other postconflict situations. The large capital bases of international banks greatly reduce the threat of insolvency. The country in which the foreign bank is headquartered also supervises and examines the operations of the bank, providing a level of oversight impossible for the nascent monetary authorities in postconflict countries.

The monetary authorities also need to create an efficient payment system. Security, speed, and accuracy are the most important characteristics of these systems. Electronic payment systems are the fastest, most secure systems for ensuring transfers. Donor funds are usually necessary for that part of the system utilized by the central bank and its branches. Commercial banks should finance their own connections. Rudimentary systems can be developed even in countries with poorly functioning electric power and telecommunication systems by using cell phones, laptops, and backup generators.

The monetary authorities also face the challenge of resuscitating or closing down insolvent banks inherited from the conflict. Until these banks are liquidated or recapitalized, the financial system will be weighed down by the bad loans on their balance sheets. The most effective policy for dealing with insolvent banks is to bring in outside audit teams that go through the bank, loan by loan, classifying them according to the likelihood of repayment. If a substantial number of loans is likely to be repaid, two new banks can be created out of the assets of the old: a solvent bank that is given the good assets and a corresponding deposit base and a "bad" bank into which the bad loans are dumped. Both banks are then recapitalized. The "good" bank operates as a normal commercial bank. The goal of the "bad" bank is to recover what it can and sell off its assets for whatever they are worth. Once it disposes of its assets, the bank is liquidated and the government receives whatever value remains. Because state-owned banks often play major roles in postconflict nations, funding and initiating the process of recapitalizing the banking sector is an important, if secondary, priority for donors and the host government. Because this process is long and complex, it is a task that does not need to be tackled immediately.

The government must also make decisions on the extent to which depositors are to be compensated. This is an especially sensitive issue in postconflict societies, as state-owned banks may be associated with one or another of the parties to the conflict. Deposits may include funds stolen during the conflict. Because the origin of large deposits is opaque, it is usually best to discriminate by the size of the deposit: The government (through assistance from the international community) pays small depositors in full while larger depositors receive only partial compensation. Because of the potential for fraud through the creation of "ghost" accounts, depositor compensation programs need to be monitored carefully, and, in some instances, they should be run by a trusted outside agency. Transactions also need to be audited.

Although these methods for dealing with insolvent banks have generally worked well, cleaning up in the aftermath of the collapse of a banking system is expensive, often running in the range of several percentage points of GDP. The host government should be intent on ensuring that the experience is not repeated by closely monitoring the emerging financial system and quickly taking action when a problem begins to emerge.

Creating an Environment Conducive to Economic Growth

Eliminating Price Controls. The removal of government controls on prices is key to creating an environment conducive to economic growth. Prices are the signals by which economic actors make decisions. When controls distort prices, this sends the wrong message to consumers and producers, resulting in wasted resources, slower growth, and pressure on the budget as the government foregoes potential tax revenues or provides subsidies. Below-market prices encourage overconsumption and smuggling, resulting in shortages. Price controls are often defended as a means of subsidizing purchases by poor households. They are an ineffective and expensive form of subsidization. They discriminate against the poor in favor of the rich: In most countries, upper-income households consume more subsidized products than do lower-income households.

During conflicts, most governments are unable to maintain price controls. They lack the funds to subsidize controlled-price goods and the ability to control borders to stop the smuggling of these products out of the country. After the conflict, the intervening authorities can help forestall the reimposition of controls by selling products other than humanitarian relief supplies at market prices and encouraging competing sources of supply. The intervening authorities can also work with the World Bank and other international donors to devise poverty-reduction strategies that address concerns about the affordability of food and fuels without resorting to price controls. For example, centers can be set up where poor families can request food assistance.

Government Regulation. In many parts of the world, regulations are frequently designed and used to seek bribes. The intervening authorities can help postconflict governments to revamp their regulatory systems so as to reduce opportunities for requesting bribes and to improve the efficacy of the system by adopting best-practice principles for writing and issuing regulations:

1. Focus first on introducing the procedures and regulations necessary to get the government up and running and to protect the lives of citizens. These include registration procedures for key potential taxpayers (larger companies and organizations and wage-earning citizens) and regulations on sanitation to prevent the spread of disease.
2. Create clear, transparent procedures for making rules. Insist on well-advertised public hearings during the process, even during the initial days after conflict. Stipulate that only rules listed in a national registry are valid and that only rules made according to stipulated procedures can be listed in the registry.
3. Designate an ombudsman to review regulations before they are issued to ensure that they are easy to understand and implement.
4. Separate inspections from enforcement. This forestalls the emergence of groups within the bureaucracy that prey on citizens and developing businesses. Make sure that inspectors are supervised closely and that their activities are subject to periodic review. As the government becomes more capable, establish administrative courts to review charges of violations of rules.

5.   Keep penalties commensurate with the size of the offense. Major violations should be penalized with more than a small fine; small infractions should not be penalized heavily. For example, importers who deliberately sell large volumes of contaminated food should be shut down, heavily fined, or, if the action was deliberate, face criminal charges. Small vendors that have failed to register should not pay substantial fines.

6.   Where possible, adopt existing regulations and standards issued by the United States or the European Union. Although neither set is perfect, regulations in these countries undergo a great deal of scrutiny and generally have an underpinning based on research, an activity that postconflict societies cannot afford. Products that have passed muster by either entity should not have to undergo additional testing or evaluation before being sold in the country.

Private-Sector Development. Over the last several decades, assistance agencies have funded a wide spectrum of programs designed to foster economic growth. In recent years, these programs have emphasized the private sector. Programs focus on transferring technologies in agriculture, manufacturing, communications, and other sectors, improving the operation of local markets, and fostering the development of financial institutions.

Because of the depressed state of the economy following a conflict, assistance agencies can contribute to jump-starting private-sector economic activity through the judicious selection of programs. However, the record of these programs has been mixed: Some have been effective in spurring economic growth in communities that have been devastated by conflict; others have not. In most postconflict situations, quality seeds and simple agricultural equipment may be in short supply. Programs to provide these inputs for free or at subsidized prices can help stimulate a recovery in agriculture. Well-run microcredit programs in postconflict environments can target groups that have been most severely affected, such as people living in conflict zones, demobilized combatants, or the physically or psychologically impaired. On the other hand, the donor community and the host government have to weigh programs carefully on the basis of complexity, timing, cost, and likely effectiveness. In 2004, the U.S. government provided assistance to restart the Baghdad stock market. Although trading now takes place, the stock market plays little role in fostering domestic economic activity and investment. In light of all the other challenges in Iraq, this money was ill spent.

A key principle in choosing among programs to fund is not to try to do too much. The capacity of the intervening authorities, the donor community, and the host country to manage projects is even more limited in the chaos following a conflict than under normal circumstances. Everything demands attention. Private-sector development programs that entail substantial involvement by officials need to be assessed carefully in terms of value added. Projects that need to be scaled up to have widespread impact, that involve substantial engagement by foreign staff, or that do not generate an immediate economic payoff are to be avoided. Even if such programs promise long-term benefits, they should be delayed until other problems are less pressing and the capacity of the host-country bureaucracy to implement them has improved. This said, donors do need to be attentive to perceptions of equity. All groups that were party to the conflict should receive some benefits, though in terms of effectiveness and equity, programs should be targeted at those groups that are worse off.

Operating, Reconstructing, and Investing in Utilities, State-Owned Enterprises, and Infrastructure

Utilities. Once the lights have been turned on and water has begun to flow in those areas where service had been available prior to the conflict, the host government and international community must turn to creating an institutional and commercial environment for the efficient provision of utilities. The equitable, efficient provision of utilities can be an important stimulus for growth and quality of life.[5] However, where governments attempt to provide utilities at tariffs that fail to cover costs, using the argument that buyers cannot afford to pay

---

[5] World Bank, *World Development Report 2006: Equity and Development*, Washington, D.C. and New York: World Bank and Oxford University Press, September 2005, p. 168.

higher tariffs, systems tend to be stunted, they cover a small area of the country, and they are prone to frequent breakdowns in delivering services. If revenues fail to cover costs, the budget must pick up the difference, reducing resources available for other government services such as health care and education.

Utilities need to be able to generate enough revenue to cover costs, and utility managers need incentives to improve efficiency and operations. Utilities that operate inefficiently impose high economic costs. Businesses, households, and hospitals invest in expensive alternative sources of power and water or suffer the consequences of sudden outages that may result in the destruction of expensive machinery, the spoilage of products that need refrigeration, or, in the case of hospitals, the loss of life. When sewage systems back up due to the failure of pumps, drinking water is polluted, contributing to the spread of disease. Because loss-making utilities lack funds for expansion, service is confined to existing customers, many, if not most, of whom are richer than the average citizen. Poorer households are forced to turn to expensive, less efficient alternatives, such as purchasing clean water from trucks or power from privately operated diesel generators, often at a cost several times what households and businesses with access to well-run systems pay.[6]

To operate utilities in a manner that fosters growth and improves human welfare, the host government, with the assistance of the intervening authorities, should create managerial and corporate incentives to expand output and minimize costs, to introduce competition wherever possible, and to create an environment in which utilities are self-financing. These are all difficult tasks, but they are well worth pursuing. They are also politically demanding, as government officials see state-run utilities as sources of jobs for supporters or as a means of subsidizing voters.

---

[6]   Mukami Kariuki and Jordan Schwartz, "Small-Scale Private Service Providers of Water Supply and Electricity: A Review of Incidence, Structure, Pricing and Operating Characteristics," World Bank Policy Working Paper 3727, Washington, D.C.: World Bank, October 2005.

The first task following the initial restoration of service is the reconstitution or creation of personnel systems and the restoration or introduction of physical and financial control systems. Once these systems are up and operating, managers are able to hire and pay employees and regulate the flow of electric power, water, telephone traffic, and other such services. They can also track the number and duties of employees, payroll numbers, and other costs. The utility also needs to review job descriptions, creating a list of tasks and jobs by department. The list should not be drawn up by the departments, but should be assembled by a task force answerable to the director of the utility and supervised by the donor community. This list will become the basis for controlling employment, a crucial management step in many countries.

Subsequently, the host government, in conjunction with the utility's management and the assistance of the donor community and outside consultants, should carefully reorganize the utility to create cost and profit centers focused on operations. For example, in the electric power sector, generating plants, the transmission system and the distribution networks should become separate cost or profit centers. As part of this process, costs will have to be calculated and allocated so as to create an effective system of internal pricing so that each unit faces meaningful price signals. In the process of reorganization, the utility should be incorporated, if it is not already, and a transparent system for appointing a board of directors set up. It is advisable to appoint outside directors recommended by international financial institutions, including foreign nationals, so as to benefit from their expertise and provide an additional means of monitoring the utility's management. Reorganization should be accompanied by the creation of bonus and promotion schemes for managers, tied to increasing profits or reducing costs in their centers. Where possible, the utility should contract out ancillary and support functions, contributing to the development of private sector suppliers of these services.

As soon as service begins to be restored, management needs to turn to billing and collecting for services. Utility services are consumed just like vegetables or shoes. If consumers do not pay for the service, the utility cannot provide it. The costs of failing to put utilities in a commercial status are high, as demonstrated by the case of Kosovo. The Kosovar electric power company is perennially short of funds to purchase fuel, maintain facilities, and invest in new plants because it is overstaffed and poorly managed, and it does not collect payments. Not surprisingly, electricity service is subject to frequent blackouts and the Kosovar economy suffers as a consequence. In contrast, early attention to payment systems and procurement practices have helped spur the development of electric power in East Timor.[7]

Best-practice policies for collecting payments include devolving the responsibility to local distribution companies. These can be run by the utility itself, private companies, municipalities, or cooperatives. In all instances, the utility needs to have the ability, legal and physical, to cut off service to the distribution company and its customers if payments are not made so as to enforce payment discipline. Devolving collection to local companies makes it easier to use social pressure and suasion as well as commercial measures to enforce payment discipline. When a neighborhood is cut off because one neighbor steals power, social pressures help force compliance.

How can utilities be made affordable for the poorest in postconflict societies? In the immediate aftermath of a conflict, collection can be introduced gradually, community by community, beginning with wealthier neighborhoods. If donors believe that it is a useful expenditure of funds, donors can cover part of the bills for lower-income people. For many utilities (for example, electric power, water, sewage) up-front costs of connection can be high, preventing poorer consumers from connecting to the system. Amortizing connection costs over a few years or spreading connection costs across the existing subscriber base can help defray these costs. In some cases, the donor community or host government may wish to cover part of the costs of connection for poorer families. Lifeline rate structures also help by keeping prices low for the first kilowatt-hours or units of water consumed and then increasing tariff rates as consumption rises. Rewarding managers

---

[7] Klaus Rohland and Sarah Cliffe, "The East Timor Reconstruction Program: Successes, Problems, and Tradeoffs," CPR Working Paper No. 2, Washington, D.C.: World Bank, November 2002.

for economizing can be an efficient means of preventing costs from escalating.

Following a conflict, regulatory issues such as connection charges and rate setting are often handled on an ad hoc basis: Interim decisions are made by the government or the intervening authorities. As utility operations stabilize, the host country should set up a regulatory agency responsible for network industries, such as telecommunications, and for natural monopolies. In countries with few people with experience in regulation, it is often more sensible to set up one agency with a few well-paid, skilled administrators than separate agencies for each sector, capitalizing on available talent and experience. This approach also serves to keep regulatory approaches similar across industries, making implementation and enforcement of regulations easier.

A useful measure to encourage full recognition of capital costs in setting rates is to transfer some government debt, commensurate with the value of the utility's assets, to the utility's balance sheet. The transfer reflects the cost of past investments, often financed by government borrowing. By imposing loan obligations on the utility, this measure forces the government, regulators, and the utility to recognize capital costs in the rate structure. The shift also reduces the debt burden of the government and attaches a potential stream of revenue from the sale of electricity or water to be used to finance this debt.

As service expands, the host government, the utilities, and the donor community should employ World Bank and UNDP methodologies to conduct more detailed needs assessments for the provision of their services than was possible immediately following the conflict.[8] These needs assessments provide a basis for planning for investments in capacity improvements and additions and for making trade-offs between the sector and other investments in the economy. Once the needs assessment has been completed, the utility, in conjunction with the planning ministry, the donor community, and leaders of the most important political factions, should begin to design an investment plan. The staff of the utility should be in charge of the plan, but it is important to include representatives of major political groups as well so

---

[8]   Kievelitz et al. (2004).

that all parties are reassured that they will receive access to service in a reasonable amount of time. Planning committees that include donor representation should improve the capacity of the utility and the government to plan investments more effectively. Over time, the government should withdraw from directly participating in investment planning; this responsibility should devolve to the utility managers. If the utility remains in state hands, state control should be exercised through a board of directors despite the likely opposition of government leaders. Making donor funds contingent on establishing independent utilities is a useful means of separating utilities from political pressures.

Once investments have been selected, they should be funded through project finance. Project finance imposes discipline absent from projects funded with grant aid. It forces all parties to address issues related to the appropriate size of the facility, operating and capital costs, and repayment, which in turn lead to concrete projections of solvent demand and the resolution of issues concerning rate setting, collections, and taxation of utility services. By conducting careful financial analysis and insisting on loan or equity finance, project finance pushes utility managers to evaluate trade-offs between investing in additional production capacity, distribution systems, or solutions other than capacity additions such as reducing losses or turning to alternative sources of supply. For example, brownouts and blackouts are generally perceived as reflecting too little generating capacity. Although investment in additional physical capacity is often important, improvements in operating procedures, such as reducing line losses, forestalling theft of power, introducing time-of-day pricing for major industrial consumers, or increasing tariffs, may do more to reduce power disruptions than would installing new generating capacity. Project lending also helps reduce corruption, as lenders can insist on international financial contracting procedures and payments from revenues.

In contrast, grant aid is a pernicious use of funds for investing in utilities. It fails to impose discipline for evaluating trade-offs in terms of size, timing, repayment, or other alternatives. Because the utility does not pay for the cost of the capital it is using, the value of capital is often not fully incorporated into the tariff structure, distorting current and future investment and operating decisions. In Iraq, for example, the grantor, in this case the United States, has not used best-practice contracting procedures for distributing funds, contributing to corruption.[9]

State-Owned Enterprises. Some postconflict societies inherit state-owned enterprises and other assets—for example, a flour mill and the port authority in Haiti and a refined oil product distribution company in Liberia. Because state-owned enterprises are often in key sectors, they can severely hamper economic growth if poorly managed. The high cost of transit for goods through Haiti's ports has made assembly operations economically infeasible, stunting manufacturing. In most instances, the society would be better off if such state-owned enterprises were sold to the private sector. But privatization of large companies is a complicated, lengthy process, difficult in any country, and it is nigh impossible in the aftermath of conflict. As long as these enterprises remain in state hands, the host government needs to manage them well. To do so, the intervening authorities and the host government need to adopt the following practices:

1. Restart operations of those enterprises that produce marketable goods and services as soon as possible. Typically, this entails finding and rehiring staff, repairing equipment, and providing financial resources so that wages can be paid and supplies and parts purchased. Billing and collection must begin as soon as possible so that the enterprise starts generating its own revenues.

2. Remove barriers to entry for firms that compete with state-owned enterprises. If the private sector can produce a good or service more efficiently and cheaply, it should be at liberty to do so. Subsidizing the operation of state-owned enterprises penalizes private-sector entrepreneurs and wastes scarce resources.

3. Devolve management responsibility and authority to the director of the state-owned enterprise. If the enterprise is expected to compete against the private sector, its managers must have simi-

---

[9] Inspector General for Iraq Reconstruction, *Iraq Reconstruction: Lessons Learned in Contracting and Procurement*, Washington, D.C.: U.S. Government Printing Office, July 2006.

lar authority and responsibility while facing the same market discipline. Managers of state-owned enterprises cannot work effectively if they are second-guessed and overruled by ministers or other government officials. Managers should be rewarded on the basis of profitability.

4. Managers should be subject to strict financial controls. The intervening authorities should insist on creating accurate accounting systems for state-owned enterprises.

5. Contract with outside auditors and financial analysts to assess the viability of the state-owned enterprises. Those enterprises deemed unviable should be placed on a list for eventual liquidation or sale.

6. Privatization is politically sensitive, especially the sale of larger enterprises. The host-country government should take the lead on privatization. If the host-country government possesses large holdings of farmland or owns small businesses, the intervening authorities should work with the host country to devise a system of land grants or auctions to give or sell these assets to private individuals on an equitable basis. If political opposition to privatizing larger enterprises is strong, the intervening authorities should focus their efforts on improving the operations of the state-owned enterprises, not on privatizing them.

Infrastructure. Infrastructure includes transportation systems, public buildings, and facilities for the provision of public services. The term is also frequently used to describe investments in utilities. Because utilities generate services that are more easily marketable than roads, for example, we have chosen to confine our discussion of infrastructure here to roads, public buildings, and other investments needed to provide public services.

In the aftermath of a conflict, infrastructure has usually been severely damaged or destroyed. Not all of these structures need to be rebuilt immediately, and some not at all. Rather, after a first round of reconstructing schools, restoring the operation of key ports, and fixing major roads, the intervening authorities and the host government should conduct a more thorough needs assessment of roads and public services, then put together a capital budget, rank-ordering the most important projects by region and sector. Political considerations should play a role in developing this list. A road project in a region that has suffered from conflict may look less economically attractive than a project in a more prosperous region that avoided the conflict. However, constructing the road is likely to play a key role in accelerating economic growth in the region of conflict and restoring commercial and personal connections to the rest of the country, thereby cementing the peace.

Infrastructure is expensive to construct; once constructed, it is too often poorly maintained. International donors should work with the government to assign responsibilities to ministries or agencies, such as a road administration, for the construction and maintenance of infrastructure. These entities should not employ their own workforces, but should contract out design, repair, and construction work to private contractors. In many cases, the entities may choose to make local communities responsible for maintaining their own roads, schools, and clinics. In these instances, the government should help local communities raise funds or transfer funds from the national budget to cover these costs. Road and other administrations also need to develop the capability to conduct physical audits (which can also be contracted to third parties) to ensure that payments are made only for work that has been satisfactorily completed.

Constructing and repairing roads, schools, and clinics are highly useful donor-funded activities in postconflict societies. Roads connect isolated regions to the rest of the country, linking communities to national markets. They improve security by making remote communities more accessible to security forces, thus depriving spoilers of safe havens. Schools and clinics are preconditions for providing important public services. When construction projects are contracted and built locally, they pump money into local economies, generating incomes outside the major cities. Local involvement teaches contracting, project management, and construction skills. Local projects increase demand for local construction materials such as gravel, bricks, and timber. Transparent, honest contracting procedures signal that the new government has changed for the better, limiting corrupt practices.

Although investment in additional physical capacity is often important, improvements in operating procedures can be just as or even more beneficial. For example, ports and border crossings often create bottlenecks. By streamlining procedures or moving to a 24-hour-a-day operating schedule, the government may do more to speed transit times than it would through the construction of facilities or routes.

Despite the importance of providing utilities and the symbolism of constructing major projects or public works, rarely does it make sense to invest in major infrastructure or utility projects in regions where conflict continues. As shown by the experience in Iraq, construction costs during periods of conflict may run several times those in peacetime because of the additional security costs and delays and the destruction of newly built installations. High-profile projects become magnets for spoilers: The destruction of a newly built bridge can have a deeper psychological impact than its completion. In such situations, funds are better spent on restoring security and planning projects than initiating project work. Exceptions to this admonition include infrastructure needed to transport key commodities to major markets, such as railroads or ports, or installations that can be easily repaired after sabotage, such as crude-oil pipelines.

Immediately following the conflict, donors can usefully jump-start housing reconstruction by ensuring the provision of building materials, sometimes gratis or below cost. However, in the second stage of the conflict, donors should refrain from directly funding housing construction. Housing is a significant capital investment everywhere in the world—usually the largest single investment made by individuals. Because of its cost, donors lack the resources to make a substantial contribution to this sector. What monies are granted are likely to be skewed toward a small group of individuals, eliciting envy from others. Moreover, local communities have the capacity to provide for much of their own housing, making donor funds more valuable elsewhere.

Improved housing is a longer-term development goal that is of lower priority than providing utilities or infrastructure. Assistance in this area should be targeted at reducing transaction costs and creating institutions that establish a long-term basis for financing and purchasing housing. Granting titles to plots of land and buildings through the establishment of a single property register; simple, fair, and cheap procedures for claiming title; and simple adjudication procedures have long been emphasized as important steps to creating property and capital markets in developing countries. The same applies to postconflict societies. Separate administrative courts with elected judges can be utilized to adjudicate property disputes, including those that emerge because of the conflict, and to create the basis for accountable judges and greater trust in the law.

Donors should not provide subsidized lending for housing or jump-start housing finance. Because housing finance by necessity needs to be long-term, until inflation rates and nominal interest rates decline and the economy becomes more stable, mortgage finance remains a nonstarter. Attempting to circumvent financial development through subsidies or specialized mortgage programs is a waste of time and money.

Outcomes

As shown in Figure 9.1, most postconflict societies have succeeded in moving from an initial period of rapid recovery to extended periods of sustained and, in some cases, accelerated economic growth. Bosnia, Germany, and Sierra Leone averaged double-digit growth rates in the first five years after the end of their respective conflicts. Growth in Cambodia and Mozambique has also been rapid and accelerated in their respective second five-year postconflict periods.

Other postconflict societies have not done as well. Growth in Congo and Haiti was disappointing, but it can be explained in great part by the failure of both countries to establish security or follow sensible economic policies. The rates for East Timor and Kosovo have been restrained by a rapid decline in levels of assistance. The two entities received the highest levels of assistance as a share of GDP among our group of postconflict interventions. In Kosovo, assistance ran 70 percent of GDP in the second year following the conflict; it fell to 26 percent four years later. In East Timor, assistance fell from 86 percent

Figure 9.1
Economic Growth Following Conflict

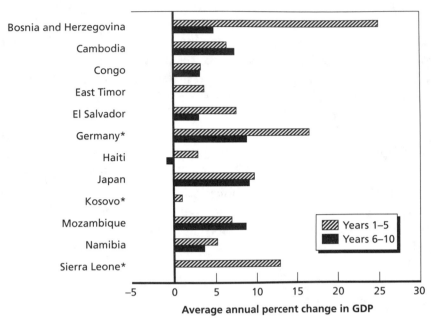

SOURCE: International Monetary Fund, International Financial Statistics Browser; Mitchell (1992, 1998); International Monetary Fund (2005b, p. 31); Demekas, Herderschee, and Jacobs (2002, p. 6); Moalla-Fetini et al. (2005, p. 81); International Monetary Fund (2000, p. 118); International Monetary Fund, "Bosnia and Herzegovina: First Review Under the Stand-By Agreement and Request for Waiver of Performance Criteria," IMF Country Report No. 03/4, Washington, D.C., January 2003, p. 29; International Monetary Fund (2005a, p. 34).

NOTE: An asterisk (*) denotes that data are for the second year after the intervention (Germany, 1947; Kosovo, 2001; and Sierra Leone, 2001) because of lack of data or because the immediate aftereffects of the conflict resulted in continued declines in output during the first year.

RAND *MG557-9.1*

of GDP in the first year following the conflict to 57 percent two years later. While non–assistance-related economic activity enjoyed healthy growth in both countries, the drawdown in assistance spending and associated economic activity kept aggregate growth rates lower than in other postconflict countries.

As noted in Chapter Seven, the rate of growth in the first year following a conflict is highly correlated with the cumulative decline in output during the conflict.[10] To some extent, this carries through during the first years following the conflict, but this initial condition becomes less important over time. In the longer run, differences in rates of economic growth in postconflict societies are driven by better policies and institutions, not by initial conditions.[11]

Key Actors

As in the initial period of stabilization, the IMF should take the lead in working with the monetary authorities of the host country to create a well-functioning monetary policy framework and a healthy financial system. The World Bank, in conjunction with the IMF, should take the lead in establishing budgeting, financial information, and auditing systems.

Donor committees with host-country participation should continue to coordinate assistance during this stage. Such committees should be chaired by the individual in charge of the intervening authorities or by a designated alternate until the mission ends, at which time a representative of the World Bank or one of the regional development banks should become the chair.

The World Bank or a regional development bank should take the lead in assisting the host government in setting up personnel, contracting, and procurement systems. For assistance with individual ministries such as health, education, or justice, the World Bank may wish to devolve responsibility to one of the national assistance programs. How-

---

[10] The correlation is −0.69.

[11] See, for example, World Bank, *World Development Report 2002: Building Institutions for Markets*, Washington, D.C., and New York: World Bank and Oxford University Press, September 2001b; World Bank, *World Development Report 2005: A Better Investment Climate for Everyone*, Washington, D.C., and New York: World Bank and Oxford University Press, September 2004; Craig Burnside and David Dollar, "Aid, Policies, and Growth," *American Economic Review*, Vol. 90, No. 4, September 2000, pp. 847–868 [p. 964]; Paul Collier and David Dollar, "Aid Allocation and Poverty," Policy Research Working Paper No. 2041, Washington, D.C.: World Bank, draft of October 20, 1998; and Paul Collier and Anke Hoeffler, "Aid, Policy, and Growth in Post-Conflict Societies," Policy Research Working Paper No. 2902, Washington, D.C.: World Bank, October 2002.

ever, financial and personnel systems need to be standardized across ministries. The World Bank has experience in assisting in contracting with countries of widely varying capabilities and is adept at tailoring procedures to those of host governments, even in postconflict situations. The host country should adopt the procurement manuals, regulations and rules, and draft contracts from the World Bank.[12] It should also request technical assistance from the World Bank in setting up and implementing these contracting procedures and in granting major contracts.

Host governments should be encouraged to permit a variety of suppliers for services, especially utilities. Where possible, private-sector provision and competition should be encouraged for utilities. Local governments, NGOs, businesses, and cooperatives can all play roles in providing education, training, and health care.

The World Bank should take the lead in working with the ministries involved in planning for the construction of infrastructure. The host government with the assistance of the World Bank should be responsible for reporting on plans at donor committee meetings.

Costs

In this section, we establish rough guidelines for determining appropriate levels of effective assistance for economic development, budget support, and investment in utilities and infrastructure in countries during the first several years following a conflict. We first address the question of what overall levels of assistance postconflict societies can usefully absorb and when. We then turn to a more detailed assessment of reasonable levels of assistance for budgetary support, infrastructure, and utilities and the forms in which it is most efficacious to provide this assistance.

Overall Levels of Assistance. Figure 9.2 shows the average share of foreign assistance in terms of GDP during the first nine years following

---

[12] World Bank, *Bank-Financed Procurement Model*, Washington, D.C., draft of July 2001a.

Figure 9.2
Shares of Foreign Assistance as a Percent of GDP in Postconflict Societies

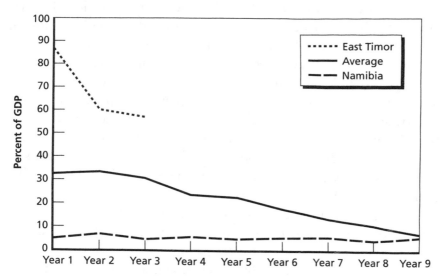

NOTE: Economies included in the averages for the first two years include
Afghanistan, Bosnia and Herzegovina, Cambodia, Congo, East Timor, El Salvador,
Haiti, Iraq, Kosovo, Mozambique, Namibia, and Sierra Leone. Because several of
these conflicts were of recent vintage, the number of countries in the sample
declines in the out years.
RAND *MG557-9.2*

a conflict for 12 postconflict societies. The average level of foreign
assistance for the group in the first three years following the conflict
was about 30 percent of GDP, after which it gradually declined to
13 percent in the seventh year. The figure also shows the country that
received the highest share of assistance (East Timor) and the country
with the lowest (Namibia). At least initially, levels of assistance vary
dramatically: Assistance to East Timor in the first year following the
conflict ran 86 percent of its much-reduced GDP; for Kosovo, this
figure was 70 percent. In contrast, assistance to Namibia and El Salvador fluctuated between 2 percent and 7 percent of GDP throughout
the postconflict period.

These figures show what the international community has chosen to provide, not what these postconflict societies could have usefully absorbed. Paul Collier and Anke Hoeffler (2002) tackle this latter question. They conclude that, following a conflict, the international community can provide effective assistance equivalent to upwards of 40 percent of GDP, measured at market exchange rates to countries, or roughly double the share of assistance in GDP that other developing countries can absorb without experiencing sharp declines in the effectiveness of additional assistance.[13] Collier and Hoeffler also find that the efficacy of assistance varies over time. They argue that assistance has its greatest impact on growth between the fourth and seventh years following the conflict, after which it declines. During that period, the country has developed to a point at which it can effectively absorb larger quantities of assistance. After seven years, private investment takes over as the driver of growth and aid has a relatively smaller impact.

Reviewing past patterns of assistance and drawing on Collier and Hoeffler's work, we have developed the following guidelines for determining an effective level of assistance after a conflict. As a general rule, we advocate providing assistance in the amount of one-third to two-fifths of GDP in the first three years following a conflict, levels that have been fairly common in better-funded interventions but that reflect higher-than-average assistance levels. For very low-income countries or those badly devastated by conflict, we advocate increasing this share to 70 percent for the first year after a conflict. We then advocate a gradual reduction in the share of assistance to 20 percent of GDP by the seventh year following the conflict. The decline in assistance levels as a share of GDP does not necessarily imply an immediate decline in absolute levels of aid. The primary reason for the declines in assistance as a share of GDP shown in Figure 9.2 is growth in the denominator, GDP. In many postconflict societies, GDP grows very quickly in the first years following a conflict. Consequently, even if donors sustain or increase the dollar amount of assistance, assistance as a share of GDP falls.

---

[13] Collier and Hoeffler (2002, p. 7).

In Table 9.1, we compare actual assistance levels to what this pattern of assistance would have looked like if applied to Namibia and Mozambique. We use two sets of parameters. For Namibia, a lower-middle–income developing country, we posit assistance equal to 33 percent of GDP for the first three years after the conflict and then gradually reduce it to 20 percent. For Mozambique, one of the world's poorest countries, we use a rate equal to 70 percent of GDP in the first year following the conflict. We then gradually reduce the share of assistance as a share of GDP to 20 percent by the seventh year following the

Table 9.1
Comparison of Actual and Suggested Levels of Assistance in Namibia and Mozambique

Country	Year 1	Year 2	Year 3	Year 5	Year 7
Namibia					
Actual assistance ($ millions)	154.6	224.3	172.7	159.2	208.5
Posited assistance ($ millions)	1,028.6	1,048.6	1,165.2	910.2	774.5
Actual assistance as a share of GDP (%)	5.0	7.1	4.9	4.6	5.4
Posited assistance as a share of GDP (%)	33.0	33.0	33.0	26.5	20.0
Mozambique					
Actual assistance ($ millions)	1,388.6	1,384.0	1,202.6	1,034.4	856.1
Posited assistance ($ millions)	2,181.9	1,636.5	1,165.2	1,133.5	1,277.9
Actual assistance as a share of GDP (%)	32.7	36.9	30.3	40.7	27.2
Posited assistance as a share of GDP (%)	70.0	51.5	33.0	33.0	33.0

SOURCE: Foreign aid data, World Bank, World Development Indicators Database; GDP data, International Monetary Fund, International Financial Statistics Browser; other indicators, RAND calculations.

NOTE: All dollar amounts are in constant 2002 U.S. dollars. Amounts may not sum due to rounding.

conflict. As can be seen, assistance flows would have been substantially greater for both Namibia and Mozambique under these assumptions.

What would the additional assistance have achieved? In a recent paper, Clemens, Radelet, and Bhavnani evaluate the effectiveness of budget and balance-of-payments support, investments in utilities and infrastructure, and aid to productive sectors such as agriculture or industry in spurring growth.[14] They find that, on average in developing countries, an additional percentage point of assistance as a share of GDP results in an additional 0.31 percentage points of annual growth in GDP.[15] Applying this parameter to the assistance levels posited in the table, by the seventh year after the conflict, GDP would have been 40 percent higher in Namibia and 17 percent higher in Mozambique if higher levels of assistance had been provided. Like Collier and Hoeffler, Clemens, Radelet, and Bhavnani find that, at a certain point, the effectiveness of additional assistance declines, eventually capping the amount of assistance that can be utilized effectively.

Utilities and Infrastructure. Building utilities and infrastructure is expensive. In the case of utilities, the user must be connected to the network to obtain service. Consequently, the network has to be constructed up front; returns come as services are provided over time and more users are connected. Constructing and improving ports, railroads, and public buildings also entail significant investment.

In developing countries, the cost of making these investments in infrastructure and utilities may add up to several percentage points of GDP. For example, in 2004, China with its booming economy and underdeveloped infrastructure invested 4.2 percent of its GDP in utilities and an additional 5.6 percent in transportation, primarily infrastructure, for a total of 9.8 percent of GDP.[16] In developed countries, where utilities and infrastructure have already been constructed, public investment is correspondingly lower. The United States invested only

---

[14] Michael A. Clemens, Steven Radelet, and Rikhil Bhavnani, "Counting Chickens When They Hatch: The Short-Term Effect of Aid on Growth," Working Paper No. 44, Washington, D.C.: Center for Global Growth, December 2, 2004.

[15] Clemens, Radelet, and Bhavnani (2004, p. 40).

[16] *China Statistical Yearbook 2005*, China Statistics Press, 2005, pp. 52, 187.

0.6 percent of its GDP in electric power and telecommunications in 1997; investment in public infrastructure ran 2.5 percent of GDP, for a total of 3.1 percent.[17]

More than with other types of assistance, investments in utilities and infrastructure take time to ramp up. Projects need to be designed and sized carefully so that they provide sufficient capacity to meet future needs but do not waste investment funds because they are too large. Sites have to be selected and prepared, buildings constructed, and equipment ordered and installed. Once constructed, the project has to be linked with existing systems. All this takes time. In an evaluation of 19 major investment projects, the World Bank found that, on average, 14 percent of total project costs were expended in the first year of disbursement, rising to 22 percent in the second year and 23 percent in the third (see Figure 9.3). The bank's analysis underlines the difficulties of spending massive amounts of money on infrastructure projects quickly and effectively. The sorry record of U.S. reconstruction expenditures in Iraq corroborates the bank's lessons.[18]

What do these lessons imply for appropriate levels of investment in utilities and infrastructure following a conflict? In the first year following a conflict, the host country and the international community should focus on restarting and repairing existing systems and setting up proper maintenance and management procedures for their current and future operation. At this juncture, programs focusing on the repair of roads, both national and local, are a good expenditure of funds. Importing and stockpiling critical components and establishing efficient maintenance procedures for electric power and water systems are also key tasks. Although these activities cost money, they are not as expensive as new infrastructure projects.

The host country and the donor community also need to begin planning and designing the renovation or construction of facilities

---

[17] Bureau of Economic Analysis, National Economic Accounts, National Income and Product Account Tables: Section 5, Saving and Investment, Tables 5.3.5.A and 5.8.5.A. (Detailed data were for 1996 and 1997 only.)

[18] Inspector General for Iraq Reconstruction (2006).

Figure 9.3
Disbursement Patterns of World Bank Loans

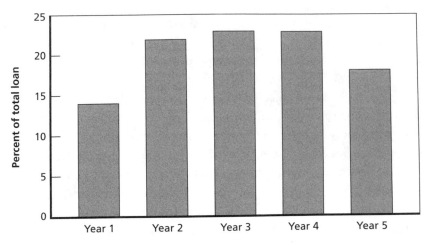

SOURCE: United Nations Development Group and World Bank, *United Nations/World Bank Joint Iraq Needs Assessment*, Washington, D.C., October 2003, pp. 56–57.
RAND *MG557-9.3*

and other infrastructure. These activities are less expensive, but they are as important as construction. Poorly designed projects can hinder development: They may saddle a country with electric power and water systems subject to frequent breakdowns, result in perennially congested road networks, or impose debts that cannot easily be repaid.

As project designs and assessments are completed, construction can be gradually ramped up in the third and fourth years following the conflict. Initially, most postconflict states encounter bottlenecks in terms of moving material and equipment and organizing construction. For example, Afghanistan has had difficulty in absorbing reconstruction assistance. In 2004–2005, the donor community offered assistance equal to 13 percent of Afghanistan's GDP; total disbursements were only 2.9 percent of GDP.[19] To prevent construction delays and keep costs under control, the host government, especially the ministry in charge of planning and development, and international donor community need to carefully coordinate projects so as not to generate

---

[19] International Monetary Fund (2005d, p. 22).

backlogs at ports and key transportation nodes. As the country's capacity to absorb investment rises, it will be able to absorb larger inflows of foreign assistance for infrastructure development.

This assistance should come in the form of loans or equity investment, not grant aid. If projects are well designed, the social and economic rates of return on these investments are likely to be high, especially in postconflict societies in which much of the capital stock has been destroyed or neglected. For example, the payback period on investments in mobile telephone service in Somalia has been as rapid as three years.[20] Grant aid is better spent in covering operating expenditures of the government than in financing the provision of utilities.

Despite our emphasis on project finance for utilities and infrastructure projects, the donor community still has a key role in facilitating loans or equity investment. Postconflict economies are risky: The probability of political turmoil or a return to conflict is high; the government has little ability to raise revenues; and the nascent private sector lacks the experience, management capacity, and capital to plan, build, and finance significant projects. The donor community can play a useful role in financing the construction and operation of utilities and infrastructure by providing guarantees or loans from official loan programs or from international financial institutions.

Although loans from the international community are useful, a focus on providing subsidized loans ignores the larger and, in our view, more important task of reducing the level of risk for all investors, private and government, in the postconflict society. First and foremost, this entails ensuring the security of people and property in both the immediate postconflict period and, through the development of an effective system of justice, the ensuing years. Second, the donor community needs to work with the host-country government to create institutions and laws that reduce regulatory risk and the threat of corruption. This is a hard task; no society has mastered it in full. However, some best practices have been identified. Focusing assistance and, just

---

[20] John Bray, "International Companies and Post-Conflict Reconstruction," Conflict Prevention and Reconstruction, Social Development Paper No. 22, Washington, D.C.: World Bank, February 2005, p. 12.

as importantly, donor attention on the development of these institutions and practices is far more important than donating funds for the construction of a new hospital or university.

Because it is one of the best-funded and better-documented cases, we have used Bosnia as a model again for suggested levels of assistance for infrastructure. Figure 9.4 shows total investment and reconstruction aid as a share of GDP in Bosnia between 1995, the last year of the conflict, and 2005. As shown in the figure, reconstruction aid played a very important role early on in boosting investment from 20 percent to over 40 percent of GDP. It accounted for three-fourths of total investment in 1996, the first postconflict year. Reconstruction aid became progressively less important both in dollar terms and as a share of Bosnian GDP during the subsequent decade. We note that Bosnia's figures for gross investment as a share of GDP in the fourth and later years following the conflict are somewhat low compared to other developing

Figure 9.4
Gross Investment and Reconstruction Aid as a Share of Bosnia's GDP

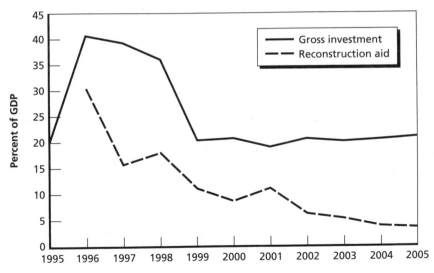

SOURCE: International Monetary Fund (2000, p. 139; 2005a, p. 39).

countries.[21] Many rapidly growing developing countries invest close to 30 percent of GDP. However, the figures are similar to or higher than those in other postconflict societies such as Cambodia, Mozambique, Namibia, and Sierra Leone.

In Table 9.2, we again apply these patterns of investment and reconstruction assistance to Namibia and Sierra Leone to illustrate appropriate levels of reconstruction aid to these two countries. Using the investment and assistance path illustrated in Figure 9.4 as a guide, reconstruction aid would cover most investment in the first year following the conflict, then fluctuate between 40 percent and 50 percent for the next five years, falling to about a quarter of the total in the seventh year. As the economy grows and commercial sources of capital become more available, financing shifts from assistance to domestic and commercial sources of finance.

---

[21] However, the IMF suspects that the Bosnian numbers are underestimated (International Monetary Fund, "Bosnia and Herzegovina: Selected Economic Issues," IMF Country Report No. 04/54, Washington, D.C., March 2004, p. 12).

Table 9.2
Estimated Gross Fixed Capital Investment and Reconstruction Assistance in Namibia and Sierra Leone

Country	Year 1	Year 2	Year 3	Year 4	Year 5
Namibia					
GDP ($ millions)	3,117.1	3,177.6	3,530.8	3,215.1	3,434.9
Gross fixed capital investment as a share of GDP (%)	40.3	39.2	36.0	20.0	20.6
Gross fixed capital investment ($ millions)	1,257.7	1,244.5	1,270.2	643.0	707.6
Reconstruction aid as a share of GDP (%)	30.2	15.6	17.7	10.9	8.4
Recommended reconstruction aid ($ millions)	941.6	496.6	623.4	351.6	287.3
Sierra Leone					
GDP ($ millions)	661.9	819.0	936.0	971.9	1,030.8
Gross fixed capital investment as a share of GDP (%)	40.3	39.2	36.0	20.0	20.6
Gross fixed capital investment ($ millions)	267.1	320.8	336.7	194.4	212.3
Reconstruction aid as a share of GDP (%)	30.2	15.6	17.7	10.9	8.4
Recommended reconstruction aid ($ millions)	199.9	128.0	165.2	106.3	86.2

SOURCE: RAND calculations.

NOTE: All dollar amounts are in constant 2002 U.S. dollars. Amounts may not sum due to rounding.

CHAPTER TEN

Conclusion: The Cost of Nation-Building

This volume is intended to help those mounting nation-building operations in designing, assembling, and employing the necessary components. It should also assist journalists, legislators, and other interested observers in evaluating the planning and implementation of any such mission. Each preceding chapter contains simple formulas for estimating the required size and likely cost of the various mission elements. This chapter addresses the overall costs.

Two types of variables have been used throughout this volume to predict costing requirements. The first are the more or less immutable facts on the ground, such as the size of the population, its degree of urbanization, and its level of income, factors that cannot be immediately affected by the intervention. The second are societal conditions that may, over time, be influenced and the goals for doing so. In this latter category are the levels and types of conflict within the society and the scope of reforms being attempted.

Most historical nation-building operations have fallen into one of two categories. The first are peacekeeping missions mounted on the basis of prior agreement among the warring parties. The second are peace enforcement operations launched over the opposition of one or more of the indigenous factions. Interventions of the first type have typically been led by the United Nations, those of the second by a major global or regional power or by an alliance of such powers. Peace enforcement actions of this latter type have proved much more expensive than peacekeeping operations, and particularly so for the leading participants.

Table 10.1 shows the requirements for the two types of operations in the same hypothetical country. The nation in question is rather small and very poor, with a population of 5 million and a per capita income of $500, thus similar in size and level of development to Haiti, Sierra Leone, or Liberia. The light peacekeeping operation assumes a permissive entry, acquiescent population, and some level of remaining local capacity for governance and security. The heavy peace enforcement mission assumes a forced entry, a more hostile or divided population, and little or no immediately available indigenous capacity for governance and security.

Table 10.1
The Costs of Nation-Building

Sector	Light Peacekeeping Number of Personnel Local	Int'l	Cost (millions of US$)	Heavy Peace Enforcement Number of Personnel Local	Int'l	Cost (millions of US$)
Military	15,000		50	15,000		50
		8,000	360		65,000	13,000
Police	11,000		18	11,000		18
		1,000	170		8,000	1,250
Rule of law			18			18
Humanitarian			170			170
Governance			260			260
Economic stabilization			30			30
Democratization			50			50
Development and infrastructure			390			750
Total	26,000	9,000	1,520	26,000	73,000	15,600

NOTE: Data are based on operations in a hypothetical country of 5 million people with a per capita GDP of $500. Costs may not sum due to rounding.

In both cases, the society is assumed to be generating no significant government revenue, thus requiring that nearly all public services be funded initially by the intervening authorities. More prosperous postconflict societies are usually able to fund some appreciable share of their own government operations, but their reconstruction may nevertheless pose a larger burden on external donors because public services in such societies are more expensive to provide due to higher wage rates. Thus, somewhat counterintuitively, nation-building can be more expensive in relatively developed societies, such as Bosnia or Iraq, than in highly underdeveloped ones, such as Afghanistan or Sierra Leone.

A light peacekeeping operation in this hypothetical society is estimated to require 9,000 international soldiers and police at a total cost of $1.5 billion per year. A heavy peace enforcement mission could require 80,000 personnel and cost $15 billion per year.[1]

---

[1] In three instances, the projections differ substantially. The size, capability, and cost of the international military force that intervenes under the heavy peace enforcement operation are substantially greater than in the light peacekeeping scenario, consistent with the international community's experience with these two types of operations. For the heavy peace enforcement scenario, we calculated the number of soldiers using the average number of international military personnel deployed in the first year of eight peace enforcement operations (in East Timor, Eastern Slavonia, Japan, Somalia, Haiti, Bosnia, Kosovo, and Iraq; we excluded the two outliers—Germany on the high end and Afghanistan on the low end—from the average). For the light peacekeeping scenario, we used the average number of soldiers in the first year of six peacekeeping operations (in Congo [in the 1960s], Namibia, Cambodia, Mozambique, Sierra Leone, and El Salvador).

Numbers of international police officers also differ. For the heavy peace enforcement scenario, we computed the number of police officers using the average number of international police officers deployed in the first year in three operations: Bosnia, East Timor, and Kosovo. (The average was 161 per 100,000 inhabitants; Afghanistan, Germany, and Japan were excluded from the average because no civilian international police force was deployed to these three countries). For the light peacekeeping scenario, we used the average number of police in the first year of eight less ambitious operations with international police components (in Congo [in the 1960s], Namibia, El Salvador, Cambodia, Somalia, Mozambique, Haiti, and Sierra Leone).

Finally, we assumed that the willingness of foreign donors to fund infrastructure development was less in the peacekeeping than in the peace enforcement scenarios. For the peacekeeping scenario, we assumed that the international community would fund reconstruction in the range of 16 percent of GDP, the level provided in Bosnia during the second year after the end of the conflict. For the peace enforcement scenario, we assumed that the interna-

These figures are consistent with the actual costs and staffing levels of UN-led peacekeeping and U.S.-led peace enforcement operations over the past several decades. Over this period, heavy nationally or alliance-led peace enforcement missions have proved, on average, to require approximately 10 times more personnel and money, on a per capita basis, than lighter UN-led peacekeeping missions.

The expense of any nation-building mission is shared among troop contributors, aid donors, and the international community as a whole according to various burden-sharing formulas. The costs of UN-led operations are spread most widely. Those of nationally led peace enforcement missions fall more heavily on the lead nation and its principal allies.

As a practical matter, therefore, full-scale peace enforcement actions are feasible only when the intervening authorities care a great deal about the outcome and, even then, only in relatively small societies. Thus, the effort needed to stabilize Bosnia and Kosovo has proved difficult to replicate in Afghanistan or Iraq, nations that are eight to 12 times more populous. It would be even more difficult to mount a peace enforcement mission in Iran, which is three times more populous than Iraq, and nearly impossible to do so in Pakistan, which is three times again more populous than Iran. Considerations of scale, therefore, suggest that the transformational objectives of interventions in larger societies should be sharply restrained to account for the relatively much more modest resources likely to be available for their achievement.

Even the lighter, more consensual, less ambitious approach to nation-building epitomized by UN peacekeeping operations represents an expensive enterprise, though it is not more expensive than allowing a conflict, once halted, to be renewed. Put differently, conflicts generally impose greater costs on the international community than the expense necessary to ensure that the cycle of violence, once halted for whatever reason, is not renewed. While it may be prohibitively expensive to forcefully halt a civil war in full swing, experience has shown

---

tional community would fund reconstruction at a high level: 30 percent of GDP, the level provided in Bosnia during the first year after the end of the conflict.

that interventions intended to consolidate and perpetuate a tentative peace are cost-effective.[2]

It has been said that no war plan can survive first contact with the enemy. Similarly, no plan for nation-building is likely to survive first contact with the nation to be rebuilt. The true test of any such plan, therefore, is not its ability to predict every twist and turn of the resultant operation, but rather its success in matching ends to means. If the planners have given the operators what they need to succeed, they have done their jobs. If operations are mired in shortcomings and attention cannot be focused exclusively on the mission at hand, the planners have not met their obligations. This guide should help meet that crucial test.

---

[2] Collier and Hoeffler (2004, p. 3); Dobbins, Jones, et al. (2005, p. 247).

Bibliography

Ball, Howard, *Prosecuting War Crimes and Genocide: The Twentieth-Century Experience*, Lawrence, Kan.: University Press of Kansas, 1999.

Barro, Robert J., "Democracy and Growth," *Journal of Economic Growth*, Vol. 1, No. 1, March 1996, pp. 1–27.

Barry, Jane, and Anna Jefferys, "A Bridge Too Far: Aid Agencies and the Military in Humanitarian Response," Network Paper No. 37, London: Humanitarian Practice Network, January 2002.

Bass, Gary Jonathan, *Stay the Hand of Vengeance: The Politics of War Crimes Tribunals*, Princeton, N.J.: Princeton University Press, 2000.

Benomar, Jamal, "Constitution-Making After Conflict: Lessons for Iraq," *Journal of Democracy*, Vol. 15, No. 2, April 2004, pp. 81–95.

Bornemisza, Olga, and Egbert Sondorp, *Health Policy Formulation in Complex Political Emergencies and Post-Conflict Countries: A Literature Review*, London: London School of Hygiene and Tropical Medicine, November 7, 2002. Online at http://www.lshtm.ac.uk/hpu/conflict/publications/LiteratureReviewonhealthpolicyformulationinCEandP.pdf?section=news&wwwID=1704 (as of October 6, 2006).

Bray, John, "International Companies and Post-Conflict Reconstruction," Conflict Prevention and Reconstruction, Social Development Paper No. 22, Washington, D.C.: World Bank, February 2005. Online at http://lnweb18.worldbank.org/ESSD/sdvext.nsf/67ByDocName/InternationalCompaniesandPost-ConflictReconstructionCross-SectoralComparissons/$FILE/WP22_RevisedWeb.pdf (as of October 18, 2006).

Bureau of Economic Analysis, National Economic Accounts, National Income and Product Account Tables: Section 5, Saving and Investment. Online at http://www.bea.gov/bea/dn/nipaweb/index.asp (as of October 18, 2006).

Burkhart, Ross E., and Michael Lewis-Beck, "Comparative Democracy: The Economic Development Thesis," *American Political Science Review*, Vol. 88, No. 4, December 1994, pp. 903–910.

Burnside, Craig, and David Dollar, "Aid, Policies, and Growth," *American Economic Review*, Vol. 90, No. 4, September 2000, pp. 847–868.

Call, Charles T., "Democratisation, War and State-Building: Constructing the Rule of Law in El Salvador," *Journal of Latin American Studies*, Vol. 35, No. 4, November 2003, pp. 827–862.

Callwell, C. E., *Small Wars: Their Principles and Practice*, Wakefield, UK: EP Publishing Ltd., [1906] 1976.

Carothers, Thomas, *Aiding Democracy Abroad: The Learning Curve*, Washington, D.C.: Carnegie Endowment for International Peace, 1999.

———, ed., *Promoting the Rule of Law Abroad: In Search of Knowledge*, Washington, D.C.: Carnegie Endowment for International Peace, 2006.

Central Intelligence Agency, *The World Factbook 2006*, Washington, D.C.: 2006. Online at https://www.cia.gov/cia/publications/factbook/index.html (as of October 6, 2006).

Chesterman, Simon, *You, The People: The United Nations, Transitional Administration, and State-Building*, New York: Oxford University Press, 2004.

China Statistical Yearbook 2005, China Statistics Press, 2005.

Clemens, Michael A., Steven Radelet, and Rikhil Bhavnani, "Counting Chickens When They Hatch: The Short-Term Effect of Aid on Growth," Working Paper No. 44, Washington, D.C.: Center for Global Growth, December 2, 2004. Online at http://www.cgdev.org/content/publications/detail/2744 (as of October 18, 2006).

Collier, Paul, and David Dollar, "Aid Allocation and Poverty," Policy Research Working Paper No. 2041, Washington, D.C.: World Bank, draft of October 20, 1998. Online at http://www.worldbank.org/html/dec/Publications/Workpapers/wps2000series/wps2041/wps2041.pdf (as of October 18, 2006).

Collier, Paul, and Anke Hoeffler, "Aid, Policy, and Growth in Post-Conflict Societies," Policy Research Working Paper No. 2902, Washington, D.C.: World Bank, October 2002. Online at http://www-wds.worldbank.org/ external/default/WDSContentServer/WDSP/IB/2002/11/01/0000 94946_02101904245026/Rendered/PDF/multi0page.pdf (as of October 18, 2006).

————, "The Challenge of Reducing the Global Incidence of Civil War," Copenhagen Consensus Challenge Paper, Oxford: Centre for the Study of African Economies, Oxford University, April 23, 2004. Online at http://www.copenhagenconsensus.com/Files/Filer/CC/Papers/Conflicts_ 230404.pdf (as of October 2, 2006).

Counterpart International, *Afghanistan Civil Society Assessment*, Washington, D.C., June 3, 2005.

Dahl, Robert A., *Polyarchy: Participation and Opposition*, New Haven, Conn.: Yale University Press, 1971.

Demekas, Dimitri G., Johannes Herderschee, and Davina F. Jacobs, *Kosovo: Institutions and Policies for Reconstruction and Growth*, Washington, D.C.: International Monetary Fund, 2002. Online at http://www.imf.org/ external/pubs/ft/kosovo/2002/eng/iprg/iprg.pdf (as of October 17, 2006).

Diamond, Larry, "Promoting Democracy in Post-Conflict and Failed States: Lessons and Challenges," paper presented at the National Policy Forum on Terrorism, Security, and America's Purpose, Washington, D.C., September 6–7, 2005. Online at http://www.stanford.edu/~ldiamond/papers/ PromotingDemocracy0905.htm (as of October 17, 2006).

Dobbins, James, Seth G. Jones, Keith Crane, Andrew Rathmell, Brett Steele, Richard Teltschik, and Anga Timilsina, *The UN's Role in Nation-Building: From the Congo to Iraq*, Santa Monica, Calif.: RAND Corporation, MG-304-RC, 2005. Online at http://www.rand.org/pubs/ monographs/MG304/ (as of October 2, 2006).

Dobbins, James, John G. McGinn, Keith Crane, Seth G. Jones, Rollie Lal, Andrew Rathmell, Rachel M. Swanger, and Anga Timilsina, *America's Role in Nation-Building: From Germany to Iraq*, Santa Monica, Calif.: RAND Corporation, MR-1753-RC, 2003. Online at http://www.rand. org/pubs/monograph_reports/MR1753/ (as of October 2, 2006).

Doyle, Michael W., *Ways of War and Peace: Realism, Liberalism, and Socialism*, New York: W. W. Norton, 1997.

Doyle, Michael W., and Nicholas Sambanis, "International Peacebuilding: A Theoretical and Quantitative Analysis," *American Political Science Review*, Vol. 94, No. 4, December 2000, pp. 779–802.

Fallon, Richard H., Jr., "'The Rule of Law' as a Concept in Constitutional Discourse," *Columbia Law Review*, Vol. 97, No. 1, January 1997, pp. 1–56.

Federal Statistical Office, Yugoslavia, *Statistical Yearbook of Yugoslavia 1997*, Belgrade, 1997.

Fischer, Stanley, Ratna Sahay, and Carlos Végh, "Modern Hyper- and High Inflations," IMF Working Paper 02/197, Washington, D.C.: International Monetary Fund, January 31, 2003. Online at http://www.imf.org/external/pubs/ft/wp/2002/wp02197.pdf (as of October 17, 2006).

Fukuyama, Francis, *State-Building: Governance and World Order in the 21st Century*, Ithaca, N.Y.: Cornell University Press, 2004.

Galula, David, *Counterinsurgency Warfare: Theory and Practice*, New York: Praeger, 1964.

Gleditsch, Kristian Skrede, *All International Politics Is Local: The Diffusion of Conflict, Integration, and Democratization*, Ann Arbor, Mich.: University of Michigan Press, 2002.

Gleichman, Colin, Michael Odenwald, Kees Steenken, and Adrian Wilkinson, *Disarmament, Demobilization and Reintegration: A Practical Field and Classroom Guide*, Frankfurt, Germany: Druckerei Hassmuller Graphische Betriebe, 2004.

Goreux, Lois, "Conflict Diamonds," Africa Regional Working Paper, No. 13, Washington, D.C.: World Bank, March 2001. Online at http://www.worldbank.org/afr/wps/wp13.pdf (as of October 17, 2006).

Gormley, William T., Jr., and David L. Weimer, *Organizational Report Cards*, Cambridge, Mass.: Harvard University Press, 1999.

Hagman, Lotta, and Zoe Nielson, "A Framework for Lasting Disarmament, Demobilization, and Reintegration of Former Combatants in Crisis Situations," paper presented at International Peace Academy–United Nations Development Programme Workshop, New York, December 12–13, 2002. Online at http://www.ciaonet.org/wps/hal07/hal07.pdf (as of October 19, 2006).

Hatry, Harry P., *Performance Measurement: Getting Results*, Washington, D.C.: Urban Institute Press, 1999.

Hayek, Friedrich A., *Law, Legislation, and Liberty, Volume 1: Rules and Order*, Chicago: University of Chicago Press, 1973.

Headquarters, U.S. Department of the Army, *Military Police Operations*, FM 3-19.1, Washington, D.C., 2002.

———, *Stability Operations and Support Operations*, FM 3-07, Washington, D.C., 2003.

———, *Counterinsurgency Operations*, FMI 3-07.22, Washington, D.C., 2004.

Hippel, Karen von, *Democracy by Force: U.S. Military Intervention in the Post–Cold War*, New York: Cambridge University Press, 2000.

Horowitz, Donald L., *Ethnic Groups in Conflict*, Berkeley, Calif.: University of California Press, 1985.

———, *A Democratic South Africa? Constitutional Engineering in a Divided Society*, Berkeley, Calif.: University of California Press, 1991.

Human Security Centre, University of British Columbia, *Human Security Report 2005: War and Peace in the 21st Century*, New York: Oxford University Press, 2005. Online at http://www.humansecurityreport.info/content/view/28/63/ (as of October 4, 2006).

Huntington, Samuel P., *The Third Wave: Democratization in the Late Twentieth Century*, Norman, Okla.: University of Oklahoma Press, 1991.

IFES, Election Guide: Macedonia, guide for 2006 Macedonia parliamentary elections, Washington, D.C., 2006. Online at http://www.electionguide.org/election.php?ID=913 (as of October 17, 2006).

IFES, and United Nations Development Programme, *Getting to the Core: A Global Survey on the Cost of Registration and Elections*, Madrid and Washington, D.C., 2006. Online at http://www.ifes.org/publication/4242624b9711806527bcec1133059faf/CorePublcolor.pdf (as of October 17, 2006).

Inspector General for Iraq Reconstruction, *Iraq Reconstruction: Lessons Learned in Contracting and Procurement*, Washington, D.C.: U.S. Government Printing Office, July 2006. Online at http://www.sigir.mil/reports/pdf/Lessons_Learned_July21.pdf (as of October 18, 2006).

International Crisis Group, "Afghanistan: Judicial Reform and Transitional Justice," Asia Report No. 45, Kabul and Brussels, 2003. Online at http://www.crisisgroup.org/library/documents/report_archive/A400879_28012003.pdf (as of October 19, 2006).

International Federation of Red Cross and Red Crescent Societies, "Code of Conduct for the International Red Cross and Red Crescent Movement and NGOs in Disaster Relief," Geneva, Switzerland, 1994. Online at http://www.ifrc.org/publicat/conduct/index.asp (as of October 6, 2006).

International Institute for Strategic Studies, *The Military Balance, 2004–2005*, London: Taylor and Francis, 2004.

International Monetary Fund, International Financial Statistics Browser, available by subscription through the International Monetary Fund.

————, "Bosnia and Herzegovina: Selected Issues and Statistical Appendix," IMF Staff Country Report No. 00/77, Washington, D.C., June 2000. Online at http://www.imf.org/external/pubs/ft/scr/2000/cr0077.pdf (as of October 17, 2006).

————, "Bosnia and Herzegovina: Statistical Appendix," IMF Country Report No. 02/60, Washington, D.C., March 2002. Online at http://www.imf.org/external/pubs/ft/scr/2002/cr0260.pdf (as of October 16, 2006).

————, "Bosnia and Herzegovina: First Review Under the Stand-By Agreement and Request for Waiver of Performance Criteria," IMF Country Report No. 03/4, Washington, D.C., January 2003. Online at http://www.internationalmonetaryfund.com/external/pubs/ft/scr/2003/cr0304.pdf (as of October 18, 2006).

————, "Bosnia and Herzegovina: Selected Economic Issues," IMF Country Report No. 04/54, Washington, D.C., March 2004. Online at http://www.imf.org/external/pubs/ft/scr/2004/cr0454.pdf (as of October 18, 2006).

————, "Bosnia and Herzegovina: 2005 Article IV Consultation—Staff Report; Staff Supplement; Public Information Notice on the Executive Board Discussion; and Statement by the Executive Director for Bosnia and Herzegovina," IMF Country Report No. 05/199, Washington, D.C., June 2005a. Online at http://www.imf.org/external/pubs/ft/scr/2005/cr05199.pdf (as of October 16, 2006).

————, "Democratic Republic of Timor-Leste: 2005 Article IV Consultation—Staff Report; Public Information Notice on the Executive Board Discussion; and Statement by the Executive Director for the Democratic Republic of Timor-Leste," IMF Country Report No. 05/245, Washington, D.C., July 2005b. Online at http://www.imf.org/external/pubs/ft/scr/2005/cr05245.pdf (as of October 16, 2006).

————, "Iraq: Statistical Appendix," IMF Country Report No. 05/295, Washington, D.C., August 2005c. Online at http://www.imf.org/external/pubs/ft/scr/2005/cr05295.pdf (as of October 17, 2006).

————, "Islamic Republic of Afghanistan: Fifth Review Under the Staff-Monitored Program and Request for an Extension," IMF Country Report No. 05/371, Washington, D.C., October 2005d. Online at http://www.imf.org/external/pubs/ft/scr/2005/cr05371.pdf (as of October 17, 2006).

————, "IMF Emergency Assistance: Supporting Recovery from Natural Disasters and Armed Conflicts," fact sheet, Washington, D.C., December 2005e. Online at http://www.imf.org/external/np/exr/facts/conflict.htm (as of October 17, 2006).

————, Country Statistical Information Database, information current in mid-2006. Online at http://www.imf.org/external/country/index.htm (as of November 15, 2006).

————, reports by country, information current in mid-2006. Online at http://www.imf.org/external/country/index.htm (as of October 7, 2006).

Jones, Seth G., Lee H. Hilborne, C. Ross Anthony, Lois M. Davis, Federico Girosi, Cheryl Benard, Rachel M. Swanger, Anita Datar Garten, and Anga Timilsina, *Securing Health: Lessons from Nation-Building Missions*, Santa Monica, Calif.: RAND Corporation, MG-321-RC, 2006. Online at http://www.rand.org/pubs/monographs/MG321/ (as of October 6, 2006).

Jones, Seth G., Jeremy Wilson, Andrew Rathmell, and K. Jack Riley, *Establishing Law and Order After Conflict*, Santa Monica, Calif.: RAND Corporation, MG-374-RC, 2005. Online at http://www.rand.org/pubs/monographs/MG374/ (as of October 19, 2006).

Kariuki, Mukami, and Jordan Schwartz, "Small-Scale Private Service Providers of Water Supply and Electricity: A Review of Incidence, Structure, Pricing and Operating Characteristics," World Bank Policy Working Paper 3727, Washington, D.C.: World Bank, October 2005. Online at http://www-wds.worldbank.org/external/default/WDSContentServer/IW3P/IB/2005/09/23/000016406_20050923090807/Rendered/PDF/wps3727.pdf (as of October 18, 2006).

Kievelitz, Uwe, Thomas Schaef, Manuela Lonhardt, Herwig Hahn, and Sonja Verwerk, *Practical Guide to Multilateral Needs Assessments in Post-Conflict Situations*, New York: United Nations Development Programme, World Bank, and United Nations Development Group, August 2004. Online at http://lnweb18.worldbank.org/ESSD/sdvext.nsf/67ByDocName/PracticalGuidetoMultilateralNeedsAssessmentsinPost-ConflictSituationAJointUNDGUNDPandWorldBankGuidepreparedbyGTZwiththesupportofBMZ/$FILE/PCNA.Tool.pdf (as of October 18, 2006).

Langton, Christopher, ed., *The Military Balance, 2006*, London: International Institute for Strategic Studies, 2006.

Lijphart, Arend, "Constitutional Democracy," *World Politics*, Vol. 21, No. 2, January 1969, pp. 207–225.

———, *Patterns of Democracy: Government Forms and Performance in Thirty-Six Countries*, New Haven, Conn.: Yale University Press, 1999.

Lipset, Seymour Martin, "Some Social Requisites of Democracy: Economic Development and Political Legitimacy," *American Political Science Review*, Vol. 53, No. 1, March 1959, pp. 69–105.

MacNeil, Michael, Neil Sargent, and Peter Swan, eds., *Law, Regulation, and Governance*, New York: Oxford University Press, 2002.

Mansfield, Edward D., and Jack Snyder, *Electing to Fight: Why Emerging Democracies Go to War*, Cambridge, Mass.: MIT Press, 2005.

Mao Zedong, *Selected Military Writings of Mao Tse-Tung*, Peking, China: Foreign Languages Press, 1963.

Marten, Kimberly Zisk, *Enforcing the Peace: Learning from the Imperial Past*, New York: Columbia University Press, 2004.

McKechnie, Alistair J., "Humanitarian Assistance, Reconstruction and Development in Afghanistan: A Practitioners' View," CPR Working Paper No. 3, Washington, D.C.: World Bank, March 2003. Online at http://lnweb18.worldbank.org/ESSD/sdvext.nsf/60ByDocName/Humanitarian AssistanceReconstructionandDevelopmentinAfghanistanAPractitioners ViewSouthAsiaRegionCPRWorkingPaper3March2003PDF94KB/ $FILE/WP-No3.pdf (as of October 7, 2006).

Miller, Laurel, and Robert Perito, *Establishing the Rule of Law in Afghanistan*, Special Report No. 117, Washington, D.C.: United States Institute of Peace, March, 2004. Online at http://www.usip.org/pubs/specialreports/sr117.html (as of October 19, 2006).

Mitchell, B. R., *International Historical Statistics: Europe 1750–1988*, 3rd ed., New York: Stockton Press, 1992.

——, *International Historical Statistics: Africa, Asia, and Oceania 1750–1993*, 3rd ed., New York: Stockton Press, 1998.

Moalla-Fetini, Rakia, Heikki Hatanpää, Shehadah Hussein, and Natalia Koliadina, *Kosovo: Gearing Policies Toward Growth and Development*, Washington, D.C.: International Monetary Fund, 2005. Online at http://www.imf.org/external/pubs/ft/kosovo/2005/GPGD.pdf (as of October 16, 2006).

Morrow, Jonathan, and Rachel White, "The United Nations in Transitional East Timor: International Standards and the Reality of Governance," *Australian Year Book of International Law*, Vol. 22, Canberra, Australia: Centre for International and Public Law, Australian National University, 2002, pp. 1–46.

Mueller, John, *The Remnants of War*, Ithaca, N.Y.: Cornell University Press, 2004.

National Security Presidential Directive 44, "Management of Interagency Efforts Concerning Reconstruction and Stabilization," Washington, D.C.: White House, December 7, 2005. Online at http://www.fas.org/irp/offdocs/nspd/nspd-44.pdf (as of December 8, 2006).

Oakley, Robert B., Michael J. Dziedzic, and Eliot M. Goldbert, eds., *Policing in the New World Disorder: Peace Operations and Public Security*, Washington, D.C.: National Defense University, 1998. Online at http://www. ndu.edu/inss/books/books%20-%201998/Policing%20the%20New%20 World%20Disorder%20-%20May%2098/PNW.pdf (as of October 6, 2006).

Oliker, Olga, Richard Kauzlarich, James Dobbins, Kurt W. Basseuner, Donald L. Sampler, John G. McGinn, Michael J. Dziedzic, Adam Grissom, Bruce R. Pirnie, Nora Bensahel, and A. Istar Guven, *Aid During Conflict: Interaction Between Military and Civilian Assistance Providers in Afghanistan, September 2001–June 2002*, Santa Monica, Calif.: RAND Corporation, MG-212-OSD, 2004. Online at http://www.rand.org/pubs/ monographs/MG212/ (as of October 2, 2006).

Olson, Mancur, *The Logic of Collective Action: Public Goods and the Theory of Groups*, Cambridge, Mass.: Harvard University Press, 1971.

Orr, Robert C., ed., *Winning the Peace: An American Strategy for Post-Conflict Reconstruction*, Washington, D.C.: Center for Strategic and International Studies, 2004.

Paris, Roland, *At War's End: Building Peace After Civil Conflict*, New York: Cambridge University Press, 2004.

Perito, Robert M., *The American Experience with Police in Peace Operations*, Clementsport, Canada: Canadian Peacekeeping Press, 2002.

———, *Where Is the Lone Ranger When We Need Him? America's Search for a Postconflict Stability Force*, Washington, D.C., United States Institute of Peace Press, 2004.

Posen, Barry, "The Security Dilemma and Ethnic Conflict," in Michael E. Brown, ed., *Ethnic Conflict and International Security*, Princeton, N.J.: Princeton University Press, 1993, pp. 103–124.

Presidential Decision Directive 56, "Managing Complex Contingency Operations," Washington, D.C.: White House, May 1997. Online at http:// www.fas.org/irp/offdocs/pdd56.htm (as of October 2, 2006).

Przeworski, Adam, *Democracy and the Market: Political and Economic Reforms in Eastern Europe and Latin America*, New York: Cambridge University Press, 1991.

Przeworski, Adam, and Fernando Limongi, "Moderization: Theories and Facts," *World Politics*, Vol. 49, No. 2, January 1997, pp. 155–183.

Ramsbotham, Oliver, and Tom Woodhouse, *Encyclopedia of International Peacekeeping Operations*, Santa Barbara, Calif.: ABC-CLIO, 1999.

Rohland, Klaus, and Sarah Cliffe, "The East Timor Reconstruction Program: Successes, Problems, and Tradeoffs," CPR Working Paper No. 2, Washington, D.C.: World Bank, November 2002. Online at http://www-wds.worldbank.org/external/default/WDSContentServer/WDSP/IB/2003/07/22/000090341_20030722090808/Rendered/PDF/263610PAPER0Colon0wp0no20East0Timor.pdf (as of October 18, 2006).

Russett, Bruce, *Grasping the Democratic Peace: Principles for a Post–Cold War World*, Princeton, N.J.: Princeton University Press, 1993.

Sen, Amartya, *Development as Freedom*, New York: Anchor Books, 2000.

Smith, Bradley F., ed., *The American Road to Nuremberg: The Documentary Record, 1944–1945*, Stanford, Calif.: Hoover Institution Press, 1982.

Snyder, Jack, *From Voting to Violence: Democratization and Nationalist Conflict*, New York: W. W. Norton, 2000.

Sphere Project, *The Sphere Handbook*, Geneva, Switzerland, 2004. Online at http://www.sphereproject.org/handbook/ (as of October 6, 2006).

Strohmeyer, Hansjörg, "Building a New Judiciary for East Timor: Challenges of a Fledgling Nation," *Criminal Law Forum*, Vol. 11, No. 3, September 2000, pp. 259–285.

———, "Collapse and Reconstruction of a Judicial System: The United Nations Missions in Kosovo and East Timor," *American Journal of International Law*, Vol. 95, No. 1, January 2001, pp. 46–63.

Stromseth, Jane, David Wippman, and Rosa Brooks, *Can Might Make Rights? The Rule of Law After Military Interventions*, New York: Cambridge University Press, 2006.

Trinquier, Roger, *Modern Warfare: A French View of Counterinsurgency*, Daniel Lee, trans., New York: Praeger, 1964.

UK Ministry of Defence, *The Military Contribution to Peace Support Operations*, Joint Warfare Publication 3-50, London, 2004.

United Nations, *Managing Arms in Peace Processes: Cambodia*, New York, 1996.

———, *Managing Arms in Peace Processes: Nicaragua and El Salvador*, New York, 1997.

United Nations Department of Peacekeeping Operations, *Disarmament, Demobilization and Reintegration of Ex-Combatants in a Peacekeeping Environment: Principles and Guidelines*, New York, December 1999. Online at http://www.un.org/Depts/dpko/lessons/DD&R.pdf (as of October 19, 2006).

United Nations Development Group, and World Bank, *United Nations/ World Bank Joint Iraq Needs Assessment*, Washington, D.C., October 2003. Online at http://siteresources.worldbank.org/IRFFI/Resources/ Joint+Needs+Assessment.pdf (as of October 18, 2006).

———, *An Operational Note on Transitional Results Matrices: Using Results-Based Frameworks in Fragile States*, New York, January 2005. Online at http://www.undg.org/documents/5532-Operational_Note_on_ Transitional_Results_Matrices_-_Results_Matrix_Guide.pdf (as of October 6, 2006).

United Nations Development Programme, *Human Development Report 2004*, New York, 2004. Online at http://hdr.undp.org/reports/global/ 2004/?CFID=318490&CFTOKEN=91993609 (as of October 7, 2006).

United Nations General Assembly, "United Nations Standard Minimum Rules for the Administration of Juvenile Justice ('The Beijing Rules')," A/RES/40/33, 96th plenary meeting, November 29, 1985. Online at http://www.un.org/documents/ga/res/40/a40r033.htm (as of October 6, 2006).

———, "Performance Report on the Budget of the United Nations Mission in Liberia for the Period from 1 August 2003 to 30 June 2004: Report of the Secretary-General," A/59/624, 59th session, agenda item 134, December 20, 2004a. Online at http://daccessdds.un.org/doc/UNDOC/ GEN/N04/656/06/PDF/N0465606.pdf?OpenElement (as of October 6, 2006).

———, "Performance Report on the Budget of the United Nations Mission in Sierra Leone for the Period from 1 July 2003 to 30 June 2004: Report of the Secretary-General," A/59/635, 59th session, agenda item 136, December 21, 2004b. Online at http://daccessdds.un.org/doc/UNDOC/ GEN/N04/663/63/PDF/N0466363.pdf?OpenElement (as of October 6, 2006).

————, "Performance Report on the Budget of the United Nations Organization Mission in the Democratic Republic of the Congo for the Period from 1 July 2003 to 30 June 2004: Report of the Secretary-General," A/59/657, 59th session, agenda item 127, March 4, 2005a. Online at http://daccessdds.un.org/doc/UNDOC/GEN/N04/663/92/PDF/N0466392.pdf?OpenElement (as of October 6, 2006).

————, "Budget for the United Nations Stabilization Mission in Haiti for the Period from 1 July 2005 to 30 June 2006 and Expenditure Report for the Period from 1 May to 30 June 2004: Report of the Secretary-General," A/59/745, 59th session, agenda item 155, March 18, 2005b. Online at http://daccessdds.un.org/doc/UNDOC/GEN/N05/276/81/PDF/N0527681.pdf?OpenElement (as of October 6, 2006).

United Nations Interim Administration Mission in Kosovo, Regulation No. 1999/1, "On the Authority of the Interim Administration in Kosovo," July 25, 1999. Online at http://www.usig.org/countryinfo/laws/Kosovo/re99_01.pdf (as of October 6, 2006).

United Nations Office for Coordination of Humanitarian Affairs, Financial Tracking Service, Web-based, global humanitarian aid database, updated daily. Online at http://ocha.unog.ch/fts/index.aspx (as of October 6, 2006).

United Nations Office on Drugs and Crime, *The Eighth United Nations Survey on Crime Trends and the Operations of Criminal Justice Systems*, Vienna, 2002. Online at http://www.unodc.org/unodc/crime_cicp_survey_eighth.html (as of October 6, 2006).

United Nations Security Council, Resolution 1272, on the situation in East Timor, 4,057th meeting, October 25, 1999. Online at http://daccessdds.un.org/doc/UNDOC/GEN/N99/312/77/PDF/N9931277.pdf?OpenElement (as of October 7, 2006).

————, Resolution 1542, on the question concerning Haiti, 4,961st meeting, April 30, 2004. Online at http://daccessdds.un.org/doc/UNDOC/GEN/N04/332/98/PDF/N0433298.pdf?OpenElement (as of October 7, 2006).

United Nations Transitional Administration in East Timor, Regulation No. 2000/1, "On the Organization of Courts in East Timor," March 6, 2000. Online at http://www.un.org/peace/etimor/untaetR/Reg11.pdf (as of October 6, 2006).

U.S. Army, Marine Corps, Navy, and Air Force, *Peace Ops: Multi-Service Tactics, Techniques, and Procedures for Conducting Peace Operations*, FM 3-07.31, MCWP 3-33.8, AFTTP 3-2.40, 2003. Online at http://www. globalsecurity.org/military/library/policy/army/fm/3-07-31/fm3_07x31. pdf (as of October 19, 2006).

U.S. Congress, Congressional Budget Office, *Estimated Costs of Continuing Operations in Iraq and Other Operations of the Global War on Terrorism*, Washington, D.C., June 25, 2004. Online at http://www.cbo.gov/ftpdocs/ 55xx/doc5587/Cost_of_Iraq.pdf (as of October 6, 2006).

U.S. Defense Science Board, *Transition to and from Hostilities*, Washington, D.C.: Office of the Under Secretary of Defense for Acquisition, Technology, and Logistics, December 2004. Online at http://www.acq.osd. mil/dsb/reports/2004-12-DSB_SS_Report_Final.pdf (as of October 19, 2006).

U.S. Department of the Army, *Strength of the Army*, weekly report series, STM-30, Washington, D.C., December 1, 1946.

U.S. Department of State, *Occupation of Germany: Policy and Progress, 1945– 1946*, Washington, D.C.: U.S. Government Printing Office, 1947.

———, *Rule of Law in Afghanistan*, Washington, D.C.: U.S. Department of State, International Narcotics and Law Enforcement Affairs, 2006.

U.S. Joint Chiefs of Staff, *Joint Tactics, Techniques, and Procedures for Foreign Internal Defense (FID)*, Joint Publication 3-07.1, Washington, D.C., April 30, 2004. Online at http://www.dtic.mil/doctrine/jel/new_pubs/jp3_07_ 1.pdf (as of October 19, 2006).

U.S. Marine Corps, *Small Wars*, Washington, D.C., 2004.

Weart, Spencer R., *Never at War: Why Democracies Will Not Fight One Another*, New Haven, Conn.: Yale University Press, 1998.

Whitehead, Laurence, ed., *The International Dimensions of Democratization: Europe and the Americas*, New York: Oxford University Press, 1996.

Wilensky, Robert J., *Military Medicine to Win Hearts and Minds: Aid to Civilians in the Vietnam War*, Lubbock, Tex.: Texas Tech University Press, 2004.

World Bank, World Development Indicators Database, available by subscription through the World Bank.

————, *Bank-Financed Procurement Model*, Washington, D.C., draft of July 2001a. Online at http://siteresources.worldbank.org/PROCUREMENT/Resources/pm7-3-01.pdf (as of October 18, 2006).

————, *World Development Report 2002: Building Institutions for Markets*, Washington, D.C., and New York: World Bank and Oxford University Press, September 2001b. Online at http://www.worldbank.org/wdr/2001/fulltext/fulltext2002.htm (as of October 18, 2006).

————, *World Development Report 2005: A Better Investment Climate for Everyone*, Washington, D.C., and New York: World Bank and Oxford University Press, September 2004. Online at http://siteresources.world bank.org/INTWDR2005/Resources/complete_report.pdf (as of October 18, 2006).

————, *World Development Report 2006: Equity and Development*, Washington, D.C., and New York: World Bank and Oxford University Press, September 2005. Online at http://www-wds.worldbank.org/external/default/WDSContentServer/IW3P/IB/2005/09/20/000112742_20050920110826/Rendered/PDF/322040World0Development0Report02006.pdf (as of November 15, 2006).

Ziemke, Earl F., *The U.S. Army in the Occupation of Germany, 1944–1946*, Washington, D.C.: U.S. Army Center of Military History, 1975. Online at http://www.army.mil/cmh/books/wwii/Occ-GY/ (as of October 6, 2006).

Index

About the Authors

James Dobbins directs the RAND Corporation's International Security and Defense Policy Center. He has held U.S. State Department and White House posts, including Assistant Secretary of State for Europe, Special Assistant to the President for the Western Hemisphere, Special Adviser to the President and Secretary of State for the Balkans, and Ambassador to the European Community. He has handled a variety of crisis management assignments as the Clinton administration's special envoy to Somalia, Haiti, Bosnia, and Kosovo, and the Bush administration's first special envoy to Afghanistan. He is lead author of RAND's two-volume *History of Nation-Building*. Dobbins graduated from the Georgetown School of Foreign Service and served three years in the U.S. Navy.

Seth G. Jones is a political scientist at the RAND Corporation and an adjunct professor at Georgetown University's Edmund A. Walsh School of Foreign Service. He is the author of *The Rise of European Security Cooperation* (Cambridge University Press, 2007). He has published articles on a range of national security subjects in *The National Interest*, *Political Science Quarterly*, *Security Studies*, *Chicago Journal of International Law*, *International Affairs*, and *Survival*, as well as such newspapers and magazines as the *New York Times*, *Newsweek*, *Financial Times*, and *International Herald Tribune*. He received his M.A. and Ph.D. from the University of Chicago.

Keith Crane is a senior economist at the RAND Corporation, where he works on issues pertaining to Eastern Europe, Russia, international development and trade, China, Iraq and the Middle East, as well as postconflict nation-building. In fall 2003, he served as an economic policy advisor to the Coalition Provisional Authority in Baghdad. More recently, he was a member of the Reconstruction and Economics Working Group serving the Baker-Hamilton Commission on Iraq. He received his Ph.D. in economics from Indiana University.

Beth Cole DeGrasse is a senior program officer in the Center for Post-Conflict Peace and Stability Operations at the U.S. Institute of Peace (USIP). Prior to joining USIP, she held a variety of positions in the executive, legislative, and nonprofit sectors. She worked on arms control issues for many years, including assignments at the U.S. Arms Control and Disarmament Agency and the Foreign Affairs and National Defense Division of the Congressional Research Service. She received her B.A. in political science and French from the University of Vermont and completed Kent State University's program on international organizations in Geneva, Switzerland.